THE IMPACT OF MICHEL FOUCAULT ON THE SOCIAL SCIENCES AND HUMANITIES

D0558003

The Impact of Michel Foucault on the Social Sciences and Humanities

Edited by

Moya Lloyd
Lecturer in Politics
Queen's University
Belfast

and

Andrew Thacker
Lecturer in English
University of Ulster
at Jordanstown

First published in Great Britain 1997 by
MACMILLAN PRESS LTD
Houndmills, Basingstoke, Hampshire RG21 6XS
and London
Companies and representatives
throughout the world

A catalogue record for this book is available
from the British Library.

ISBN 0–333–63126–9 (hardcover)
ISBN 0–333–68432–X (paperback)

First published in the United States of America 1997 by
ST. MARTIN'S PRESS, INC.,
Scholarly and Reference Division,
175 Fifth Avenue,
New York, N.Y. 10010

ISBN 0–312–16429–7

Library of Congress Cataloging-in-Publication Data
The impact of Michel Foucault on the social sciences and humanities /
edited by Moya Lloyd and Andrew Thacker.
p. cm.
Includes bibliographical references and index.
ISBN 0–312–16429–7
1. Foucault, Michel—Contributions in social sciences.
2. Foucault, Michel—Contributions in humanities. 3. Social
sciences—Philosophy. 4. Humanities—Philosophy. I. Lloyd, Moya,
1960– . II. Thacker, Andrew, 1962– .
H61.I5157   1996
300—dc20   96–27849
                                                                CIP

10 9   8   7   6   5   4   3   2   1
05 04 03 02 01 00 99 98 97 96

Printed and bound in Great Britain by
The Ipswich Book Co. Ltd, Ipswich, Suffolk

Contents

Preface and Acknowledgements

This book aims to survey the impact of the work of the French thinker Michel Foucault (1926–84) upon a number of different subjects and disciplines in the social sciences and humanities. Given the constraints of producing one smallish volume upon this topic we have eschewed any attempt to be all-inclusive. We have, instead, tried to cover a significant range of subject areas, a range that will best illustrate the profound effect that Foucault's thought has had upon a very wide – and expanding – number of academic areas of study. We hope that the chapters in this book go some way to charting how Foucault's work has produced problems and challenges for subjects such as politics, philosophy, history, feminism and so on, and that the book also indicates some directions for the continuing influence of Foucault's ideas on such topics as power, knowledge and subjectivity.

This book grew out of a Foucault reading group that both editors, and a number of the contributors, were involved with in Wolverhampton in the early 1990s. Many of the ideas and arguments that appear here might be traced back – in discontinuous fashion of course – to those often challenging, always enjoyable, meetings. We would like to thank the other members of this group who, at various times, contributed to the success of the group, especially Sue Brock and Steve Tombs. All of the chapters here were circulated to the other contributors for comments and all contributors would like to thank the other authors for their helpful advice. In addition the following people read and provided useful and detailed comments upon a number of the chapters: John Benson, Mike Cunningham and Iain MacKenzie. Final editorial responsibility lies with the editors alone, and we would, in the spirit of mutual back-slapping, like to thank each other for help and support.

Moya Lloyd and Andrew Thacker
Belfast 1996

Notes on Contributors

Alan Apperley is Lecturer in Politics at the University of Wolverhampton. He is primarily interested in issues around community and identity, and is currently engaged in a study of liberal theory and its response to cultural pluralism.

Bob Carter is a Senior Lecturer in Sociology at Worcester College of Higher Education. He has published extensively on racism, immigration and politics in post-war Britain and is currently working on a realist critique of sociologies of 'race' and 'race relations'.

Davina Cooper is a senior lecturer in the Law School, University of Warwick. Her research is mainly in the area of feminist political theory, urban studies and socio-legal analysis. She is the author of *Sexing the City: Lesbian and Gay Politics Within the Activist State* (Rivers Oram, 1994) and *Power in Struggle: Feminism, Sexuality and the State* (Open University, 1995). She is currently completing a book on space, governance and community.

Kimberly Hutchings is a lecturer in Political Theory at the University of Edinburgh. Her interests include Kantian and post-Kantian social and political theory, including feminist theory and international relations theory. She is the author of *Kant, Critique and Politics* (Routledge, 1995).

Moya Lloyd teaches Politics and Women's Studies at Queen's University, Belfast. She has published on various aspects of Foucault and feminist theory, including work on Judith Butler. She is currently working upon a book entitled *A Feminist Politics of Difference* (Sage).

Kevin Magill is Lecturer in Philosophy at the University of Wolverhampton. He is the author of *Freedom and Experience: Self-Determination Without Illusions* (Macmillan, 1996), and has written articles and papers on free will, causation and determinism, agency, punishment, realism in the social sciences and conservatism. He is a member of the editorial collective of *Radical Philosophy*.

Andrew Thacker lectures in English at the University of Ulster at Jordanstown. He has published on Foucault and aesthetics, gender and modernism, and modernist little magazines. His current research is upon theories of space and place in the modernist novel.

Introduction: Strategies of Transgression

Moya Lloyd and Andrew Thacker

> In attempting to uncover the deepest strata of Western culture, I am
> restoring to our silent and apparently immobile soil its rifts, its instability,
> its flaws; and it is the same ground that is once more stirring under our
> feet. (Foucault, 1970, xxiv)

It is impossible to deny that Michel Foucault has had a profound impact upon
many subjects and disciplines within the humanities and social sciences.
Evaluating the value and worth of this impact is, of course, a different matter
and it is perhaps far too early an endeavour to accomplish with any degree
of success. However, even a cursory glance at the range of disciplines in which
books are emerging that engage with Foucauldian ideas suggests that his work
will affect the intellectual landscape within which much academic work is
conducted. Books entitled 'Foucault and ...' are a simple indication of this
trend: Jan Goldstein's *Foucault and the Writing of History* (1994), Simon
During's *Foucault and Literature: Towards a Genealogy of Writing* (1992),
Alan Hunt and Gary Wickham's *Foucault and Law: Towards a Sociology
of Law as Governance* (1994), and Jon Simons' *Foucault and the Political*
(1995) are but a few instances. Foucault's influence has also been noted in
areas of enquiry that do not always fit such traditional disciplinary paradigms:
the literature on Foucault and feminism is burgeoning (see Lloyd in this
volume), as are texts devoted to queer theory (see Butler, 1991; 1993a;
Cohen, 1991) and post-colonial theory (see Young, 1995) that often bear the
imprint of Foucault's thought. Sometimes it appears that there is every
danger, to the chagrin no doubt of its author, of there emerging a Foucauldian
methodology or approach to issues and problems in specific disciplines and
areas of investigation. The man who wrote 'in order to have no face'
(Foucault, 1972a: 17) and whose work sought to reveal the self to be
constituted by 'the difference of masks' (1972a: 131) would probably have
had a few rebarbative comments to make upon texts espousing a Foucauldian
approach.

Foucault once stated that 'we are difference' (1972a: 131); different selves
in different discourses and different times and spaces. Difference is not,
however, to be valorised into an explanatory principle: 'That difference, far
from being the forgotten and recovered origin, is this dispersion that we are
and make' (1972a: 131). To suggest, then, that there could be a Foucauldian
methodology that can be applied in social policy, and then dusted down ready

for application in art history would make a nonsense of this appeal to difference. We cannot just apply a ready-made Foucauldian methodology, rather we must actively and creatively use his work and ideas. The uses of Foucault amongst the many disciplines of the humanities and social sciences are legion, and to try to neatly homogenise them would be to offend against what Deleuze saw as one of the key points of Foucault's work, that is, 'the repudiation of universals' (Deleuze, 1992: 162). The mapping of the applications of Foucault's ideas should perhaps be seen, in Deleuze's description of a *dispositif* (apparatus), as that of 'a tangle, a multilinear ensemble' (Deleuze, 1992: 159) where lines of influence, specific concepts, ideas and questions are taken from his work in multiple ways and along varying trajectories.

This book cannot hope to traverse all of these tangled pathways, and indeed certain readers may immediately feel that their particular area of interest or study is underrepresented, badly represented or not represented at all. Our aim, however, is not to attempt merely to be representative but rather to show how Foucault's texts have been and might be used in specific parts of particular disciplines, without prescribing how they should be applied. We wanted to see how Foucault's work might stir up and stretch, sometimes to breaking point, the disciplinary stories a subject, whether sociology or philosophy or international relations, tells of itself. The book aims, therefore, to show how Foucault's work poses probing questions to particular areas of study, without necessarily offering glib solutions to how such studies might alter fundamentally their conduct; how Foucault questions whether an academic subject necessarily *progresses* in its knowledge of an object of study; and how Foucault's work, as is inevitable given his own plurality of interests, interrogates the boundaries of certain disciplines, problematising the borders around their methods and methodologies, their theoretical frameworks and empirical objects of investigation.

This may make the book, and our interpretations of Foucault's impact upon the social sciences and humanities, appear remorselessly negative, finding fault and error within the accepted paradigms and contents of traditional subjects and disciplines. But there is, we believe, a reconstructive side to this project, a side that cannot be dissociated from this element of a more traditional criticism found in Foucault's work. We have tried to use the attitude of questioning found in Foucault's thought, to ask what makes and maintains a discipline as a particular discipline? In this we echo Bernauer's claim that Foucault's works 'exhibit the style of what he took teaching to be: an incessant interrogation in the interest of examining how an issue is cast in the form of a problem' (Bernauer, 1990: 3).

A discipline, for Foucault, is a 'principle of control over the production of discourse' (Foucault, 1980g: 61). One such element of control is that of truth: in order for a discourse to be included within a disciplinary framework it must function within what that discipline regards as the realm of truth: 'one is "in the truth" only by obeying the rules of a discursive "policing" which one has to reactivate in each of one's discourses' (1980g: 61). A discipline 'fixes limits for discourse by the action of an identity which takes the form of a permanent re-actuation of the rules' (1980g: 61). Any academic discipline constantly surveys its own borders, allowing only certain discourses to be included within it, as part of a process designed to maintain its own identity and status: too many aberrant discourses allowed within the portals of a discipline would threaten the boundaries of the subject but would also threaten the principle of order and organisation that maintains the self-identity of a discipline. Any discipline *disciplines* the discourses it allows within it because of a fear of how new and different discourses might disrupt the contours of the subject of study: 'It is just as if prohibitions, barriers, thresholds and limits had been set up in order to master, at least partly, the great proliferation of discourse, in order to remove from its richness the most dangerous part, and in order to organise its disorder according to figures which dodge what is most uncontrollable about it' (1970: 66).

Questioning in this Foucauldian fashion does not, however, remain at the level of patiently outlining the constraining mechanisms by which disciplines operate. Foucault also wished to examine the points at which the discursive policing of discourses break down, the limits whereby the ordinary values, practices and beliefs of a discipline can be transgressed in order that new or different discourses can emerge. Disordering the organisation of a discipline is also an eminently Foucauldian project. In the essay 'The Order of Discourse' (1980g) Foucault described this latter project as the genealogical aspect of his work, whilst the analysis of the policing of discourses is called the 'critical' side or, we might say, the more archaeological part of his work.[1] Genealogy complements the analysis of 'instances of discursive control' (1980g: 71) by studying 'the effective formation of discourse either within the limits of this control, or outside them, or more often on both sides of the boundary at once' (1980g: 71). To study discourses that cross disciplinary boundaries is thus to analyse modes of transgression, to examine discourses that push up against and cross the limits or borders of a discipline. This is an activity first outlined in Foucault's early essay 'A Preface to Transgression' (1977b) and which continues in a modified form as a theme into his final writings, with the notion of philosophy as 'work on our limits' (1984a: 50) contained in 'What is Enlightenment?':

This philosophical ethos may be characterized as a *limit-attitude*. We are not talking about a gesture of rejection. We have to move beyond the outside-inside alternative; we have to be at the frontiers. Criticism indeed consists of analyzing and reflecting upon limits. But if the Kantian question was that of knowing what limits knowledge has to renounce transgressing, it seems to me that the critical question today has to be turned back into a positive one: in what is given to us as universal, necessary, obligatory, what place is occupied by whatever is singular, contingent, and the product of arbitrary constraints? The point ... is to transform the critique conducted in the form of necessary limitation into a practical critique that takes the form of a possible transgression. (1984a: 45)

Transgression, however, should not be reified into a universal principle, such that every transgressive act or practice should be praised just by dint of being transgressive; Foucault's words point to the *possibility* of transgression, if it is required. The content of an act of transgression is, in a sense, not of intrinsic value. Any action or discourse repeated endlessly inevitably loses its transgressive force, as the rapid recuperation within the art establishment of modernist painting amply demonstrates. Foucault's point is not to ascribe any universal value to transgression, but rather to indicate the contemporary necessity of having the option of transgressing a particular discourse, sexual practice, disciplinary knowledge and so on. Transgression, curiously for some, no doubt, must proceed with caution or at least with a degree of realism, for it must 'put itself to the test of reality, of contemporary reality, both to grasp the points where change is possible and desirable, and to determine the precise form this change should take' (Foucault, 1984a: 46).

The transgression of particular disciplines recently has become more than a theoretical point for many subjects in the humanities and social sciences. The call for work termed interdisciplinary and cross-disciplinary has become a common feature in academic journals, conferences and names of degrees. Indeed it is the fundamental principle underlying, for example, Women's Studies (see Bowles and Klein, 1983). In addition, disciplines have also begun to address issues typically outside what Foucault calls their 'statutory domain' (1984f: 386), and here Foucault's work on the body, sexuality, governmentality and the nature of the human sciences has been particularly influential in 'problematising' both the questions disciplines ask of themselves and the answers they accept. Foucault himself indicated that we should pay attention to how disciplinary discourses appear as 'discontinuous practices, which cross each other, are sometimes juxtaposed with one another, but can just as well exclude or be unaware of each other' (1980g: 67).

Foucault's work has also influenced the terminology and conceptual apparatus of many subjects, with increased attention being paid, for example, to the role of discourses in constituting and maintaining social relations and subjects, or to the ways in which relations of power are implicit in the construction of specific forms of knowledge and truth. Perhaps the key influence Foucault has had for many people, and one which is shown in a number of the chapters in this book, is to draw attention to the ambivalent nature of terms such as 'subject' or 'discipline'. For Foucault a discipline is both an area of knowledge, a space to conduct enquiry and to probe for answers to novel questions, and a practice that systematically controls and orders that knowledge by a whole panoply of power relations that are implicit even in the smallest, and apparently most neutral and disinterested enquiry into knowledge. The message of texts such as *Discipline and Punish* is that the growth of knowledge – whether in reforms to prisons or the arrangement of school classrooms – always runs parallel with what Foucault termed 'the intensification of power relations' (Foucault, 1984a: 48). For academics today this kind of 'intensification' is felt in any number of disciplinary gatekeeping practices such as reviews of research output, monitoring of teaching quality, and peer-review of scholarly activity.

A number of the chapters here explore this ambiguous view of the idea of a discipline, some finding it a challenging and productive approach to the chosen area of study, others arguing that viewing power and knowledge as always combined in some agonistic fashion highlights major difficulties for Foucault's work and its applicability in other areas of study.

Apperley's chapter provides an overview of what Foucault offers in the way of a methodology for subjects in the humanities and social sciences. Unlike many earlier theorists, argues Apperley, the usefulness of Foucault consists in his 'openness to method', that is, his refusal to articulate any unified methodological principles other than a strategic use of different discourses and approaches. Apperley illustrates this argument by examining Alasdair MacIntyre's critique of Foucault. For MacIntyre, Foucault's work is characterised by an unsustainable and contradictory method of study (genealogy). Apperley shows how we cannot faithfully describe the entire work of Foucault as genealogical, due to the plurality of methods he utilised at various times. Trying to ascribe such a unity to his work simply misses the force and nuance of Foucault's challenge to orthodox notions of how an academic discipline operates. Foucault is an exemplar whose work, in Apperley's words, 'troubles the academy'.

This theme is continued in Thacker's account of how Foucault's work has been, or might be, taken up within a central discipline within the humanities and social sciences, that of history. After delineating Foucault's various comments upon history and historiography from the *Archaeology of Knowledge* onwards, the chapter examines how ideas such as historical discontinuity, the role of discourses in the writing of history, and of the need for sustained self-reflection by the historical writer have been used in what has become known as the 'post-modern turn' in social and economic historiography. Thacker suggests that the full implications of Foucault's challenge to the writing of history have perhaps not yet emerged, except in some versions of feminist history, and his chapter attempts to show how Foucault's transgressive idea of an 'historical ontology of the self' might be applied to recent debates in Irish historiography. Foucault's problematic notion of the 'history of the present' offers a set of challenges, argues Thacker, not only for history as a discipline but for any area of study that uses historical concepts and practices. As Foucault himself put it: 'History constitutes ... for the human sciences, a favourable environment which is both privileged and dangerous' (Foucault, 1970: 371).

These two chapters are weighted towards fairly detailed accounts of Foucault's own ideas whereas the next three chapters offer fuller applications of his work to other significant theoretical debates in the social sciences and humanities: the philosophical idea of freedom, feminist theory and feminist politics, and theories of international relations.

Magill's chapter focuses upon the problems raised by Foucault for one central problem in philosophy, the question of freedom. One traditional philosophical position argues that in order for an individual or a collectivity truly to be free there must be an absence of power relations, or at least a sufficient diminishment of them in order that freedom can be articulated fully. Foucault's work questions this assumption and Magill examines Foucault's ambivalent attitude towards the relationship between freedom and power by situating his work within the philosophical tradition of Stoicism. For the Stoic tradition freedom is a quality obtained through certain practices of goodness and reason which are identified as a person's essential self. Foucault's work challenges this idea in his insistence that there is no essential self, only a self constructed as an effect of power by modern disciplinary technologies, and thus hampered in their ability to be a 'free self'. Magill offers a strong defence of the Stoic conception of freedom by identifying weaknesses in Foucault's account of power and subjectivity. Despite these criticisms Magill suggests that philosophical conceptions of freedom have much to learn from Foucault's work: if we cannot escape from power perhaps we are able to utilise the monitoring mechanisms of modern forms of power in order to create new forms of freedom. Foucault's work, concludes Magill, reminds us that philosophical questions such as the nature of freedom must be framed within a discussion of what we are, and what we might become, as human subjects.

Lloyd's chapter presents a different approach to questions of subjectivity raised by Foucault by examining the political rather than philosophical consequences of his later theories for contemporary feminism. For Lloyd the issue is not who we are as free or unfree subjects but what it means to be a gendered and sexed subject. A number of feminist critics have argued that Foucault's work undermines much of the essence of feminism by querying the notion of a unitary political subject or agent (Woman) around which a feminist politics should be organised. Lloyd, however, shows that Foucault's later work on ethics (Volumes 2 and 3 of *The History of Sexuality*) offers feminism a different political agenda and a more productive conception of the subject. She traces how the same 'textual openness' in Foucault identified by Apperley has been used by feminists working in three areas: Elspeth Probyn in cultural studies, Rosalyn Diprose in ethics and Judith Butler in political philosophy. Lloyd argues that Foucault's examination of Greek ethics, 'the care of the self', helps identify potential strategies of transgression in the present world that may be of much political use to contemporary feminism. One example of this is Butler's notion that gendered identity is performative, extending Foucault's theory of an 'aesthetics of existence'. Lloyd shows how such developments of Foucault's ideas – sometimes transgressing fundamentally his own thinking – help destabilise current identities and point forward to transformed identities as gendered and sexed subjects. In this way, Lloyd shows how feminist politics might use Foucault's work to forge a way forward that avoids either a glibly universalising feminist subject (Woman) or a fractured and disabling form of identity politics.

If feminism has had an ambivalent relationship to Foucault's work then this is in marked contrast to the subject of international relations within political studies which has, until relatively recently, hardly engaged with Foucault or with any other form of post-structuralist or post-modernist thought. Hutchings' chapter presents an overview of a number of critics within international relations who are turning to Foucault in order to present more sophisticated accounts of the discipline, accounts that push beyond the current theoretical orthodoxies (such as realism and idealism). In particular Hutchings examines how writers such as Der Derian and Bartelson use Foucault's notion of genealogy to understand the role of the international relations theorist; and how Keeley and Forbes try to utilise Foucault to reassess problems in, respectively, regime theory and normative theory. Hutchings shows how all of these writers try to adapt Foucault's notion of transgressive critique, where the critic challenges, for example, the seemingly self-evident theoretical boundaries of the discipline as they are drawn by key concepts in international relations such as the idea of a 'regime', the notion of 'sovereignty', or the focus on 'inter-state relations'. Hutchings' assessment of these applications demonstrates, yet again, the problematic legacy of Foucault's ideas, shown in the way that different theorists are able to use Foucault either to enhance traditional understandings of international relations such as that of realism, or to radically overthrow orthodox theories.

The book then concludes with two case-studies which try to elucidate the impact of Foucault's theories for academics working on topics with a more immediately practical basis: immigration and 'race' relations in Britain since 1945, and recent government legislation on religious education in schools. Although both writers indicate difficulties with any easy assimilation of Foucault's ideas for their chosen area of study, together these chapters illustrate the rich and continuing challenge of his thought both for theoretical reflection and for issues of practical import.

Carter's chapter takes a critical stance on Foucault's usefulness for sociology, specifically the sociology of 'race'. This is an area in which, surprisingly, little work has, so far, been carried out using Foucault's ideas. Carter shows how such work might proceed, arguing that racism inscribes the body with a form of Foucauldian 'bio-power', where colour signifies a particular interpretation of the subject underneath their skin. Carter, however, also draws out the inherent tensions in Foucault's work for anyone trying to use it for the development of an anti-racist politics. Although Foucault offers much support for analyses of how in the contemporary world we become subjects for whom 'race thinking' is normal, and for whom 'race' is one form of 'truthful identity', Carter suggests that Foucault's refusal to specify an evaluative position disables any practically based political resistance to 'racism'. To illustrate this argument Carter discusses post-war British policies towards black immigration, showing how spurious 'regimes of truth' based upon the surveillance of black immigrants in Britain influenced subsequent government policies on citizenship and immigration legislation. Carter's historical analysis concludes by suggesting that Foucault's work is 'frustratingly abstract' when it comes to articulating how resistance to these racist 'regimes of truth' might proceed.

Cooper uses Foucault to explore the impact of legislation around worship and religious education in contemporary Britain, and argues that, to an extent, certain forms of centralised governmental action – such as the 1988 Education Act – have paradoxically empowered those most under attack by the actual legislation. Cooper's point is to demonstrate Foucault's conception of power as fluid and relational, focusing upon how law functions as a generative form of power rather than in a merely repressive or dominating fashion. She stresses how we need to examine the complexity of the effects of legislation which prescribed that Christianity should be central for both the compulsory daily act of worship in schools and the syllabuses of religious education. Rather than simply viewing it as a blanket means whereby the State extends its control over another aspect of daily life, and marginalises other religious faiths and beliefs in the context of an attack upon multiculturalism, Cooper shows how educationalist and community activists have organised tactically as a direct consequence of this legislation. By investigating how these disparate groups opposed to government legislation have proceeded, Cooper's microanalysis illustrates Foucault's point that resistance can occur through a discourse, here a legal one, which is not only 'an instrument and effect of power' but also 'a starting point for an opposing strategy' (Foucault: 1978, 101).

Although this book concentrates on the impact of Foucault's work on the humanities and social sciences, its authors do not advocate a canonical reading of Foucault. Rather, they argue, to different degrees, for an interpretation of Foucault's work as open, not just hermeneutically but in terms of its applicability to spheres of activity outside the confines of academia. This is exemplified most clearly in the chapters on race, the law and education, and feminism, where concerns of a broader political nature are to the forefront. However, it is also implied in most of the chapters in terms of reflections upon what we do as academic practitioners. Perhaps the dominant impact of Foucault's work has been to expose the rifts, instabilities and flaws in many diverse disciplines in the humanities and social sciences, leading to the sorts of fresh and alternative modes of analysis and enquiry demonstrated in this book. But Foucault's work also reveals that the position from which academics speak and work, within the borders of a discipline or the norms and values of a particular institution, is also ground that stirs and shifts and might, upon reflection, be ripe for transgression.

NOTE

1. Clearly Foucault's use of the term 'critical' changes after the writing of this text, for he also avers that genealogy is itself a 'critical' project (see Foucault, 1984b; 1988b).

1   Foucault and the Problem of Method

Alan Apperley

What, do you imagine that I would take so much trouble and so much pleasure in writing, do you think I would keep so persistently to my task, if I were not preparing – with a rather shaky hand – a labyrinth into which I can venture, in which I can move my discourse, opening up underground passages, forcing it to go far from itself, finding overhangs that reduce and deform its itinerary, in which I can lose myself and appear at last to eyes that I will never have to meet again. (Foucault, 1972a: 17)

Introduction

Michel Foucault can be all things to all people. Indeed, this is something Foucault himself acknowledged, and apparently endorsed (Foucault, 1984e: 376; 1984f: 383–4). Despite this 'protean'[1] aspect of Foucault's work, he has nevertheless come to be associated primarily with a genealogical approach to the study of the human sciences. One writer who endorses this association is Alasdair MacIntyre. In his *Three Rival Versions of Moral Enquiry* (1990), MacIntyre continues and advances his account of the Enlightenment Project begun in *After Virtue* (1981). Of the three versions of moral enquiry identified in the later text, two – the encyclopaedic and the genealogical – are clearly related to the Enlightenment Project.[2] But whilst the encyclopaedic tradition upholds the Enlightenment aspiration to universal standards of truth and rationality, the genealogical tradition seeks, or so MacIntyre claims, to subvert this aspiration. It is in the context of the genealogical tradition that MacIntyre discusses Foucault.

I am not concerned in this chapter to defend the general account MacIntyre gives of the Enlightenment Project. I do, however, wish to defend Foucault against MacIntyre's attempt to implicate him in the genealogical tradition. This will seem odd to those, like MacIntyre, for whom Foucault is primarily a genealogist. Nevertheless, I will argue that Foucault's thoughts and comments on questions of method problematise genealogy itself sufficiently to prevent any straightforward association between Foucault and genealogy. In order to establish my claim, it will be necessary to examine the relationship in Foucault's work of three key issues – power, subjectivity and method.

The social sciences and humanities have always been troubled by questions of method. While the natural sciences study a mechanical, law-governed universe, the social sciences and humanities have as their object the social life of self-interpreting human beings. In studying such beings, the investigator must at some point address and compensate for the constraints that are perceived to operate on self-understanding, whether institutional, structural or psychological. But at some point, of course, the social scientist must also confront those institutional, structural and psychological constraints acting not just upon the objects of investigation, but also upon the investigator. Here we encounter a reflexive problem, for there might be no guarantees that the investigator can either adequately identify or sufficiently compensate for those constraining factors in his or her own self-analyses.

Into this fraught arena of debate we might introduce, as one potential defence against this reflexive problem, the integrity of a particular method. For it might be possible to develop a method of enquiry that offers some guarantee of objectivity, of truth amongst a welter of interpretations. Some such hope is at least one characteristic of the Enlightenment Project. It is therefore with MacIntyre's account of the Enlightenment Project that I begin.

MacIntyre: Enlightenment and Method

In *After Virtue* (1981) MacIntyre characterises the Enlightenment Project as the attempt to provide 'an independent rational justification of morality' (1981: 38); independent, that is, both of any social, historical and cultural context and of any specific account of the Good Life for humankind.[3] In 1988 MacIntyre delivered the Gifford Lectures at the University of Edinburgh. That venue's associations with the key figures of the Scottish Enlightenment prompted MacIntyre to reflect upon the implications of his arguments concerning the fate of the Enlightenment Project within academia. The results of MacIntyre's reflections were published as *Three Rival Versions of Moral Enquiry* (1990).

In this text MacIntyre develops his account of the Enlightenment Project in terms of a tradition to which he assigns the label 'encyclopaedic'. The premises upon which the encyclopaedic tradition rests are broadly speaking those identified with the Enlightenment Project in *After Virtue*. These premises include a 'unitary conception of rationality and of the rational mind' such that 'all rational persons conceptualize data in one and the same way' (1990: 16–17). This unitary view of rationality had implications for the pursuit of knowledge, for it underpinned a belief that knowledge itself could be unified. The task of science was precisely to demonstrate this unity through the methodical application of reason to facts. What is more, the successful outcome of this process led to 'continuous progress in supplying ever more adequate unifying conceptions which specify ever more fundamental laws' (1990: 20). Thus science had a history, 'one of relatively continuous progress' (1990: 20). These aspects of the Enlightenment Project are, MacIntyre claims, encapsulated in and exemplified by the Ninth Edition of the *Encyclopaedia Britanica*. The encyclopaedic intellectual posits: 'a single framework within which knowledge is discriminated from mere belief, progress towards knowledge is mapped, and truth is understood as the relationship of *our* knowledge to *the* world' (1990: 42, emphases in original). The Enlightenment Project also gave rise to a specific understanding of the role of method in the pursuit of universal truth and knowledge. According to MacIntyre, encyclopaedic knowledge and truth is obtained 'through the application of those methods whose rules are the rules of rationality as such' (1990: 42).

MacIntyre's claim at this point concerns, not the unity of knowledge as such – for that is the *aspiration* of scholarly endeavour – but rather the unity of *method*. As he puts it, sciences in the nineteenth century were 'generally taken to be individuated by their subject matter, not by their methods' (1990: 19). The Enlightenment Project's aspiration to the unity of truth and knowledge depended upon the development of a secure rational method, the application of which to the diversity of facts would yield the rational unity that lay behind that apparent diversity. Encyclopaedists believed, MacIntyre claims, that 'methodical reflection upon the facts' would supply the 'unifying synthetic conceptions' that comprised comprehensive, encyclopaedic knowledge (1990: 20).

Although MacIntyre locates his discussion of the encyclopaedic tradition in the nineteenth century, the aspiration to develop an incorrigible method with which to guide one's investigations can be observed running through many of the canonical texts of the seventeenth, eighteenth and nineteenth centuries. The aspiration is there in the work, for example, of a seminal Enlightenment figure such as Descartes who, perhaps better than anyone else, characterises both the concern with finding an incorrigible method with which to proceed, and recognition of the potential such a method might have in terms of explanatory scope. For Descartes, truth will not emerge spontaneously, nor will it emerge through an untutored reason. That all men have the capacity to reason is, for Descartes, an uncontentious starting-point (Wilson, 1969: 107). But it does not follow that all men reason alike, for the 'natural light' of reason is confounded by 'unregulated inquiries and confused reflections' condemning its possessors to walk in darkness (Wilson, 1969: 44). In order to avoid this darkness, it is important for Descartes that reason proceed *methodically*. Reason is a loose cannon without a method to guide it, and a method, for Descartes, is straightforwardly a set of 'simple rules' (Wilson, 1969: 44).[4]

Descartes, of course, is not the only Enlightenment precursor who sought to protect the integrity of rational enquiry through the imposition of a set of rules or guidelines. Bacon's *Novum Organon* (1620), Hobbes' *Leviathan* (1651) and Spinoza's *On the Improvement of the Understanding* (1660) all attest to the importance of method as a defence against confusion, error and superstition. Indeed, so important was method deemed to be that even when erroneous conclusions were reached, a thinker could still be admired and respected for proceeding methodically. As Voltaire remarked of Descartes (Voltaire, 1980: 72): 'He was wrong, *but at least methodically*.'[5] For enlightened thinkers such as Voltaire, an incorrigible method would provide the thread that would eventually lead them out of the labyrinth and into the light.

MacIntyre: Subversion and Genealogy

Against the encyclopaedic tradition with its aspirations to comprehensive-ness and universality, MacIntyre posits the genealogical tradition. What distinguishes this latter tradition from the former is its conviction that truth, knowledge and rationality are always evidence of 'membership in a culture' (1990: 35). The genealogist 'takes there to be a multiplicity of perspectives within each of which truth-from-a-point of view may be asserted, but no truth-as-such, an empty notion, about *the* world, an equally empty notion' (1990: 42, emphasis in original).

MacIntyre's point here is that the genealogist aspires not to provide an alternative 'truth' to that of the encyclopaedist but rather to show how canons of truth and rationality such as those presupposed by the encyclopaedic perspective function to mask the play of power in human relationships.[6] Nietzsche's 'The Genealogy of Morals' shows us, for example, how morality, itself a human artefact, had been both transformed and distorted in the service of Christianity.

In contesting the existence of universal truth, the genealogist simultaneously contests the status of academic endeavour as it has come to be practised by encyclopaedic intellectuals working within the humanities and social sciences. MacIntyre's claim is that genealogy aspires to be subversive of those institutions and practices that embody this aspiration to comprehensiveness and unity. In fact, MacIntyre claims that the subversiveness of genealogy, if taken seriously, ultimately drives the genealogist out of the citadel: 'To be, and not to rebel against being, a member of the professoriate or of its disciples is to be a deformed person ... [complicit] in a system of suppressions and repressions' (1990: 35). Thus Nietzsche removed himself from the academic life when he resigned his chair at Basel in 1879, signalling the incom-patibility of the encyclopaedic aspirations of the academy with those of the genealogist. In the late twentieth century, the situation as characterised by MacIntyre is such that the genealogical project – like the encyclopaedic project to which it is a counterpart (1990: 43) – has itself failed.[7] The reasons for this failure are internal to the genealogical project itself and turn, MacIntyre claims, on 'standards of reason-giving, reason-accepting, and reason-rejecting' (1990: 45). MacIntyre's point here is that if genealogy is to be thoroughgoing it must be able not only to put *encyclopaedic* claims to truth into question, but also to put its *own* claims into question. Yet the ability to do this, contends MacIntyre, requires 'a fixity of stance, a staying in place, a commitment to defend and to respond and, if necessary, to yield' (1990: 45). The genealogist, like the encyclopaedist, must appeal to 'impersonal, timeless standards' (1990: 45) in order to communicate with others. It is precisely the existence of such standards that MacIntyre takes the genealogist to be challenging. Moreover, the existence of such standards implies, MacIntyre argues, a fixity of self to whom those standards apply.[8] In denying this fixity – and unity – of self the genealogist undermines the intelligibility of the genealogical project, at least as MacIntyre construes this (1990: 54–5).

In challenging the Enlightenment Project's pursuit of encyclopaedic knowledge, the genealogist also challenges the project of finding an incorrigible method that would protect the integrity of truth and knowledge. If, as MacIntyre claims, the encyclopaedist makes the rules of rationality stand for the rules of method as such, then in challenging the unity of truth and reason, the genealogist at one and the same time subverts method in its 'encyclopaedic' role as a guarantor both of rational progress and, ultimately, 'of truth itself.' Thus the genealogist implicates method in the play of power, teaching us: 'That there are no rules of rationality as such to be appealed to, there are rather strategies of insight and subversion' (1990: 42).

Leaving aside, for the moment, the alleged internal difficulties of the genealogical project, it is Foucault who provides MacIntyre with a graphic illustration of what he claims is the 'progressive impoverishment' of the genealogical project (1990: 55). MacIntyre alleges that Foucault avoided progressive impoverishment in his own work only by 'drawing less and less covertly upon nongenealogical sources and methods' until finally arriving at the 'plain academic style' of *The History of Sexuality*. In the process, Foucault unfortunately restores 'Nietzsche's project to the professoriate from which Nietzsche had rescued it' (1990: 53–5).

Having outlined the role of method in MacIntyre's account of the Enlightenment Project, and having located Foucault in relation to this account, it is appropriate at this point to turn to Foucault himself. I will begin with an account of power, as Foucault understands it, before relating it to the issues of subjectivity and method.

Foucault: Power and Method

Traditionally, knowledge has been seen as a defence against power. The classic instruments of repression have therefore usually involved restrictions on truth and knowledge in the forms of curtailment of debate, misinformation, disinformation or mystification. As a defence against such practices truth and knowledge are precious currency. But rather than seeing truth and knowledge as defences *against* power, Foucault implicates them *in* power: '[T]ruth isn't outside power, or lacking in power ... it is produced only by virtue of multiple forms of constraint. And it induces regular effects of power' (1980d: 131). Orthodox accounts of power have tended to see it as a property, of groups, individuals, classes – that is, of *agents* – or as the property of *structures*. Foucault, however, locates power at the level of discursive formations which make possible specific truths and knowledges and which also make possible specific kinds of agents and structures. It is, as Foucault says, 'in discourse that power and knowledge are joined together' (1978: 100). Foucault therefore does not see power as fixed in particular individuals, classes, structures or institutions for it 'ends by forming a dense web that passes through apparatuses and institutions' (1978: 95–6; 1977a: 26–7). Such power is thoroughly pervasive 'not because it embraces everything, but because it comes from everywhere' (1978: 93). Power as Foucault understands it is not located at a central point such as the State, nor is it located in sovereign individuals or classes. The fact that orthodox accounts of power take it to be so is itself to be understood as an *effect* of power.

Foucault understands the orthodox view to hold that power has solely a repressive or negative function. Foucault does not deny that power has this repressive function, but believes that power also has productive and positive capacities (Foucault 1980b: 59). What is more, power constitutes a set of conditions whose repressive or productive aspects are not given in advance of their instantiation in a particular institutional setting, or in a particular practice or set of practices. We cannot say of any particular institution or practice that it is *necessarily* repressive (as, for example, an anarchist might of the State) for power has productive aspects too. Power, for example, produces also the possibility of *resistance* to power (1978: 95–6). Like power itself, points of resistance to power traverse 'social stratifications and individual unities' and are therefore themselves 'mobile and transitory' (1978: 96). It is for this reason that Foucault can claim that 'everything is dangerous' (1984d: 343).

Foucault's reluctance to identify power as the property of powerful individuals, groups or classes can lead to the criticism that Foucault diverts attention away from actual power struggles. But this is to miss Foucault's point, for if it is the case that power can be positive as well as negative, productive as well as repressive, it is also always fragile and liable to be thwarted (1978: 101). Thus Foucault's claim that power is not monopolised within the traditional, sovereign centres such as the State, if taken seriously, might actually be empowering, for if everything *is* dangerous, 'then we always have something to do. So my position leads not to apathy but to a hyper- and pessimistic activism' (1984d: 343). On this understanding of power, nothing is ever finally settled for there is always everything to play for.

Implicating truth in the play of power, as Foucault does, clearly undercuts the Enlightenment belief that truth is ultimately beyond the reach of power. But what of method? As we have already seen, in terms of the Enlightenment Project method was to have guided us out of the clutches of power into the pure realm of truth. Yet we should not be surprised to find that Foucault implicates method also in his analysis of power.

One of the possible effects of power, for example, is that it might have a disciplinary function.[9] Power normalises. We should not then be surprised to find that method is implicated itself as a normalising procedure. Indeed, for a writer like Kuhn, the characterisation of 'normal science' in part refers to the methods utilised by its practitioners (Kuhn, 1970: 10). Thus it is in part the methods that one employs that characterises one as a genuine practitioner of mature science, as opposed to a charlatan or quack. Popper, for example, recognised that one implication of his attempts to correctly characterise scientific method is the demarcation of genuine practitioners ('scientists') from charlatans ('pseudo-scientists'). Even Popper's arch-enemy, Marxism, proclaims itself to be a *scientific* socialism, producing its own demarcation line exemplified in Engels' pamphlet, *Socialism: Utopian and Scientific*.

If such methodological disputes are themselves an effect of power as Foucault understands it, then these disputes might also result in repressive or productive situations. There is, for example, no doubt that such disputes can resolve themselves in the interests of particular individuals, groups or classes. If we acknowledge Descartes' claim that methodology is regulative – effectively comprising of a set rules or codes – then we can understand Foucault's statement that 'the successes of history belong to those who are capable of seizing these rules' (Foucault, 1984b: 86).

Foucault does not mean by this that history is agent-centred, a narrative of the victors, for it is not given in advance that any particular group will be in a position to benefit from the appropriation of a methodology. The point is that in themselves '[r]ules are empty ... violent and unfinalized; they are impersonal and can be bent to any purpose' (1984b: 85–6). One does not know in advance of the resolution of a dispute, what the possibilities –

negative or positive – in the resulting situation will be. We should not therefore expect the repressive or productive aspects of method to be given in advance either. It is a matter for analysis, and specifically for an 'analytic' of power concerned with the 'singularity of events' (1984b: 76).

This tentative conclusion does not exhaust Foucault's consideration of method, for implicating method in the grids of power does not address the problem of subjectivity to which I referred at the beginning of this chapter. It is to this issue that I now turn.

Foucault: Subjectivity and Genealogy

Towards the end of his life, Foucault came to see his own work as part of a project of self-transformation, a form of aesthetic experience.[10] This might seem odd given that Foucault elsewhere appeared to challenge the very idea of the 'self', underpinned as it is by notions of subjectivity, identity and Enlightenment conceptions of personal responsibility (Foucault, 1984a: 49–50). One of the abiding images from Foucault's work is that which occurs at the very end of *The Order of Things*. It is that one day 'Man' will disappear – 'erased, like a face drawn in sand at the edge of the sea' (1970: 387). On the basis of such phrases a belief in the 'death of the subject' as such is sometimes carelessly attributed to Foucault. But whereas it is certainly the case that Foucault calls subjectivity into question, he does not preach its death as an imperative. Rather, he seeks to examine the conditions of its present constitution and the possibility of its reconstitution. Since the self is a product of specific configurations of power, it becomes a spatially and temporally located phenomenon and one that is itself shot through with both negative and positive, productive and repressive possibilities. It is no surprise to find that in putting the Enlightenment idea of the sovereign self to the question, Foucault also finds the idea of 'an author' problematic too.[11] Since it is inevitably through his writing that Foucault pursues these issues, it will be necessary to consider Foucault's statements on method in more detail. I begin this task, however, with a brief consideration of the relationship between archaeology and genealogy.

MacIntyre identifies Foucault as a representative of the genealogical tradition. Yet, as is often noted, Foucault's turn to genealogy occurs after *The Archaeology of Knowledge*, published in 1969 (Foucault, 1972a). It is also often noted that this period marks variously a turn, or return, to Nietzsche on Foucault's part; the emergence of Foucault's interest in the analysis of power, itself a prelude to Foucault's interest in subjectivity (Foucault, 1982: 209); and his prioritising of practices, institutions and normalising techniques over fields of knowledge (discourses or epistemes). The reasons for the shift to genealogy are the subject of speculation both as to why this shift occurred, and as to what the implications of the move were for Foucault's *oeuvre*. In terms of why the shift happened, some see a reflective concern with the limitations of the archaeological project (Dreyfus and Rabinow, 1982: 79–100), whilst others see in this shift a response to the failures of the 1968 'revolution' in France (Habermas, 1987a: 256; Kritzman, in Foucault 1988f: ix–xiv).[12] Foucault himself tended to reclassify his earlier works in the light of his present concerns, so that his archaeological writings became part of his genealogical concerns, which in turn became part of his aesthetico-ethical project (Flynn, 1994: 28).

It might be tempting to see in Foucault's post-archaeology shift an abandonment of the archaeological method. Such a discontinuity would not be out of place given Foucault's challenge to continuous and progressive histories (Foucault, 1984b: 88; 1972a esp. 'Introduction'; Flynn, 1994: 28).[13] However, Foucault himself indicated that archaeology and genealogy might be complementary, and hinted that each might be mapped on to a branch of the power/knowledge dyad, genealogy concerning itself with power whilst archaeology concerns itself with knowledge (Foucault, 1980c: 87; cf. 1972b, 234; Dreyfus and Rabinow, 1982: 104–5; Davidson, 1986: 221–33). On the basis of the claim that both approaches were always present in Foucault's work, some commentators have suggested that after *The Archaeology of Knowledge* it is the priority accorded to each element that is altered. Up to this point, it is suggested, archaeology had been prioritised over genealogy. But in *Discipline and Punish* and *The History of Sexuality* archaeology is 'subordinated to genealogy' (Dreyfus and Rabinow, 1982: 102–3). It has also been suggested that from this point onwards 'practice, on all levels, is considered more fundamental than theory' in Foucault's work (Dreyfus and Rabinow, 1982: 103; cf. MacIntyre, 1990: 49).

Such debates as these indicate the difficulty of fixing the place of archaeology and genealogy in Foucault's writings. Yet I think that this difficulty is increasingly recognised by Foucault himself, and put to productive use in his work. This can be illustrated via a consideration of Foucault's complex and subtle relationship to Marxism, a relationship of which he often deferred direct discussion.[14]

Foucault was especially critical of Marxism from the perspective of his account of power, arguing that both Marxism and Liberalism share a common view of power as centralised and repressive (Foucault, 1980c: 88–9; 1980d: 115–22; also Clegg, 1989: 183; Sawicki, 1991: 51–2). Yet his critical attitude on this issue belies his more general openness to Marxism.[15] One of the admirable characteristics of Marxism, for example, is its concern to take the relationship between theory and practice seriously. But despite this concern, it is sometimes the case that Marxists foreclose the possibility that their analyses might lead them beyond the parameters of a class-based politics. From this position, the relationship between theory and practice is never allowed free reign, since it is always assumed at the outset that the class dimension will reassert itself 'in the final analysis'.[16] One might say, with Poster, that the theory of class struggle has come to dominate over practice (Poster, 1984: 59).[17]

Foucault, on the other hand, is willing to allow class a role in the power relations that characterise society but not at the expense of other factors. Despite the complex relationship between theory and practice that is implicit in Marx's writings, the unwillingness to read power in anything other than class terms might be characterised as a dogmatic reluctance to admit this complexity. For Foucault, the grid of power relations is not reducible to any single explanatory characteristic but can plausibly be characterised in a number of ways. Thus Foucault does not simply shift his concerns from theory to practice, as Dreyfus and Rabinow claim, but rather allows that it is always an open question as to which assumes, or ought to be accorded, priority. Marxists will always have either the security of class struggle or 'dialectical materialism' to guide them on their travels, or they will have the harbour of communism at the end of their journey. But Foucault does not presuppose where his analysis will take him. As he remarked in the introduction to *The Archaeology of Knowledge*: 'Do not ask me who I am *and do not ask me to remain the same*' (Foucault, 1972a: 17, emphasis added).[18]

Foucault refuses the label 'Marxist' as he refuses most attempts to fix him as one thing rather than another. He is, to borrow a term from Deleuze, a *nomad* – one who continually evades the 'codes of settled people' (Deleuze, 1985: 149) – where these codes are theories such as those of Marxists and Freudians that both totalize and reassure (Foucault, 1984h: xi-xiv). Like Deleuze's Nietzsche, it is at the level of *method* that Foucault is at his most nomadic (Deleuze, 1985: 146).[19] In order to establish this claim more securely, we need to look more closely at Foucault's own comments on method. But we must also look at his methodological practices, for the question is not always one of *why* Foucault proceeds as he does but sometimes rather of *how* (Foucault, 1984h: xii).

Method as Strategy

In common with his rejection of systematic and totalising philosophies, we should not be surprised to find that Foucault's own writings avoid system and totality. This is no less the case with regard to his writings on method. By the time of his shift to genealogy Foucault had already written and published two books – *The Order of Things* and *The Archaeology of Knowledge* – that he himself would later describe as methodological (Foucault, 1991c: 28). We have already noticed that it is at this time that Foucault begins to turn his attention to the question of the nature and constitution of subjectivity and the possibility of its reconstitution (Gutting, 1994: 11–12). As we have seen already, Foucault had concluded *The Order of Things* anticipating the 'death of Man', by which we may understand him to mean the death of a particular configuration of subjectivity. But this particular 'death' opens up a range of possibilities for reconstituting subjectivity. As Foucault elsewhere acknowledged:

> It is not enough, however, to keep repeating the empty affirmation that the author has disappeared. For the same reason, it is not enough to keep repeating (after Nietzsche) that God and man have died a common death. Instead, we must locate the space left empty by the author's disappearance, follow the distribution of gaps and breaches, and watch for the openings that this disappearance uncovers. (Foucault, 1984c: 105)

Language, knowledge and the writing of history comprise the subject-matter of these 'methodological' works. It is the limiting functions of epistemes (in *The Order of Things*) and discursive formations (in *The Archaeology of Knowledge*) that raise with Foucault the problem of power as both that which limits (the repressive function) and that which facilitates the transgression of limits (the productive function). It is also through this subject-matter that Foucault encounters the limits not just of subjectivity and the self in universal terms, but of his own specific subjectivity, his own specific self. For in attempting to think through the problem of limits, Foucault directly encounters the limits of what can be thought, even if he cannot recognise precisely what those limits are because they are 'preconceptual'.[20] However, it is clear that Foucault is interested in somehow getting at the limiting elements of discourse, of finding some way of exploring the liminal regions of the discursive grid that both produces and defines 'Foucault'. That he is unclear precisely how to proceed at this point accounts for the troubled tone of some of the writing in *The Archaeology of Knowledge*, as the following passage demonstrates:

> I am trying to elucidate in itself – in order to measure it and to determine its requirements – a possibility of description that I have used without being aware of its constraints and resources; rather than trying to discover what I said, and what I might have said, I shall try to reveal, in its own regularity – a regularity that I have not yet succeeded in mastering – what made it possible to say what I did. (Foucault, 1972a: 114)

The writing of history might provide Foucault with one possible strategy for solving this problem since historical study must reveal in it traces of the present. The task, in a sense, is not to look directly at the present since this will always escape us (rather like the enemy that continually dodges behind us whenever we turn our head). Instead, we look off into the distance in order to uncover information about where we are standing (rather like those 3-D 'magic eye' images that resist direct attempts to 'see' them, the point being that if you look for them directly you don't see them). Under such circumstances it is not surprising that Foucault described his subsequent projects as histories of the present.[21]

The solution to this problem, as Dreyfus and Rabinow demonstrate at length, is contingent upon Foucault abandoning the position of detached commentator upon discourse-objects (Dreyfus and Rabinow, 1982: 102). The troubled tone of *The Archaeology* is in part then a product of Foucault's recognition that he is immersed in, and produced by, the objects he is studying. He is both the bearer of a discourse and a sign of it, and he cannot represent that discourse to himself without enacting it.[22] The liminal characteristics of discourses then are present not just in the objects of Foucault's studies in all their variety, but are interiorised in Foucault himself too – as the account of panoptic power subsequently demonstrates (1977a: 195–228; 1980e: 155).[23] To say that the discourses of power are 'interiorised' in Foucault himself might appear to presume a dichotomous relationship between interiority and exteriority. For Foucault, however, such a dichotomy would not be an *a priori* category, but would itself have been constituted by specific relations of power. This would imply the possibility of going beyond this particular dichotomy to arrive at some new configuration. Part of this 'going beyond' involves the recognition that understanding the situation in this way produces the situation as one understands it. Self-knowledge is therefore self-production, but it is production within limits. As Foucault later explicitly acknowledges: '[b]etween techniques of knowledge and strategies of power, there is no exteriority' (1978: 98). This claim extends, of course, to those techniques – methods such as archaeology and genealogy – employed by Foucault himself.

It is at this time that Foucault begins to explore the possibilities and implications of the disappearance of 'Foucault' the author, who writes precisely 'in order to have no face' (1972a: 17). Where the self has been thoroughly problematised, even self-knowledge is potentially a form of subjection to a sovereign self or to one's own identity (1982: 212).[24] Writing 'in order to have no face' therefore assumes, like the writing of history, the role of tactic in Foucault's intellectual armoury. It is a tactic which Foucault would still be resorting to over a decade later (1988e; 1988c: 52–3)[25] and one which appears to have met with a measure of success, something Foucault later acknowledged with some satisfaction (1984e: 376; 1984f: 383–4). The point needs to be stressed that Foucault's purpose in problematising notions of the self in this way is not to pass through the tyranny of an identity into some realm of limitless freedom beyond all identities. It is rather to establish the limits of the identity he has in order to explore the possibility of reconstituting those limits. One cannot locate a position beyond power but one can potentially locate and exploit the points of resistance within power in order to reconstitute the self and its environment. One cannot know in advance what the implications of this reconstitution will be (which is at least one reason why everything is dangerous), but this is no reason not to proceed: 'When you know in advance where you're going to end up there's a whole dimension of experience lacking' (Foucault, 1988c: 48).

This exploration of the limits of discourse and identity takes the strategic form of an openness towards method. Foucault, I believe, is increasingly aware that particular approaches to the study of social phenomena deliver up particular kinds of knowledges, since they are at one and the same time instantiations of the 'dense web' of power that enlaces and intersects society. But particular approaches also deliver up particular kinds of experiences, and different ways of experiencing the social world. The point is that different methods delineate particular fields of knowledge and experience. Thus 'historical materialism' as a method of approach to the study of social phenomena both produces and limits the object of analysis – productive relations – and both facilitates and names the experience of class struggle. Similarly, genealogy both facilitates and names the experience of fragmentation and discontinuity in history and social life. The existence of a plurality of methods then both facilitates and names a plurality of possible experiences. On this basis the utilisation of a particular method clearly rules out 'a whole dimension of experience'. But on the other hand the adoption of a method might make it possible to experience the world in a way that one has not yet experienced it. Openness towards method, then, is at one and the same time openness towards experience.[26]

Method and Practice

This openness can clearly be seen operating in Volume 1 of Foucault's *The History of Sexuality*. This particular text can itself be described as a methodological introduction to the series of monographs on sexuality that Foucault, at that time, was planning to write, or had begun to write. Yet it contains a short section in which Foucault puts forward, almost in a parody of Descartes' *Rules*, 'some general propositions concerning the objective, the method, the domain to be covered, and the periodizations that one can accept in a provisory way' (Foucault, 1978: 80).

These 'general' and 'provisory' propositions constitute a set of hypotheses which will situate Foucault's investigations. Moreover, he goes on to state explicitly in the section entitled 'Method' that the four methodological rules he sets out 'are not intended as methodological imperatives' but are 'at most ... cautionary prescriptions' (1978: 98). For those such as MacIntyre's encyclopaedists who expect method to act as a guide, it is disconcerting to notice that Foucault treats method itself as hypothetical. But it should not by now be surprising to find that Foucault does not expect his method to *govern* the investigation of his chosen subject-matter. The veiled presence of 'logos' in the term 'methodological' should alert us to this. After all, Foucault rejects the 'monotonous finality' (Foucault, 1984b: 76) of progressive teleology that even methodological anarchists like Feyerabend cannot bring themselves to erase from their work (Feyerabend, 1975: *passim*). In the light of our previous discussion of the position of the methodologist (perhaps 'methodician' would be more appropriate) as both constrained and produced by the relations of power, it is not surprising to find that in the section entitled 'Method', what Foucault *actually* gives us is an extended discussion of *power* (1978: 92–102).

Foucault's researches problematise method such that it is only with hindsight and on completion of a work that Foucault can 'deduce a methodology' (Foucault, 1991c: 28).[27] But this does not allow the production of a *general* method. As Foucault puts it: 'Each of my books is a way of dismantling an object, and of constructing a method of analysis toward that end' (1991c: 28). Thus the strategy of openness towards method itself requires an openness to the subject-matter to be studied (Gutting, 1994: 14). The diversity of subject-matter implies a diversity of methods. This is exemplified by the fact that in *Discipline and Punish* there are also 'four general rules' that provide a temporary framework for Foucault's study of prisons and punishment, none of which bear any relation to those found in *The History of Sexuality* since they are specific to the subject-matter of that text (Foucault, 1977a: 23–4). The question then of which methodological strategy is appropriate to an object of study cannot be divorced from the question of what is it that makes that object available to the investigator. In the case of sexuality, for example, there is an explicit answer to this latter question: 'If sexuality was constituted as an area of investigation, this was only because relations of power had established it as a possible target' (Foucault, 1978: 98).

Both the subject-matter under investigation and the methods deemed appropriate to that investigation will bear traces of the relations of power as they are presently constituted. Thus in practice there is 'no fixed, definite rule' but only a 'series of precise considerations' available to the investigator (1991c: 28). Foucault's methodological writings do not therefore comprise a general method and are not prescriptive, not even for Foucault himself (Foucault, 1991c: 29; Dean, 1994: 134).

My claim, then, is that, for Foucault, method and experience share a close interior relationship, such that openness towards method is at one and the same time openness towards experience. Rather than simply burrow deeper into an ideology – whether this be 'Bourgeois science' or 'Scientific Socialism' – Foucault's strategy is to employ a variety of methods in order to experience 'the multiplicity of force relations' (1978: 92) that enlace and intersect in 'Foucault'. Foucault explicitly recognised that his theoretical work was rooted in experience and that particular pieces of work were 'fragments of autobiography' (1988d: 156). It is not then implausible to conclude that Foucault's later experiments with drugs and sado-masochism are a practical continuation of his academic project, an attempt by Foucault to transgress the limits of his own identity utilising a variety of methods. This is no facile libertarianism, however, for as we have seen, to engage in transgressive practices is not *necessarily* to evade the repressive aspects of power.[28]

It is appropriate at this point to return to MacIntyre's critique of what he calls Foucault's (and Nietzsche's) genealogical project. There are specifically two points I wish to address: the first concerns Foucault's tactic of problematising the self; the second concerns the practice of genealogy as a subversion of traditional academic practices.

Subverting Genealogy: Foucault *contra* MacIntyre

In *Three Rival Versions of Moral Enquiry* MacIntyre mounts a critique of Foucault's attempt to problematise the self. As we have seen, Foucault at times pursued this task through the strategy of writing 'in order to have no face'.[29] MacIntyre reads this tactical move in straightforward Nietzschean terms as the successive wearing of masks:

> The problem... for the genealogist is how to combine the fixity of particular stances, exhibited in the use of standard genres of speech and writing, with the mobility of transition from stance to stance, how to assume the contours of a given mask and then to discard it for another, without ever assenting to the metaphysical fiction of a face which has its own finally true and undiscardable representation. (1990: 47)

MacIntyre's point is that any form of communication, whether between the self and others, or between the self as it presently is and the self as it was or will be, assumes a minimal metaphysical commitment on the part of that self to 'standards of reason-giving, reason-accepting and reason-rejecting' (MacIntyre, 1990: 45). But the question is just how minimal a commitment must this be? In setting out his narrative account of the self MacIntyre acknowledges that there are constraints on how we construct the story that we tell about our selves, but goes on to note that: 'within those constraints there are indefinitely many ways that it [that is, the story] can continue' (MacIntyre, 1981: 201).

We may not make our own selves just as we please, but even MacIntyre appears to agree that we are inventive enough within those constraints to reconstitute ourselves in an indefinite variety of ways. After all, if mythology is at the heart of things as MacIntyre claims (1981: 201) then it is necessary to allow inventiveness since no myth is given *a priori*, and no myth is entirely immutable.[30] Even on MacIntyre's own terms, therefore, we may come to appreciate the nature of whatever constraints exist by adopting precisely the tactic of reconstituting ourselves.[31] It is this tactic that I attribute to Foucault. As I have suggested, Foucault's use of this tactic is not designed to serve the purpose of eradicating 'Foucault' once and for all, which would be impossible. It is rather designed to explore the limits of what is possible. In this sense genealogy is 'gray' (1984b: 76) not because it involves meticulous, detailed and possibly dull work, but because it operates in a twilight zone on the border between meaning and the absence of meaning, in much the same way that Joyce's *Finnegans Wake* could be said to have done.

It remains to assess MacIntyre's critique of Foucault as academician. As we have seen, MacIntyre reads genealogy as aspiring to be subversive of the academy (MacIntyre, 1990: 32–57). Whilst Nietzsche had the good sense to remove himself from the academy, Foucault wound up as a respected member of the academy in a position of some authority. Does this fact in itself signal the failure, or at least the taming, of the genealogical project? I do not think it does, for the straightforward reason that there is no 'genealogical project' as such in Foucault's work. As we have seen, genealogy is only one amongst a variety of methodological strategies (including, as we have seen, archaeology and transgressive practices) that Foucault employed, and whose deployment depends on a variety of factors including the subject-matter under scrutiny (and no doubt also biographical facts about the investigator). As we have seen, Foucault's strategy of openness to method precludes the reductive description of Foucault as a 'genealogist'. What is more, Foucault himself recognised that genealogies 'run the risk of re-codification, re-colonisation' (Foucault, 1980c: 86) and could therefore be made to serve repressive as well as productive functions. The uses to which genealogy can be put are no more given in advance of their deployment than is the case with any other method. Contrary to MacIntyre's claim, there is nothing that is *necessarily* subversive about genealogy and there is nothing *necessarily* reactionary about occupying a position within the academy, regardless of whether or not one is a 'genealogist'.

For those of us who work within the humanities and the social sciences, the genealogical method can provide us with a tool both for exploring new subjects and for reconstituting old subjects in new ways. In this, even though Foucault does not universalise what he says or does and does not prescribe his methods to us in the form of a programme (Foucault, 1991a: 73), he is nevertheless an exemplar whose work is testament to the fruitfulness of genealogy as a method. But of course it is not the only tool available to us. What is clear, however, is that whichever method we employ we cannot use it to escape beyond the reach of power, as Foucault understands it. It is here where the encyclopaedic project is at its weakest, for it fails to recognise the potential for method to reinscribe power in the relationship between the investigator and the object of study. It is for this reason that Foucault continues to trouble the academy, for they are constant reminders to us that what we do is potentially fraught with dangers.

NOTES

1. The term is used by Kritzman in his introduction, 'Foucault and the Politics of Experience' (in Foucault 1988f: xvii).
2. The third version is a reconstructed Thomism.
3. For a critical appraisal of MacIntyre's account of the Enlightenment Project, see Wokler's chapter in Horton and Mendus (1994: 108–26).
4. Foucault (1970: 17–45) locates the intertwinement of language and nature in the Renaissance episteme. This may be read as suggesting that a methodical approach to knowledge reveals truth precisely because nature itself is orderly. If this is accepted, then Descartes' approach to method is itself made possible by the Renaissance episteme, whilst at the same time opening up the possibility of making nature subject to method and reason.
5. Emphasis added. Similarly also J.S. Mill, in his anonymously published essay 'On Bentham', argued that it was above all else Bentham's 'method, that constituted the novelty and value of what he did' (Ryan, 1987: 138–9).
6. In the case of Nietzsche, it is explicitly the *will* to power that is at play.
7. MacIntyre, in *After Virtue*, argues that Nietzsche (alongside Weber) provides one of the 'key theoretical articulations of the contemporary social order'. Indeed, the bureaucratic culture of our age is underpinned in thought by 'suppressed Nietzschean premises' (1981: 108). In the sense of diagnosing the contemporary malaise, Nietzsche's project is clearly not a failure. In the sense of providing an alternative to the Enlightenment Project and its encyclopaedic aspirations, it is.

8. This fixity of self is necessary in order for the self to communicate not only with others, but also with itself at a later point in time (MacIntyre, 1990: 46–7).

9. 'Power is not discipline; discipline is a possible procedure of power' (Foucault, 1984e: 380).

10. 'I am not interested in the academic status of what I am doing because my problem is my own transformation. That's the reason also why, when people say, "Well, you thought this a few years ago and now you say something else," my answer is, "Well, do you think I have worked like that all those years to say the same thing and not be changed?"' (Foucault, 1988a: 14).

11. Foucault explicitly links his discussion of the author to the problematic of subjectivity (1984c: 117–18).

12. Foucault himself comments on this (1980d: 109–11; 1984f: 383–4). None of these claims precludes the others.

13. Though elsewhere Foucault claimed that 'no-one was more of a continuist' than he (1991a: 76).

14. Foucault (in 1980a: 52–3) acknowledges his debt to Marx without commenting on the nature of that debt. (See also Foucault, 1988b: 43–6.)

15. He described himself as 'neither an adversary nor a partisan of Marxism' (Foucault, 1984f: 383).

16. 'For the Marxist method, the dialectical materialist knowledge of reality, can arise only from the point of view of a class, from the point of view of the struggle of the proletariat' (Lukács, 'What Is Orthodox Marxism?', 1971: 21).

17. Popper, on the other hand, argues that Marxism's problem is that it constantly makes *ad hoc* theoretical amendments to compensate for its failure to predict revolution. There are too many differences between Popper and Foucault to warrant listing them here, but suffice to say that Popper wants to consign Marxism to the ash-heap of history, whereas I take Foucault to be freeing Marxism from the constraints of its own history.

18. 'I never know at the beginning of a project what I'll think at its conclusion' (Foucault, 1991c: 28).

19. Deleuze believes that it is at the level of method that the revolutionary character of Nietzsche's work becomes apparent (Deleuze, 1985: 146).

20. On this point see 'The Formation of Concepts' (Foucault, 1972a: 56–63).

21. This is not to accuse Foucault of 'presentism' – the view that the present is an inevitable outcome of the past. Nor is it to say that the past is simply a creation of the present.

22. Foucault once remarked, 'I think to imagine another system is to extend our participation in the present system' (cited in Rorty, 1989: 64, n.23). Rorty reads this as an implausibly pessimistic position, and one which he believes grows out of a failure of imagination on Foucault's part. I would suggest that imagination is precisely one of the ways in which one might explore the limits of what is possible, and push beyond those limits. Foucault's strategy is to open up spaces where the imagination might be put to work.

23. Fraser accuses Foucault of failing to appreciate both 'the degree to which the normative is embedded in and infused throughout the whole of language at every level and the degree to which, despite himself, his own critique has to make use of modes of description, interpretation and judgement formed within the modern Western normative tradition' (Fraser, 1989: 30–1). Yet if my reading

of Foucault is plausible it is Fraser herself who fails to appreciate the extent to which Foucault is troubled by precisely this problem.

24. There are echoes of Callicles in this claim: *Gorgias,* 491–2.
25. This is not to say that Foucault saw anonymity as a goal in and of itself preferable to being identified with his work. Anonymity, if it is a tactic, is not the only tactic available to Foucault (Simons, 1995: 6–8).
26. For a discussion of Foucault's nominalism, see Flynn (1994: 39–40).
27. Note that this reverses the traditional relationship between methodology and method, where the former – a system of beliefs about how to study the world – sets the terms of appropriateness for the latter.
28. For a useful discussion of this point, see Simons (1995: 95–104).
29. But only at times, for, as MacIntyre himself recognises, Foucault gave many personal interviews, clearly eschewing on those occasions the project of self-erasure.
30. Some myths, perhaps all, may be indefinitely immutable, as James Joyce (whom MacIntyre cites in this context) demonstrated with his reworking of Homer's *Odyssey, Ulysses.*
31. I am taking MacIntyre seriously here on the point that the self is constituted in and through the story (or stories) it tells and that there is not some ghostly self, akin to the liberal unencumbered self, behind the scenes directing that story. In the absence of such a self, telling a different story about oneself really does imply that the self is different too.

2 Foucault and the Writing of History

Andrew Thacker

I am well aware that I have never written anything but fictions. I do not mean to say, however, that truth is therefore absent. It seems to me that the possibility exists for fiction to function in truth, for a fictional discourse to induce effects of truth, and for bringing it about that a true discourse engenders or 'manufactures' something that does not as yet exist, that is, 'fictions' it. One 'fictions' history on the basis of a political reality that makes it true, one 'fictions' a politics not yet in existence on the basis of a historical truth. (Foucault, 1980f: 193)

Introduction

Writing history has become a rather fraught affair. The discipline of history, in the Anglo-American world, has in the last decade or so had to contend with a 'linguistic turn' or the rise of a 'postmodern history', a series of debates that have provoked, enraged and disrupted much that was taken as a methodological consensus. Equally, many other social science and humanities disciplines have become more concerned with the historical dimension of their chosen area of study. English studies, for example, has seen numerous examinations of the historical development of the discipline as part of a questioning of the present status and orientation of how the subject is taught and thought about.[1] In this chapter I explore how Michel Foucault's work has important and challenging things to offer to history as a central discipline within the humanities and social sciences. To the study of history, Foucault's work poses disciplinary questions – of justification, of tactics, of power. These are questions about the methodology and conduct of historical research, as well as epistemological questions concerned with the very status of historical writing. Broadly, Foucault raises three sets of issues: the first about the status of history as discourse or as involving the investigation of historically constituted discourses; the second about the entwinement of historical writing with questions of power, a part of Foucault's notion of genealogy; and finally, Foucault asks questions about the relation of the present to the past, questions contained in his description of his own work as being part of a 'history of the present'. This chapter offers a detailed overview of Foucault's work on historiography before assessing how his ideas have influenced the writing of history in three areas: postmodernist history, women's history and feminist history, and revisionist histories of modern Ireland.

Foucault on History

To ascertain the overall role of history in Foucault's work I want to analyse three key texts by him: *The Archaeology of Knowledge*, the 1971 (Foucault, 1984b) essay 'Nietzsche, Genealogy, History', and the late essay on Kant, 'What Is Enlightenment?'. One starting place is his conception of historical writing as genealogical, a term which emerges after Foucault's espousal of an archaeological approach in his texts up to and including *The Archaeology of Knowledge*. I will concentrate upon these texts, rather than upon Foucault's earlier historical texts such as *Birth of the Clinic* or *Madness and Civilization*, because it is these later texts that contain the most suggestive reflections upon the processes of historical writing.[2]

It is sometimes difficult to disentangle archaeology from genealogy in Foucault's work, other than by noting the influence of Nietzsche in the latter methodology. Archaeology as a style of historical investigation appears to be replaced at the start of the 1970s by the Nietzschean-derived genealogy. Indeed, Foucault claimed in an interview originally published in 1983 that he no longer used the term 'archaeology' (Foucault, 1988f: 31). However, in the Enlightenment essay published in 1984 Foucault states that his historical work combines archaeology as a 'method', and genealogy as a 'design' (Foucault, 1984a: 46). His ambivalence to utilising a precise terminological distinction between the two is also found in an early interview, 'The Discourse of History' (1967). Here Foucault states that archaeology is not akin to a genealogy which produces 'descriptions of beginnings and sequences' (Foucault, 1989: 25); but he then goes on to state that: 'no doubt my archaeology owes more to the Nietzschean genealogy than to structuralism' (Foucault, 1989: 31). To clarify this important distinction it is necessary to look at *The Archaeology of Knowledge*. Here we repeatedly learn what archaeology is not; only rarely can we discern the positive contours of archaeological history. Two important features of archaeology do clearly stand out: first, it is an attempt to write history in terms of a notion of discontinuity; second, it is a form of writing which is rooted in the analysis of history as discourse. In his subsequent work Foucault appears, to an extent, to modify the second principle, while strengthening the role of discontinuity.[3]

Discontinuity represents a stigma to conventional history since it is that part of the past that must be eradicated by means of explanation. History presents itself to us in the form of 'dispersed events – decisions, accidents, initiatives, discoveries' (Foucault, 1972a: 8) that must be rearranged and reordered so as to reveal the essential continuity of events. For example, modules or journals in history have displayed this aversion to discontinuity simply by their titles: 'Continuity and Change in Modern Ireland' is one such instance. Change is to be incorporated into an overall view of the development, and thus the essential continuity, of history. Any event that represents 'change' must be explained and hence rendered safe and part, once more, of the continuous historical narrative.[4] In this way written history overcomes 'temporal dislocation' (Foucault, 1972a: 8) – chance meetings of significant historical actors, avenues of action not taken – so as to be able to interpret the past. Historians were always aware of the contingent nature of historical events but, argues Foucault, regarded this 'given' of history as practically 'unthinkable' (Foucault, 1972a: 8), since it challenges the essential methodology of most historical work. For Foucault discontinuity should be both a tool of the historian, and a description of the object that one is investigating (Foucault, 1972a: 9). One examines the past through the lens of discontinuity, while also being aware that what one is regarding is itself constitutionally broken and dispersed. Discontinuity is not 'an external condition that must be reduced, but ... a working concept' (Foucault, 1972a: 9) for the historian.

Foucault's dislike of continuous, or what he also terms 'total history' (Foucault, 1972a: 9), is related to his earlier critique of the transcendental subject in *The Order of Things*. It is not quite clear if he dislikes continuous history because it supports this sovereign subject, or because continuous history is itself sustained by this form of subjectivity. Indeed Foucault avoids this issue by claiming they are two sides of the same theoretical approach: 'Continuous history is the indispensable correlative of the founding function of the subject' (Foucault, 1972a: 12). Continuous history acts as a reassurance to subjectivity, promising to restore, as historical consciousness, all that is different and other to subjectivity.[5] Foucault clearly has in mind here the link of subjective consciousness and historical development found initially in Hegel and then Marx, and which he feels is revived, in a slightly different form, in the twentieth century by phenomenology (Foucault, 1988f: 23). Foucault espouses discontinuity to assist in defining 'a method of historical analysis freed from the anthropological theme' (Foucault, 1972a: 16). However, can history completely escape the question of subjectivity as foundation, as Foucault suggests? And does traditional history always rely upon a linkage of continuous history and a foundational subject? Foucault's later work addresses these problems, although he still retains discontinuity as a key principle of his historical writing even when he shifts from a solely archaeological perspective.

The other prong of archaeological analysis – its discursive focus – is, however, considerably altered. Archaeological history studies discourses rather than the objects or events to which discourses or signs refer or represent, and this is shown when Foucault states that he does not analyse discourses in order to write a 'history of the referent' (Foucault, 1972a: 47). His study of madness, for example, was not an attempt to reconstitute what madness was, before it was represented and organised in a variety of discourses. Just as the principle of discontinuity was upheld because it was more faithful to the reality of historical events, so Foucault values discourses for what they are rather than for what they represent:

> What we are concerned with is not to neutralize discourse, to make it the sign of something else, and to pierce through its density in order to reach what remains silently anterior to it, but on the contrary to maintain it in its consistency, to make it emerge in its own complexity. What, in short, we wish to do is to dispense with 'things' ... To substitute for the enigmatic treasure of 'things' anterior to discourse, the regular formation of objects that emerge only in discourse. (Foucault, 1972a: 47)

This statement raises a number of important epistemological issues for the understanding of Foucault's historiography. Prima facie, Foucault might be saying one of two things. His comments could imply that history only possesses a linguistic existence. If objects and events only emerge in discourse does that entail their having only a discursive existence? It is, therefore, historical interpretation that produces what we believe to be the events and objects of 'the past'. The second interpretation is that our only access to historical 'reality' is through specific discourses that, in various ways, describe them. This implies that 'the past' does, or rather did, exist in some non-discursive form, but that our only grasp upon it is through our own discursive interventions, and these necessarily contain our own perspectives and interests embedded into them. The first position is a form of quite radical scepticism about historical knowledge, while the second, which is closer to Foucault's own view, is perspectival or relativist, but not so sceptical. Remaining at the level of discourse when analysing history does not, however, imply treating discourses as subject only to linguistic rules. Discourses are not – as in structuralism – to be treated purely as 'groups of signs ... but as practices that systematically form the objects of which they speak' (Foucault, 1972a: 49). Archaeology studies 'discourses as practices obeying certain rules' (Foucault, 1972a: 138). Foucault does not perceive history as merely a set of discourses since history is about practices that occur under the constraints of rules. But ambiguities remain. If we understand discourses as practices does that mean we should also consider the reverse, and treat practices as discourses? Foucault's adoption of the term 'discursive practice' only complicates matters here. And how are we to regard the systematic 'rules' that constrain discursive practices? Are the rules themselves discursively constructed? The epistemological status of history as discourse is, it appears, a little obscure.

Foucault's attempt to resolve these difficulties is found in the essay 'Nietzsche, Genealogy, History', published in 1971 (Foucault, 1984b), two years after *The Archaeology of Knowledge*. Now practices are emphasised more than discourses, while the notion of discontinuity is re-emphasised, finally helping Foucault break with the structuralist vocabulary of rules of formation. History now is not primarily about discourses but about power. This is a point summarised in a slightly later interview, 'Truth and Power', when Foucault explains his distance from the structuralist perspective upon history: 'I believe one's point of reference should not be to the great model of language (*langue*) and signs, but to that of war and battle. The history which bears and determines us has the form of a war rather than that of a language: relations of power, not relations of meaning' (Foucault, 1980d: 114). One impetus for this shift from signs to power is Nietzsche's argument that signs are themselves nothing but interpretations of earlier interpretations that have been forgotten or suppressed. Rather than the anodyne theory that discourses are practices governed by innocent rules of formation, Foucault now adopts Nietzsche's view that 'everything that exists, no matter what its origin, is periodically reinterpreted by those in power in terms of fresh intentions' and that this reinterpretation is a forceful 'outstripping and overcoming' during which earlier meanings are necessarily destroyed (Nietzsche, 1956: 20). Rules of formation are now to be understood within a matrix of power relations.

'Nietzsche, Genealogy, History' attempts to revise historical enquiry in the light of this shift of emphasis.[6] It is also a vituperative attack upon the methods of conventional historical writing, a much more aggressive critique than is evident in *The Archaeology of Knowledge*. Although the target is not easily discerned, the tenor of Foucault's criticism is very clear. Foucault accuses historians of not actually paying sufficient attention to history. Historians are just not meticulous enough, as they hide their gaze from the discontinuous and contradictory clutter of the past because they desire to write history in the form of a reassuring narrative of origins, explanations and continuities. In *The Archaeology* Foucault argued that the philosophical itch for foundations manifested itself in conventional history in several ways: one was the linkage of continuous history and the transcendental subject, another was the desire to interpret signs as representations of things. Now Foucault is not content to view these as errors of method that can be corrected by prescribing procedures for analysing discursive formations. The historian's quest for origins has to be seen as a motivated desire to ignore the twisted fabric of history, part of a 'will to power' that writes history from an omniscient perspective, where the past makes sense only because the aleatory reality of that past is actually violently suppressed: 'The historian's history finds its support outside of time' (Foucault, 1984b: 87). Conventional history is more properly named a metahistory or a 'suprahistorical history' (Foucault, 1984b: 93). Historians try to uncover a 'primordial truth' behind or before 'the external world of accident and succession' (Foucault, 1984b: 78). The genealogist, in contrast, refuses these metaphysical comforts and actually 'listens to history', where he or she finds no secret essence behind historical events but rather an essence 'fabricated in a piecemeal fashion from alien forms', or discovers that 'reasonable' actions by historical actors have their origin in chance (Foucault, 1984b: 78).

Foucault, therefore, respects history too much, listens to the singular events, contingent occurrences and random beginnings too closely to reduce these 'myriad events' (Foucault, 1984b: 81) to some pre-existent or imposed narrative. Archaeology sought to split history writing from its comfortable relationship with the idea of the transcendental subject. Now Foucault realises this separation is not sufficient to free history from this influential model of subjectivity. The writing of history must, instead, be actively turned against the transcendental subject in order that the past can be properly analysed without fearing the return of a transcendental conception of subjectivity to bridle and contain the contingency of the past. Thus Foucault writes that the 'purpose of history, guided by genealogy, is not to discover the roots of our identity, but to commit itself to its dissipation' (Foucault, 1984b: 95). Genealogy is concerned with the descent rather than the evolution of events in history, a movement backwards rather than forwards in time. One such series of events is the way the self 'fabricates a coherent identity' from 'numberless beginnings' (Foucault, 1984b: 81); tracing the forward evolution of such a self would too readily produce an image of progressive unity. If we reverse the focus of historical study, and work backwards, then this fiction of a unified subjectivity is less likely, argues Foucault, to captivate us. Analysing descent 'permits the dissociation of the self, its recognition and displacement as an empty synthesis, in liberating a profusion of lost events' (Foucault, 1984b: 81). Unlike evolution, genealogical descent must never reach some point of origination, and instead seeks only 'the moment of arising' or the 'emergence' of something as a result of a struggle of forces against one another (Foucault, 1984b: 83).[7]

Here I want to explore four difficulties with Foucault's notion of genealogy as a prelude to considering his later history writing.

First, is it possible that history as descent might arrive at a point of origin? There appears a danger that the conclusion of one's descent might be regarded as a point of origin for the historical event under investigation. The difference between regarding an event as a beginning and as a point of origin seems tenuous. However, Foucault's point is that it is the attitude adopted to the event that is significant; regarding it as a beginning grants it a provisional status. There could be other beginnings, so far undiscovered by the historian, and it may be impossible to prioritise the importance of the beginnings discovered. The possibility also exists that the real beginning of some event might never be recovered. An event seen as an origin, however, suggests a fixity and an explanatory causality that Foucault refuses: there is only ever a single origin, beginnings can be plural and do not govern the subsequent course of historical events.

Second, what is it about descent that compels us to see subjectivity as dispersal and not unity? And why is it that evolutionary history is doomed only ever to produce a unified subjectivity? There appears nothing inherent in the temporal direction of history writing that completely structures what one will say of the object under investigation. Foucault's answer might be that evolutionary history is not just about temporal directions, but about an evaluative notion of progress being embedded in the subject one studies. Equally, Foucault might argue that descent, in uncovering a plurality of beginnings, brings to light the fact that subjectivity too is plural in nature and form.

Third, descent helps Foucault introduce the idea of writing a history of the present, a notion most clearly articulated in a 1984 interview: 'I set out from a problem expressed in the terms current today and I try to work out its genealogy. Genealogy means that I begin my analysis from a question posed in the present' (Foucault, 1988f: 262). Starting in the present does not confirm a direct and monolithic relationship between past and present, such that the entire key to understanding the present results from understanding how the past has inevitably shaped us. Deleuze summarises Foucault's sense of the relation between past and present by suggesting that the historical archive (or past) is about 'the drawing of what we are and what we are ceasing to be' (Deleuze, 1992: 164). The past does not just tell us who we are today, it tells us from where we might have come, and from where we will start to be different in the present.

Foucault's history of the present develops Nietzsche's point that knowledge is always a matter of perspective (Nietzsche, 1956: 255). Historians must acknowledge their own perspective on the past, their 'grounding in a particular time and place, their preferences in a controversy'. History is thus a 'curative science' whose perception is slanted, 'being a deliberate appraisal, affirmation, or negation' that examines issues in the past in order to intervene and 'prescribe the best antidote' (Foucault, 1984b: 90). The historian examining some topic in a previous era should start by asking what is it in the present that makes this topic of contemporary interest?[8] Foucault extends this point in a later definition of genealogy as concerned with the 'insurrection of subjugated knowledges', those local, illegitimate or disqualified knowledges that are opposed to what Foucault calls 'the tyranny of globalising discourses' (Foucault, 1980f: 81; 83) such as the disciplinary networks of power analysed in *Discipline and Punish*.[9] Genealogy here aims to utilise the perspectival interests of the historian in the present. Foucault's wish is to 'establish a historical knowledge of struggles and to make use of this knowledge tactically today' (Foucault, 1980f: 83). Archaeology now reappears as the method for studying and recuperating these local knowledges; genealogy refers to the tactics by which these subjugated knowledges can be freed and 'brought into play' in the present (Foucault, 1980f: 85). The question here, however, is how easy is it to utilise historically subjugated knowledges in the present? One might wish to recover a subjugated set of practices, but be unhappy at certain historical ideas attached to practices. Can one always easily be selective about which parts of subjugated knowledges one wishes to employ? This is perhaps the basis for some of the problems involved in Foucault's present-centred study of the sexuality of the classical world (see Thacker, 1993: 14–15). How selective, then, can one be in reactivating the practices or discourses of these ancient 'arts of existence'?

Fourth, the dissipation of identity celebrated by Foucault as an essential part of genealogy arises from a renewed value granted to the idea of discontinuity: 'History becomes "effective" to the degree that it introduces discontinuity into our very being – as it divides our emotions, dramatizes our instincts, multiplies our body and sets it against itself' (Foucault, 1984b: 88). Previously Foucault believed the recognition of discontinuity resided in the methods used to study history. Foucault then saw the need to turn discontinuity around upon the subject conducting historical investigation. Now Foucault realises that this violent annihilation of identity raises more problems that it resolves. It does not necessarily entail a form of history more attentive to the aleatory character of the past, because it raises the question of from where does the historian write if her or his identity is completely dissolved? Writing from the perspective of the present with a dissolved or reconfigured identity does not really address the question of who is writing, and what form of self is interested in these historical events. Maybe Foucault's rhetoric here is necessary in order to erase the transcendental subject, but it is instructive that the final, oblique, sections of 'Nietzsche, Genealogy, History' seem to reach a kind of impasse. We must not, argues Foucault, judge the past in terms of a truth only possessed in the present, but must risk 'the destruction of the subject who seeks knowledge' (Foucault, 1984b: 97). If 'all knowledge rests on injustice' and 'the instinct for knowledge is malicious' (Foucault, 1984b: 95), then the perspective of the present is also caught up in this obnoxious epistemology. The call, then, for the dissolution of the subject is for the 'destruction of the man who maintains knowledge by the injustice proper to the will to knowledge' (Foucault, 1984b: 97). The price, it appears, of the destruction of this injustice is the dissolution of the subject of knowledge. But then who is it that gazes upon the past or present and asserts that these events and knowledges are unjust?[10]

Foucault realises the need to reinstate some historical consideration of the subject that writes history in order to know, and thus move his own work beyond that of Nietzsche. In 'Truth and Power' Foucault's definition of genealogy is still that of 'a form of history which can account for the constitution of knowledge ... without having to make reference to a subject which is ... transcendental' (Foucault, 1980d: 117). But Foucault also recognises the need to produce an account of subjectivity that amounts to more than its demolition: 'One had to dispense with the constituent subject, to get rid of the subject itself ... to arrive at an analysis which can account for the constitution of the subject within a historical framework' (Foucault, 1980d: 117). It is only by dissolving the constituting subject of history that Foucault can reach a position where he can begin to study the historical constitution of the subject. And it is only after doing this that he, as an historically situated and constituted subject in the present, can turn to historical writing once more.

In 1981 Foucault commented that his intention was not to analyse power but 'to create a history of the different modes by which, in our cultures, the human being is made "subject"' (cited in O'Farrell, 1989: 113). This project is theorised quite explicitly in the essay, 'What Is Enlightenment?'. The subject that reappears is, however, thoroughly historicised, bound by chance, difference and contingency rather than possessed of a transcendental unity. This is why philosophical critique must engage in what Foucault terms an 'historical ontology of the self' (Foucault, 1984a: 46), rather than conduct ontology or history by assuming a transcendental subject position. A proper attention to history makes no assumptions about the nature of the self that appears in the past – it starts by respecting the ungivenness of human subjectivity.

In 'What Is Enlightenment?' Kant is interpreted as 'a point of departure' for what Foucault terms 'the attitude of modernity'. Modernity is an attitude, not an epoch, a 'mode of relating to contemporary reality' (Foucault, 1984a: 39). It is thus a way of relating to the present that includes thinking, feeling, acting and behaving but, most importantly, has the flavour of a 'task' or 'ethos' with two parts. Foucault now conducts a leap of historical and intellectual imagination that exemplifies his own discontinuous method of writing history. To help characterise the attitude to modernity he has outlined in Kant he produces a very un-Kantian example, the poet Charles Baudelaire. For Baudelaire, writes Foucault, modernity is an experience of the 'discontinuity of time' requiring the elaboration of an attitude grasping the eternal dwelling within the temporal. The true modern mode of subjectivity follows Baudelaire's command: 'You have no right to despise the present' (Foucault, 1984a: 39–40). Instead you must form an intimate relationship to the present, as Kant did when considering the Enlightenment. This is one part of the 'task' of relating to modernity: the formation of 'a relationship to the present' (Foucault, 1984a: 41). Clearly, then, Foucault is pulling together various elements from his previous work upon historiography: a notion of the discontinuity of history and of subjectivity; the importance of practices, seen in the 'task' of relating to the present; and the idea of an historical understanding of the present. The second part of the 'task' displayed by Baudelaire consists in elaborating 'a mode of relationship that has to be established with oneself' (Foucault, 1984a: 41). This marks the reappearance of considerations of the construction of subjectivity that Foucault had earlier wanted to dissolve in the interests of the writing of history. Now historical work must be intimately tied into a consideration of selves and subjects.

In Baudelaire Foucault identifies an instance of an Enlightenment 'attitude' worth genealogical 'reactivation' (Foucault, 1984a: 42): a critique of our words, ideas and actions through an 'historical ontology of ourselves' (Foucault, 1984a: 45). This yokes together the two parts of the task of modernity: forming a relation to the present, and forming a relation to oneself. Foucault's ontology of the subject bears the marks of historical discontinuity through and through. Unlike the earlier uses of discontinuity derived from Nietzsche, the effect now is not to blast apart subjectivity but to see how, historically, the self is put together after an initial dissolution of its transcendental conception. Another innovation is the foregrounding of autonomy in the constitution of the self. Not merely subjected by discourses or disciplined by technologies, the constitution of subjectivity is now a series of practices (the 'care of the self' or the 'aesthetics of existence') that can, within the constraints of specific technologies, be self-employed.

This self-formation of subjectivity can be seen in Foucault's notion of how we are to understand the present in terms of 'the contemporary limits of the necessary' (Foucault, 1984a: 43). Foucault once more eschews a transcendental approach to the self, conceiving his study as an historical one into 'the events that have led us to constitute ourselves' (Foucault, 1984a: 46). These events are those we now view as the limits of our ontological states. If Kant asked the negative question of what limits must knowledge remain within, Foucault poses a more positive question: in what poses as universal in our knowledge is there anything which is the result of contingent constraints and how, if desired, can these constraints be transgressed? This form of historical enquiry is still genealogical in being brought face to face with the present; it must 'put itself to the test of reality, of contemporary reality, both to grasp the points where change is possible and desirable, and to determine the precise form this change should take' (Foucault, 1984a: 46).

Foucault's final work upon the sexuality of the Greeks and Graeco-Romans thus comes to play a key part in his final vision of how one writes history. By considering the past events which have helped form us we gain a sense of the contingency of those norms and values we tend to regard as universal. History shows us diversity rather than universality, discontinuous modes of acting as 'human subjects'. Writing history is one way we can bring to prominence those restrictions upon our present subjectivities that perhaps should be transgressed, the points where change in values and action is possible. The past, then, does not merely help us understand the present, it also helps us have the courage to imagine that the present could be different from the form it manifests at the moment. Perhaps historical writing requires a certain aestheticisation, not to erode the 'truth' of our past, but to enable it to imagine the telling of radically different fictions of who we are or, more importantly, who we might become.

This 'fictioning' (Foucault, 1980f: 193) of history is precisely the point of genealogical history writing. Foucault says of the Enlightenment that what should be preserved is not faithfulness to any set of ideas, but rather the 'permanent reactivation of an attitude' which is that of a 'permanent critique of our historical era' (Foucault, 1984a: 42). Reactivation is the term used by Foucault when discussing how genealogy redeploys historically 'subjugated knowledges' in the present. Now it is not knowledges but an attitude, practices not discourses, that Foucault wishes to rescue from the past. It is an attitude that, by examining the vast 'network of contingencies' that is history, might help us 'grasp why and how that-which-is might no longer be that-which-is' (Foucault, 1988f: 37; 36). Discontinuity, then, no longer resides just in the approach to past events, or even in the very being of the subject, but now assumes a place in the present as an awareness of how the self can discontinue being a certain kind of subject and work towards some new self. As Mark Poster argues, for Foucault, 'historical writing is a form of self-determination as well as a practice of social critique' (Poster, 1992: 309). Historical writing should, therefore, be a much more self-reflective form of work, reflecting upon how the present is always folding into the future, and how the historian too might be transformed in the act of writing history.

The discontinuous traces of an approach to the writing of history are scattered throughout Foucault's texts. For the final Foucault a sense of the past involves a self-critique from the position of the present, with new forms of subjecthood being delineated by 'reactivation' of past practices and attitudes. This process is thus one important justification for historical research. However, it is the project of 'reactivation' which is perhaps most problematic for Foucault's practice of the writing of history.[11] It also presents a series of difficult questions for conventional historiography that I will now consider.

Discourses of History

In a recent article, 'The End of Social History?', British historian Patrick Joyce has argued for a complete rethinking of the practice of social history as presently conceived by British and American historians, citing as the main stimulus for this the work of Foucault. Historians have, until recently, steadfastly refused to engage with postmodernist thought, argues Joyce, viewing it with suspicion or disdain, and have therefore failed to see how the discipline of history is implicated in the norms and values of a modernity problematised by certain trends in postmodernism (Joyce, 1995: 73). Joyce argues that many of the key methodological cornerstones of social history require critique, such as those of 'the material' and 'the social', as well as the master-concept of Marxist historiography, 'class' (Joyce, 1995: 74). Joyce views social history as a 'child of modernity ... not innocently naming the world but creating it in its own political and intellectual image' (Joyce, 1995: 73), a fact insufficiently understood or theorised by the discipline itself. This echoes Foucault's reading of Nietzsche, where all historiography is a motivated discourse about the past, never a neutral exercise in objective or coherent description. If modernity is a project nearing its end, then a finish is also imminent, argues Joyce, for the traditional discourses of social history.[12] Social history is a project which assumes concepts, such as 'the social' or 'class', that the discipline should be self-reflexively investigating. A more vigorous analysis would reveal 'the categories of the material and the social ... to be idealized or essentialized "foundations", unable to bear the weight resting upon them' (Joyce, 1995: 75); this is a history where the social is conceived as a systematic totality or neutral background on which actions and actors, beliefs and practices, can be mapped. The historiography that most forcefully utilised this social totality as a backdrop, Marxism, replicates in its own discursive practice the drive to totalisation that characterised its object of study.[13]

For Joyce it is 'above all the figure of Michel Foucault which stands at the beginning of any new history of the social, for it is Foucault who has done most to identify the emergence of human subjectivity in the west' (Joyce, 1995: 77). Echoing Foucault in 'What Is Enlightenment?', Joyce argues that a new social history should focus on how discourses of subjectivity such as 'self' and 'individual' co-exist with those discourses creating the 'social'.[14] Joyce indicates Foucault's work on governmentality, and its adoption by social theorists such as Rose and Donzelot, as being the most apposite for moving beyond conventional discourses of society and the social (Joyce, 1995: 86). This focus on governmentality is a rather too narrow conception of a Foucauldian inspired historiography. It is also one Joyce's own work does not entirely bear out, given that he frequently employs terms such as 'discursive practices' (Joyce, 1995: 91) and 'technologies of the self' (Joyce, 1994: 19), and suggests that a new social history should be orientated around 'the history of power and of the regimes of knowledge that have produced ways of knowing the world' (Joyce, 1995: 74).

The influence of Foucault on contemporary historiography should be more widely conceived than Joyce seems to allow. Here I want to note a number of different historical discourses that bear the imprint of a historical practice informed, explicitly or implicitly, by Foucault, and speculate upon how Foucauldian ideas can illuminate other examples of historiography. First I consider how what has become known as the 'linguistic turn' among some historians derives from an interpretation of Foucault that is partly inaccurate. I then discuss how history as genealogy informs recent work in feminist history; and, finally, I consider how Foucauldian questions bring a fresh perspective to a contemporary historical debate, that of revisions of modern Irish history.

There has been a widespread debate among Western historians about the validity of a 'linguistic turn' in the academic study of history, much of which seems to recapitulate difficulties identified with Foucault's notion of a 'discursive practice'.[15] Theoretical debate upon this question has become stalled between one position, roughly that of postmodernist historians, such as Joyce, who wish to treat the 'real' or the 'material' as a set of discourses or languages, and a second position, that of critics of postmodernist history, who desire a rigid distinction between discursive representations and the real material of history. On the side of those who support a linguistic turn we can note, for example, James Vernon's appeal to Foucault's framework for 'an archaeology of "the social"' which involves viewing '"the social" as a discursive construct ... concerning questions of citizenship, class, sexuality, poverty, education, economics, health and so on, and not the material reflection of the mode of production' (Vernon, 1994: 88–9). Keith Jenkins, in his introductory guide to new theories of historiography, *Re-Thinking History* (1991), denies any distinction between history as the non-discursive 'past' and history as the neutral attempt to describe in discourse that 'reality'. Jenkins views all 'history as historiography' and wishes to analyse the past as a 'discursive construct' (Jenkins, 1991: 34). He also readily draws upon

Foucault, quoting from *Power/Knowledge* to form an analogy between how the concept of truth functions and the writing of history: 'History is a discourse, a language game; within it "truth" and similar expressions are devices to open, regulate and shut down interpretations' (Jenkins, 1991: 32). Patrick Joyce, in *Democratic Subjects*, responding to criticism of an earlier book of his that employed a discursive account of history, states that the main failing of the earlier book was that it did not employ a more forceful model of 'linguistic determinism' (Joyce, 1994: 11).

As an example of the negative perception of postmodernist history, particularly for its supposed reliance upon a model of language as determinate of the social or the real, we can cite Gertrude Himmelfarb's broad overview of this trend:

> Postmodernism repudiates both the values and the rhetoric of the Enlightenment. In rejecting the 'discipline' of knowledge and rationality, postmodernism also rejects the 'discipline' of society and authority. And in denying any reality apart from language, it aims to subvert the structure of society together with the structure of language. There is nothing concealed in this agenda: it is the explicit, insistent theme of Foucault and Derrida. (Himmelfarb, 1992: 14)

One would search hard to find this particular 'theme' in Foucault's work, especially in his later engagement with Kant on the Enlightenment. One fear expressed by Himmelfarb in this article is that the boundaries between the disciplines of history and literary criticism are being eroded. Critics of the 'linguistic turn' stress the problematic use of 'aesthetic' terms in historical research. Joyce, for example, draws upon the genre of melodrama to understand what he calls the 'aesthetic framing of the social' (Joyce, 1994: 176), the way that specific audiences were addressed and constituted as certain subjects by popular melodramatic narratives (Joyce, 1994: 179). The scorn devoted to using an aesthetic discourse is due to the fear that it turns the 'real' into fiction. It does, however, free history from the burden of reconstructing the 'truth' of the past, which all agree is an impossible project. It also helps focus on the role and power of interpretation and the creations of meanings.

Himmelfarb's article perhaps expresses more about the anxieties of the encounter of history with interdisciplinarity than any developed analysis of Foucault's impact upon historiography. However, her incorrect ascription of a crude linguistic determinism to Foucault actually unites her with some of those who espouse a Foucauldian-influenced historiography. As shown earlier, Foucault never upheld any simplistic reduction of history to the discursive, and his later genealogical work explicitly rejected relations of language for relations of power as a model for interpreting history. Although

Foucault may be cited by proponents of the linguistic turn, it is clear that Foucault's historical repertoire included a number of other, non-discursive, turns within it (see Noiriel, 1994: 565–6; Chartier, 1994; Young, 1990: 71). Even in his archaelogical phase Foucault always argued that language alone was not his focus: 'my object is not language but the archive, that is to say the accumulated existence of discourse. Archaeology ... is ... the analysis of discourse in its modality of archive' (Foucault, 1989: 25). Equally, Foucault's use of the term 'discursive practice', employed by both Joyce and Jenkins (Joyce, 1995: 77; Jenkins, 1991: 66), was often combined with reference to non-discursive practices and systems (Foucault, 1972a: 164; 162). Roger Chartier argues convincingly that Foucault 'maintains the exteriority and the specificity of practices that are not in themselves of a discursive nature' and that he did not, unlike certain proponents of the linguistic turn, 'assimilate social realities to discursive practices' (Chartier, 1994: 174; 175). Access to non-discursive practices can only be through discourses and texts, but the logic or rationality of these discourses is not to be identified with the logics or rationalities governing the production of non-discursive practices. For Chartier, discursive practice is 'a specific practice ... that does not reduce all other "rules of practice" to its own strategies, regularities, and reasons' (Chartier, 1994: 174–5). Chartier's point here is not to reinstate a division between reality and representation, and to thus privilege the former as the true object of historical scrutiny. Rather, he argues, Foucault 'annuls the division' between discourse and the real, representation and living experience, such that both are to be considered as equally 'real' and in need of investigation (Chartier, 1994: 176).[16] This position is borne out in a late interview with Foucault where he described one common theme in his historical studies as that of 'problematization', defined as 'the totality of discursive or non-discursive practices that introduces something into the play of true and false and constitutes it as an object of thought' (Foucault, 1988f: 257).

One preliminary conclusion is that Foucault's critique of historiography should not be restricted to a series of propositions concerning the epistemological status of history as real or as discursive. Foucault's work draws attention to the role of discourses in history, for example, in his consideration of the 'putting into discourse' of homosexuality in the first volume of *The History of Sexuality*. But the more important dimension of his work considers the implications of power and self-reflexivity that attend any historical practice.

Such an attention to the more genealogical aspects of Foucault's work has been evident in the theories of some recent feminist historians.[17] Feminists such as Joan W. Scott and Denise Riley have acknowledged the usefulness of Foucault's theories of the imbrication of power in historical discourse for rethinking some of the methodological assumptions of women's history and feminist history. Much of this work, influenced by poststructuralist feminist theory in general, finds Foucault's emphasis on discourse important. Riley specifically notes Foucault's 'refusals to make reductions of discourse to history or vice-versa' (Riley, 1992: 122) as an influence upon her own work of deconstructing the universal category of 'woman' in history (see Riley, 1988). But the point of using Foucauldian notions of discourse is not a mere epistemological one, but is intimately connected to a political project in the present. Scott's *Gender and the Politics of History* argues that categories such as 'experience' and 'gender' need to be considered as discursive constructs rather than as non-discursive bedrocks for feminist history (Scott, 1988). For Scott, historians should historicise the concept of 'experience' by challenging the notion that it is a form of given knowledge existing outside of the discourses producing it. Experience is, argues Scott, often used in women's history as an authenticating discourse, a foundational concept that also tends to homogenise different identities. Instead of this Scott offers her own analysis of how 'experience' should be used in historiography:

> Experience is at once always already an interpretation *and* something that needs to be interpreted. What counts as experience is neither self-evident nor straightforward; it is always contested, and always therefore political. The study of experience, therefore, must call into question its originary status in historical explanation. This will happen when historians take as their project *not* the reproduction and transmission of knowledge said to be arrived at through experience, but the analysis of the production of that knowledge itself. Such an analysis would constitute a genuinely non-foundational history, one which retains its explanatory power and its interest in change but does not stand on or reproduce naturalized categories. It also cannot guarantee the historian's neutrality, for the choice of which categories to historicize is inevitably 'political', necessarily tied to the historian's recognition of his/her stake in the production of knowledge. (Scott, 1991: 797, original emphasis)[18]

This conclusion, partly a gloss of Foucault's genealogy, shows how Scott refuses to take 'experience' as an unproblematic point of origin for feminist history. Women's actual historical experiences may be one beginning for historical research, but they should not be valorised as an explanatory principle without considering the contingency of such experiences, and the way that any concept of past 'experience' is itself already the construction of the historian in the present. The motivated perspective of the historian in the present is clearly acknowledged and foregrounded, as is the Nietzschean intertwining of knowledge and power. Scott's interest elsewhere in analysing the category of 'gender' is part of this genealogical approach, connecting the study of the historical past to the political present in order to effect change in the status of women, and write history as a 'curative science'. It is an account that resonates with Foucault's comment that: 'recourse to history ... is meaningful to the extent that history serves to show how that-which-is has not always been; i.e., that the things which seem most evident to us are always formed in the confluence of encounters and chances' (Foucault, 1988f: 37). The identities and experiences of women in different societies and periods clearly have this provisional status for an historian like Scott, and it is the contingent status of gendered or sexed identities in history, rather than any continuous and homogeneous narrative of women's 'experience', that offers the most hope for change in the present. Scott's account is therefore an attempt to introduce discontinuity into the concept of 'women's experience', eschewing the notion of a transhistorical female subject as the foundation for any feminist history. Such work will help feminists recognise the contingent nature of present-day gendered identities, and can be clearly related to Foucault's notion of a strategy of implementing change by engaging in 'an historical ontology' of the self.

Feminist appropriations of Foucault highlight genealogical history as part of a history of the present that necessarily involves questioning why people write *this* history in *this* particular way, and raises the question of whether a different sort of history should or could be written. This work is, along with that of the linguistic turn writers, part of a self-reflexive theorising of history prompted by Foucault's work. In order to substantiate the wider impact of Foucault's work upon historiography it is useful to consider how his ideas might be applied to an historical debate that does not consciously refer to his work, and which seems, at first, very distant from his concerns.

Revisionings of Ireland

One of the most acrimonious debates in recent Western historiography has been that of revisions of modern Irish history. Over the last decade or so Irish historians have vigorously debated not only the correct interpretation of events in their country's past, but also the role of the historian in relation to the nation, its people or audience, and the present day.[19] It is a dispute I will discuss briefly, arguing that a Foucauldian approach offers much to explain what is at stake in these often caustic academic debates.

The 'Preface' to Roy Foster's very successful *Modern Ireland 1600–1972* outlines the basic contours of the Revisionist view of modern Irish history. Writing the history of Ireland since the seventeenth century as a 'morality tale' (Foster, 1988: ix) has, argues Foster, disappeared over the last few years.

This residual version of Irish history is a tale where Ireland is perceived as a morally good agent oppressed and beset by English evils. The emergence, in the aftermath of the 1916 Easter Rising, of the Irish Free State is written as a triumphant and continuous narrative, where throwing off the English yoke leads to national self-determination. The key events of this narrative involve the initial conquest of Ireland by England, the maintenance of this colonial presence, and accounts of events such as the Great Famine of the 1840s which stress the negative effects of English economic policy as factors causing and prolonging the suffering. Foster is critical of the 'Anglocentric obsession' of this narrative which, he believes, has led Irish historians 'astray' and produced a number of 'romantic' and 'false trails' (Foster, 1988: ix) for the contemporary historian. Foster sees his book as an attempt, along with other Revisionist histories, to 'clarify some of the realities' (Foster, 1988: ix) of Irish history since 1600 by focusing upon what did happen rather than what historians felt ought to have happened, an approach which at times may reverse the roles of the morality tale. Foster thus assumes an omniscient position, becoming a neutral investigator into the past, devoted to discovering the 'reality' rather than the fiction ('the morality tale'), and refusing to offer judgements upon historical actors, such as the English for not offering more economic aid during the Famine period.

Historians such as Foster only adopted the name Revisionist after criticism from historians wishing to uphold, for various reasons, a version of the 'morality tale' interpretation of Irish history. The first sustained critique of the Revisionist school was in a 1989 article by Brendan Bradshaw, criticising a Revisionist account of early modern Ireland. Bradshaw argues that Revisionists uphold a 'value-free' approach to history in opposition to an earlier nationalist school that believed historical research should be committed, to some extent, to a postitive account of the Irish nation. The value-free approach of the Revisionists, argues Bradshaw, results in 'value-based interpretation in another guise' (Bradshaw, 1989: 337), particularly in their consistently negative attitude towards any form of Irish nationalism. This often means historical research which ignores or downplays the influence of nationalist leaders or movements upon the course of Irish history (Bradshaw, 1989: 344–5). Bradshaw argues that the adoption of a spurious neutrality and a commitment to the supposed 'reality' of history rather than nationalist myths or morality tales, can be understood as an historical response to the revival of violent nationalism in Northern Ireland in the Troubles of the late 1960s onwards (Bradshaw, 1989: 342). Aghast at the violence committed in the name of an Irish nationalism, academic historians tried to revise the 'morality tale' found in earlier academic textbooks. Rather than acknowledge their own opinions in relation to nationalism, Revisionists dressed up their work in the guise of a detached, scientific account of the 'realities' of the past, often focusing upon 'hard' statistical evidence rather than upon highly charged first-hand accounts of the Irish experience. Foster's chapter on the Famine in *Modern Ireland* is a good example of this style of writing, discussing the 'lacunae in statistical evidence' (Foster, 1988: 319) concerning how far and in which geographical areas economic relief was granted by either English or Irish landlords. Foster's dry style only once mentions the 'scrappy evidence recording how people experienced the famine' (Foster, 1988: 330),[20] and instead, in relation to a discussion of population changes and marriage statistics, notes a difference between the Revisionist 'new economic history' and the 'older variety that relied heavily on *literary* evidence' (Foster, 1988: 332, emphasis added).[21]

Bradshaw's witty criticism of the 'sheer dullness' of this 'clinical style' (Bradshaw, 1989: 337) contains an important point about the power of history as discursive practice. Revisionist history may believe that it is demythologising the pieties of Irish nationalism, shown in Ronan Fanning's claim that 'what historians are revising is not history but myth and legend' (Fanning, 1988: 16), but such an approach ignores the effectivity of nationalist historiography as a discourse in the public, rather than academic, sphere. As Bradshaw indicates, despite the efforts of professional historians to portray the 'realities' of the past, 'the communal memory retains a keen sense of the tragic dimension of the national history' (Bradshaw, 1989: 341). Nationalist historiography may be mythical – although the binary myth/history is clearly in need of deconstruction – but it is indeed too powerful to be easily swept away by a welter of statistics.[22] A Foucauldian analysis would not seek to elide such mythic discourses by juxtaposing them with a 'true' discourse, but would rather study them as part of 'the political history of the production of "truth"' (Foucault, 1988f: 112) in present-day Irish historiography, both academic and popular.

The Revisionist debate could usefully be analysed in the light of Foucault's notion of the history of the present. Part of Bradshaw's revision of the Revisionists involves arguing for a 'present-centred' (Bradshaw, 1989: 348)[23] Irish historiography that could interpret the 'positive, dynamic thrust' (Bradshaw, 1989: 349) of nationalist discourses without merely eulogising them. Such an investigation would, in Foucault's words, view 'nationalism' as a 'fictional discourse' that induces 'effects of truth' (Foucault, 1980f: 193). Nationalism as a discourse clearly operates in the present in Ireland, being part of the discursive and non-discursive practices of both Irish Republicans and Ulster Unionists loyal to the British nation. 'Nation' and 'national identity' are often used by both Unionists and Republicans as foundational discourses and a genealogical history might contribute to the 'dissipation' of such identities by exploring the discontinuities and fabricated coherences of these discourses.

The Revisionist rumpus also indicates the necessity for a genealogical approach to the role of the historian in the present as well. Foster may well bemoan the gap between the 'triumph' (Foster, 1993: 18) of the professional Revisionist historian and that of 'popular Irish history' (Foster, 1993: 19–20), but this is best viewed as a complaint that his discourse on the past is not accepted as the truth by all, and is being contested in the present. As Foucault argued, historians must acknowledge their 'grounding in a particular time and place, their preferences in a controversy' (Foucault, 1984b: 90) in the present. Fanning, for example, draws attention to how, since 1969, 'allegedly antiquated and decaying mythologies again acquired an ideological importance of the highest political significance' (Fanning, 1986: 140). The Revisionist debate, he suggests, takes its dynamic from 'the conviction of many politicians and ... intellectuals that modern Irish history is too politically important to be left to the charge of mere academic historians' (Fanning, 1986: 143). But Fanning is unable to situate the professional historian in relation to these debates, preferring to suggest that the historian must adopt the position Foucault, following Nietzsche, dubbed 'suprahistorical': 'Historians must never forget that the ideologists, and not the mythologists are their most dangerous enemies' (Fanning, 1986: 143). The historian evinces an 'open mind' as opposed to the 'closed minds' of those seeking to preserve their ideological position (Fanning, 1986: 143). For Fanning the Revisionist is involved in a 'quest for objective historical truth' (Fanning, 1988: 19), as opposed to the ideological project which ultimately results in 'invented history' (Fanning, 1986: 144). Somehow the Revisionist is able to stand outside his or her own present position, adopting an Olympian perspective upon the past, and writing a history that is not merely invented. Clearly certain Revisionist historians need attention to the dimensions of their own ideological position, to articulate that self-reflection upon the historical process that they can bring to bear upon earlier nationalist accounts, showing their motivations and perspectives, but which they seem unable to turn around upon themselves as a part of an historical ontology of the Revisionist self.

Clearly, however, a Foucauldian historiography is not to be allied simply with the anti-revisionists. Nothing could be more un-Foucauldian than Desmond Fennell's defence of a nationalist-informed historiography which 'sustains, energises and bonds a nation' by means of a 'continuous or near-continuous pattern of meaning in which the [Irish] nation ... was always, in some sense, right-minded and right-acting' (Fennell, 1988: 24). This is continuous history with a vengeance, linking the historical narrative to a teleological and transhistorical subject of consciousness which is 'the Irish nation'. A genealogical account would stress the contingent formation of the Irish nation out of a number of conflicting discourses – English, Irish, Catholic, Protestant, Anglo-Irish, assimilated English, settler, coloniser and so on – and perhaps start by querying the notion of an 'origin' to that nation. Such an account might appear tinged with Revisionism, but, unlike Foster's and Fanning's, would acknowledge the 'origin' of the historical research in the present and contain more self-reflection upon the perceived need to rewrite conventional nationalist histories.

Irish historians – whether it is Revisionists seeking an account of the Famine free of nationalist myths of mourning and vengeance, or Protestant paramilitaries seeking justification for their position by accounts of a pre-Celtic Protestant settlement in Northern Ireland[24] – start from a set of problems constituted in the present. Some of the Foucauldian questions to be asked of such historiography would be, for example, what is one trying to achieve in writing about this past in the present? Could this particular account of the past contribute to the solution of present-day problems? How can this 'fictioning' of the past contribute to a problematisation of the present political situation? Are there any 'subjugated knowledges' that can assist present-day struggles? And how can the practice of historical investigation lead to a process of self-reflection and self-transformation, as well as a practice of social critique? These are clearly not easy questions to answer, but they seem necessary if historiography is to engage fruitfully with Foucault's work. At one point Foster outlines a view of Irish historiography that unwittingly allies it with the 'critical history' of Foucault's genealogist:

> If there's one single unalloyed good that has come out of the overdone debates about historical 'revisionism', it is the idea of the historian as subversive. We should be seeking out the interactions, paradoxes and sub-cultures ... [including] speculative theories of origins, if only to rearrange the pieces in more surprising patterns. (Foster, 1993: 35)

How much subversion, however, is Foster, or any other historian, prepared to allow? The rearrangement of the pieces may be merely a different way of approaching a (Rankean) true image of the past, but it might equally demonstrate the limitations of conventional historiographical practice and reveal the need for more theoretical reflection, such as that shown by certain feminist historians using Foucault. The message of a Foucauldian historiography might be that jettisoning certain pieties of historical research is the more subversive historical action, and is one which could considerably enrich historical research.

Conclusion

Recognising the lack of impartiality of the historian in the present does not necessarily mean that knowledge and investigation of the past should be abandoned because of the perspectivism of the writing subject. Rather it entails that the historian must reflect and acknowledge their own perspective and make this acknowledgement part of the historical project.[25] A number of other general consequences for the writing of history emerge from reading Foucault.

First, more attention must be paid to Foucault's texts in order to clarify how historians can learn from his work. The lessons of the later texts, such as the notion of an historical ontology of the self in 'What Is Enlightenment?', have, aside from some feminist critics, not been fully addressed. Foucault's work on history is not, however, a methodology in any conventional sense. It aims to provoke more critical self-reflection upon the methods of historical research, especially around questions of power, the present and the role of discourses as practices, rather than offering a template for empirical work.

Secondly, historians should seek to employ his approach outside of the obvious areas of analysis suggested by Foucault's work, such as the body, sexuality, prisons, government and so on. This would develop his work in the spirit it was intended, as a 'tool-kit' to be used in a plurality of ways. It would also perhaps raise questions as to the efficacy of any simplistic application of his ideas and concepts outside the regimes of discourse in which he himself worked. My account of Irish revisionist historiography tried to show some of the ways in which such an extension of Foucault's work might develop.

Finally, there is a need for a certain aestheticisation of history as part of this development of the discipline. Foucault's work, especially the last two volumes of *The History of Sexuality,* 'fictioned' a link between aesthetics, ethics and history that was designed to unsettle how we understand ourselves as subjects. This seems an admirable extension of Roy Foster's notion of the 'historian as subversive' and, as any act of subversion should, raises more questions than it answers. Foucault's breaching of disciplinary boundaries in this late work – the sort of approach that unsettles historians and others that seek to distinguish history from fiction in any simplistic and absolute fashion – forces us to consider our own disciplinary practices as historians, literary critics, or whatever. It also produces a need to consider using ideas in disciplines that have not been their natural habitat. It is also clear that such discourses of transgression should not merely result in a postmodern eclecticism or faddish interdisciplinarity; Foucault's work calls upon us to be precise, vigilant and, above all, self-aware of how and where we use particular discourses and practices when writing history.

It might, finally, appear that I have not respected Foucault's problematising of history enough in this chapter. Have I sought false continuities, and tried to trace the evolution and origin of his thought by claiming a transcendental position? Where is the element of self-reflection that I have argued is perhaps the paramount lesson of Foucault's historical theorising? Partly I have conducted this research because I am not an historian by training, but am aware that I use many historical concepts and practices both in my academic work (mainly in literary studies) and in non-academic contexts. I wanted to see whether Foucault's ideas would help my thinking, by challenging points I might take for granted or brush aside. Perhaps I also feel I am bad at history, and felt that this project might alleviate some of those fears (or exacerbate them). I have become aware that I use and assume much about the role of history and historical practices, not only academically, but politically and personally, if we can preserve such distinctions for a moment. Foucault's work makes me think, hopefully in a productive rather than a self-absorbed way, upon my own discontinuous self-formation as a subject of, and in, many different histories; which means learning 'to what extent the effort to think one's own history can free thought from what it silently thinks, and so enable it to think differently' (Foucault, 1985: 9). Writing history is thus about trying to think and act differently, towards oneself, towards others, and towards the present more than the past.

NOTES

1. See Hunter (1988) for a Foucauldian account of the history of English studies, querying the standard account given in, say, Baldick (1983).
2. For discussions of the entire range of Foucault's historical studies see Goldstein (1994a); the most comprehensive account of the relation between history and philosophy in Foucault is O'Farrell (1989).
3. Foucault, however, refused to describe his early works as using a philosophy of discontinuity (see Foucault 1988f: 100).
4. A related point is made in Jenkins (1991).
5. For a useful consideration of identity and difference in historiography, see Cousins (1987).
6. Mitchell Dean argues that we should not take Foucault's position to be identical with the Nietzschean one outlined in this essay (see Dean, 1994: 19–20).

7. Cousins and Hussain summarise this point by arguing that Foucault's histories are concerned with beginnings rather than origins (Cousins and Hussain, 1984: 4).

8. For a discussion of problems associated with the idea of a history of the present, see Castel in Goldstein (1994a: 239–40).

9. *Discipline and Punish* was thus, as Foucault himself noted, related to his work for prison reform in France in the early 1970s. For details of Foucault's activism in this regard, see Macey (1994: 323–52).

10. One other problem might be that the transcendental re-emerges here, not in terms of subjectivity, but as part of the viewpoint of the present. Perhaps the present, as well as the past, needs to be seen through the lens of discontinuity.

11. The problem for Foucault's genealogy seems to revolve around what is meant by the 'reactivation' or 'insurrection' of subjugated knowledges. It may be that Foucault merely means that in drawing attention to past differences or forgotten forms of knowledge (the writings of the institutionalised, for example) in order to show the provisional nature of present forms of subjectivity or knowledge. But the concept seems to have a more developed aspect, as shown in an interview where Foucault notes that among ancient Greek cultural practices 'there is a treasury of devices, techniques, ideas, procedures, and so on, that cannot exactly be reactivated, but at least constitute, or help to constitute a certain point of view which can be very useful as a tool for analysing what's going on now – and to change it' (Foucault, 1984g: 349–50). However, this still raises the question of how choosy one can be with these 'tools' and their functions today.

12. This is not a position espoused by Foucault, who remained quizzical of any easy division between modern and postmodern (see Foucault 1988f: 35).

13. For a discussion of the role of the concept of totality in Marxist theory in general see Martin Jay, *Marxism and Totality* (1984).

14. This is precisely the sort of approach taken by Joyce himself in his recent book, *Democratic Subjects* (Joyce, 1994). A similar argument is advanced by Keith Michael Baker, in his exploration of the possibility of a Foucauldian history of the French Revolution using the notion of *eventalisation*. In such an account society 'becomes not an ultimate cause but a postive effect of the discourses and practices by which it is constructed or produced' (Baker, 1994: 193).

15. The literature on the 'linguistic turn' in history is burgeoning. Overviews can be found in the pages of the journals *History Workshop*, *Social History* and *Past and Present* from 1991 onwards. See in particular Vernon, 1994; Samuel, 1991; 1992; Stone, 1991; Jenkins, 1991; Speigel, 1991. For accounts of Foucault's general impact upon historical research, see the essays in Goldstein, 1994a; Megill, 1987; O'Brien, 1989; Poster, 1982.

16. A similar point, on how archaeology treats discourses as real, is made by Dean (1994: 16).

17. For a brief overview of uses of Foucault by feminist historians, see Hesse (1994: 81–3).

18. For a partial critique of some of Scott's points, see Canning (1994).

19. For an overview of the development of Irish Revisionist and counter-Revisionist history, see Curtis (1994). Curtis traces one beginning of the debate to be a lecture by T.W. Moody in 1978 on the need for historians to demolish certain myths about the Irish past.

20. For the reference to those who walled themselves into cabins to die, see Foster (1988: 327).
21. For Foster's own use of literary evidence, see his use of a Trollope novel (Foster, 1988: 337).
22. For just such a deconstruction, see Deane (1991).
23. Bradshaw's impetus for this approach is not, however, Foucault, but the Whig historian George Butterfield's concept of 'purposeful unhistoricity', where 'the nicely chosen past' is 'conveniently and tidily disposed for our purposes' (Butterfield, 1944: 6).
24. For a brief account of Northern Irish Protestant uses of history in the present, see Buckley (1991).
25. For Foucault's own reflections upon his historical work, see Foucault (1985: 8). It is important to note the differences between Foucault's self-reflective approach and the fairly common acknowledgement by many traditional historians that their interpretations of the past are coloured by their own personal or social values. Such acknowledgements are made, but then the historian moves on, keeping intact their overall conception of historiography. A classic example of this is found in Rudé's introductory comments to *Debate on Europe* (see Rudé, 1972).

3   Surveillance-Free-Subjects
Kevin Magill

> Power is exercised only over free subjects, and only insofar as they are free. By this we mean individual or collective subjects who are faced with a field of possibilities in which several ways of behaving, several reactions and diverse comportments may be realized. Where the determining factors saturate the whole there is no relationship of power; slavery is not a power relationship when man is in chains. ... Consequently there is no face to face confrontation of power and freedom which is mutually exclusive (freedom disappears everywhere power is exercised), but a much more complicated interplay. In this game freedom may well appear as the condition for the exercise of power (at the same time its precondition, since freedom must exist for power to be exerted, and also its permanent support, since without the possibility of recalcitrance, power would be equivalent to a physical determination). (Foucault, 1982: 221)

Foucault's analyses of the emergence and proliferation of modern relationships of power have been widely regarded as presenting substantial obstacles to projects of individual or collective emancipation and for any attempt to develop a coherent theory of how we are or can be free. Foucault himself, on the other hand, did not regard the ubiquitousness of relationships of power as necessarily antithetical to freedom, and even saw his own work as making possible a better understanding of how freedom can be pursued. In his examination of the ancient practices of 'care for the self', one of Foucault's principal aims appears to be to recapture an idea of freedom as a creative project of making and remaking the self. He explicitly disavows any suggestion that he is offering an alternative project of emancipation, or an alternative conception of freedom, to modern conceptions of liberation and freedom in which the realisation of truth and the knowing subject have occupied a central place (Foucault, 1988i: 14). His goal (although nowhere very clearly stated) appears to have been to develop different ways of understanding and relating to the modern preoccupation with truth and authenticity that will open up ways of changing what we are, and do and say (Foucault, 1988i: 14–15, 1984a: 46; and see also 1980f: 133).

The reasons for dissatisfaction with Foucault's pronouncements about the relationship between his work and the goal of freedom are well known. In the first place, although, as he states in the above quote, there is a complex interplay between power and freedom, involving possibilities of resistance and transgression, since in his view there can be no complete escape from the identities in which power involves us, he ought, it seems, to have had an account of why the replacement of one identity by another, or even the strategic modification or renegotiation of identities, should be thought preferable to soldiering on with those identities that education, legal systems, customs, systems of health care, and so on, have lumbered us with, or of why this should be thought as giving us a greater measure of freedom. If freedom is to be found within 'a relationship of self to self' (Foucault, 1988i: 19), involving practices that experiment 'at the limits of ourselves' (Foucault, 1984a: 46), this seems to presuppose a distinction between what is (more) essential and what is contingent about us, since without it there is no point to experimentation and no reason for becoming otherwise than we are. But such a distinction would be alien to the anti-essentialism that runs throughout Foucault's writings, and would have been seen by him as implying just another set of fixed identities in which to become ensnared. It appears to be no accident, therefore, that Foucault offers no positive account of freedom, and that freedom is, for him, an 'undefined work' (1984a: 46).

Further reasons for doubt and dissatisfaction with what Foucault has to say about freedom hinge on his accounts of the relationship between, on the one hand, truth and knowledge, and, on the other, power and rules of discourse. Although in his later work he appears to modify the Nietzschean perspectivism about truth and knowledge to be found in some of his earlier writings (involving the idea that truth is a mere construct: something imposed rather than discovered), his account of them is sketchy and his attitude towards them ambiguous. Commenting on the relationship between the practices of liberty/care for self of the ancient world and the idea of truth, he says:

> One cannot care for self without knowledge. The care for self is of course knowledge of self – that is the Socratic-Platonic aspect – but it is also the knowledge of a certain number of rules of conduct or of principles which are at the same time truths and regulations. To care for self is to fit one's self out with these truths. (1988i: 5)

The status or force of these truths, as truths, is not made clear, but in any case, whatever the relationship between truth and care for self was in the ancient world, none of this gets us anywhere in understanding or conceptualising what the relationship between truth and modern practices of liberty is or should be.

Finally, despite Foucault's insistence, in the quote with which we began, and elsewhere (1988i: 12), that power and freedom are not exclusive, the relationship between them is depicted by him, at the very least, as ambivalent.

Foucault's accounts of the development of systems and relations of power have continually stressed the objectives of normalisation and control, involving regimentation and codification of populations and the denial of freedoms. Inasmuch as we have freedom in relation to systems of power, Foucault talks of our having freedom 'within' them (Foucault, 1984a: 48), in their interstices, or in the form of 'transgression' (1984a: 45). What is at stake in his work is how we can disconnect 'the growth of capabilities ... from the intensification of power relations' (1984a: 48). Nowhere is there any acknowledgement, reversing the dependency in the opening quotation, that power might be a condition or a precondition of freedom. If power is not always a fetter on freedom, it is always a problem for it.

My aim in this chapter will not be to determine whether Foucault had, or ought to have had, a coherent conception of freedom and what is required for it, but rather to examine various analyses, themes and arguments from Foucault's work in relation to a philosophical tradition of thinking about freedom: a tradition within which some have thought that Foucault himself belongs. The tradition is most famously associated with the Stoics, although it has long outlived them and predated them by several centuries.[1]

The Stoic Tradition

According to the Stoic tradition, freedom is neither a natural property (something we have just in virtue of being human or conscious) nor a product of favourable environmental circumstances,[2] but a quality acquired through practices of right thinking and good conduct. The uneducated man thinks of freedom negatively: as an absence of obstacles to getting what he desires; but the wise man knows that freedom is to be found and made within himself. We acquire freedom by being able to determine ourselves to act in accordance with goodness and reason and by gaining self-mastery or self-determination through that. Goodness and reason are not to be understood as external norms, however, but are identified with a person's true, better or essential self (Marcus Aurelius, 1983, bk vi, sect. 58; Spinoza, 1910, pt iv, prop. 18, note: 155). In learning to adapt ourselves to what is right and reasonable, we realise our true or essential natures. Self-realisation, thus conceived, is a project or ideal, pursued in opposition to the enslaving promptings of the baser self and its desires: the true self is affirmed against those things that are alien to it. Goodness and reason are found through reflection, self-knowledge, and acquiring good habits of thought and action and attitudes of equanimity and detachment in the face of fortune.

There have been shifts and discontinuities in the tradition. The significance and content of self-knowledge for Athenians and Stoics, according to

Foucault, was given by rules and practices aimed at care for the self. The modern idea that self-knowledge is directed at a hidden self, illuminated by introspective scrutiny, is a product of the long historical emergence of confessional techniques and mechanisms commencing in early Christian asceticism (Foucault, 1988g: 16–49). The Stoics were also less troubled than their modern successors by the problem of reconciling the freedom of the individual, her conscience and private interests, with the existence of laws and institutional authority.

Despite the discontinuities and changes, however, there is enough continuity to make it possible to think about and discuss an ongoing and unified tradition. What has persisted throughout the Stoic tradition is an idea that freedom is to be understood as self-mastery, self-determination or self-control. The idea of self-control depends, in turn, on a supposed opposition between the better self (which controls) and a lesser self that is base, contingent and ephemeral (which is to be mastered, or denied). The identification of freedom with goodness and reason has persisted,[3] despite shifts and discontinuities in what these terms have meant. The point of viewing the Stoic tradition as a tradition, moreover, is not to claim authority for any favoured ideas about freedom that might be derived from it, but to treat it as a repository of ideas about a set of problems that have at least a family resemblance, which can serve to illuminate and provide a framework for contemporary thinking about freedom. Despite their peculiarly modern meanings, the Enlightenment notion that freedom and power are increased through knowledge (as well as related ideas about release from self-repression), and the quest for authenticity, have important roots in the Stoic tradition.

In what follows I will look at several difficulties that Foucault's work raises for the Stoic conception of freedom, and whether these difficulties can be resolved in a way that preserves what is valid and enduring in the Stoic tradition.

Foucauldian Objections to the Stoic Tradition

It is not difficult to see that each of the themes I have identified as marking out the Stoic tradition are apparently undermined or thrown into doubt by various claims and themes from Foucault's writings (and those of his interpreters), especially the accounts of the development of the human sciences, of normalising institutions and technologies, and his genealogy of the modern subject. The notion that there is a better, essential or true self is belied by the discontinuities Foucault has identified in what the various members of the Stoic tradition have taken the essential self to be. The differences between ancient and Stoic conceptions of self as a locus of disciplinary practices and exercises (Foucault, 1988g: 34) and ascetic and modern notions of self as something hidden deep within us, seem to be too wide to allow that all have been talking about one object whose nature they have disagreed about. Moreover, our modern idea that there is an essential self ('the real me') whose truth may be revealed by psychology and related disciplines, is undermined by Foucault's Nietzschean claims that the modern self is a creation rather than a natural kind awaiting discovery. The sciences do not discover their objects: they create them, by ordering and manipulating the world in ways that assume their existence and constantly supply evidence of it. At the same time as science reveals, it occludes and obscures, by reducing our sensitivity to phenomena that do not fit its 'disciplinary matrixes' (Kuhn, 1970: 182). As already noted, Foucault has been particularly concerned with the ways in which the human sciences ensnare us in identities that limit what we can do and be, which exclude possibilities for what we are and can become (Dews, 1987: 187).

The search for authenticity (the modern inheritor of the Stoic tradition's preoccupation with the true self) has locked us into 'regimes of truth', most notably (in Foucault's work) the discourses on sexuality, involving a restless and unending quest to testify and confess. Foucault rejects the view, which he associates with the 'repressive hypothesis' (the idea that in the nineteenth century particularly, there took place a concerted repression of our sexual nature and its expression (Foucault, 1978: 1–49)), that truth is opposed to power and can liberate us from it, on the grounds that truth and authenticity are themselves created by power relations and techniques and help to sustain them (Dreyfus and Rabinow, 1982: 127).

The modern subject is also a product of confessional, surveillance and disciplinary technologies, which have been centuries in the making (and which have provided the basis for the development of the supposedly disinterested and independent human sciences). The subject is not self-determining, but an effect of power. The more the modern subject seeks to know herself, and the more she seeks to resist power and be self-determining, the more effectively she will be enmeshed in power (Dreyfus and Rabinow, 1982: 127). And just as power encloses, constitutes and sustains the subject, it is also intertwined with the supposed means of her emancipation: knowledge. All the means of acquiring self-knowledge – reflection, introspection and self-scrutiny, inference, analysis and so on – will involve models or identities that serve to sustain and develop the mechanisms of power.

The idea that freedom is acquired by learning to think and act in accordance with what is right and reasonable runs up against a Nietzschean insistence in Foucault's work that such terms mask strategies of exclusion, normalisation and domination (Dreyfus and Rabinow, 1982: 109). Reason and virtue are not transhistorical givens, but bear the marks of methods, systems of observation and treatment, and institutions, which have sought ever tighter control over formerly errant and uncontrollable sections of the population. This also brings into question another of the themes identified above: that self-determination or self-mastery contrasts the true self with what is alien to it. The idea that self-determination stands in opposition to determination by what is alien or extrinsic identifies it again as a normalising discourse, resting on categories of other – the delinquent, the incontinent, the madman – which have been imposed on hoards of disparate and resisting minds and bodies.

Lastly, Foucault's insights into the operation of power can be used to argue that the preoccupation, to be found among the modern continuants of the Stoic tradition (and beyond it), with reconciling individual self-determination with laws and institutions of authority can also be seen to reflect deeper preoccupations about normalisation and control. The reconciliation of individual interests and conscience with legally imposed norms is sought through an ideal of individual self-determination which is manageable, law-abiding, predictable and controllable: one in which freedoms formerly enjoyed by unmanageable groups and classes are excluded or eliminated; possibly motivated by a desire to ensure those freedoms enjoyed by the educated and wealthy.[4] Perhaps none of this should be surprising, given that the (mostly) men who have made up the Stoic tradition have largely been drawn from narrow and privileged sections of society. It is a tradition of wise and detached men. It may also be one whose members have not sought to bring liberation, but rather to reorder the world according to their narrow social horizons.

Can the Stoic tradition about freedom meet these criticisms?[5] Or can anything of value be preserved from it? In what follows I will examine, in turn, what Foucault has had to say about power and normalisation, surveillance and knowledge, and what are the consequences of each for the possibility of freedom.

Power, Normalisation and Freedom

Power, according to Foucault, has hitherto been negatively conceived by the juridico-political model as repressive, punitive, denying and so on (Foucault, 1978: 82–91). But it should also be understood positively as productive and creative (Foucault, 1977a: 194). If power is creative and productive, then to that extent one would also expect it to be, in various ways, enabling and even liberating. But as I mentioned above, despite his injunction to view power positively, where Foucault does refer to possibilities for emancipation it is characteristically in terms of opposition or resistance to power and power-imposed identities. From his chronicling of the seditious discourses of delinquents, madmen and anarchists, to his later attempts to recapture something of the ancient *ars erotica* and care of the self, Foucault has tended to identify emancipation with 'recalcitrance' (see opening quote), resistance, refusal or renegotiation of power, and the exploration of possibilities of existence that transgress or modify power relationships and identities. In arguing that power is not always and everywhere a monolithic relationship of domination, Foucault's characteristic tendency is to see power as something to be resisted, exposed or thwarted.[6]

In *Discipline and Punish* Foucault depicts power as a collection of proliferating technologies for normalisation, which have gradually brought disparate and anarchic populations under centralised regimens (Foucault, 1977a: 200–1). Operating through central institutions such as the prison and the clinic, power has spread its tentacles among the population at large by means of welfare programmes, health care monitoring, and control and isolation of deviant groups. The system of 'bio-power' (Foucault, 1978: 141–4; Dreyfus and Rabinow, 1982: 133–42) achieves its aims by dividing, classifying and recording increasingly minute details of individual and family life (Foucault, 1977a: 211–12). The same compartmentalising observation and analysis has been performed on the human body (Foucault, 1977a: 135–41, 164). In achieving this, power turns individuals into productive and efficient units, and this is power's real interest in individuals. The State, as one locus of power, is concerned with the health and welfare of individuals only to the extent that it requires the individual's health and welfare for its own reasons (Foucault, 1988h: 152). The prison system enables control of the movement of the delinquent population at large, and is able to put this to use in isolating delinquency from the wider population (making them fear it and being associated with it), in making crime manageable, by creating a strike-breaking reserve work-force and in profiting economically from the work of prostitutes (Foucault, 1977a: 271–87).

As power turns individuals into its creatures, it must deny former freedoms and ways of life that are antithetical to its mechanisms and purposes. A population whose members formerly engaged in occasional, diverse and unmanageable illegality are now dragooned, on the one hand, into delinquent groups who are forced into a monitored and controlled life of crime (Foucault, 1977a: 278 and 290–2), and, on the other, into the law-abiding, who must ceaselessly monitor and modify their behaviour to avoid joining the ranks of delinquents on the road to ruin (Foucault, 1977a: 285–7, 299).

The disciplinary images of power called to mind by such processes are those of the army, the machine and the social insect; images in which regimentation, order, efficiency and minute specialisation are set to work in the service of a larger purpose. Small wonder then that Foucault's inclination was to locate freedom within resistance to power and refusal of power-imposed identities, or that any possibilities for emancipation his work might offer have typically been understood in this way. But is resistance the only source of freedom in relation to power? Again, if power is creative and productive, if it trains and develops skills in individuals, why should it not be thought of as sometimes enabling and extending the options of individuals (even as it closes off others)?

The emergence of the systems of power Foucault describes can be seen as a solution to the fundamental problem of government: namely, 'how are people to live together?' (cf. Foucault, 1977a: 221). The development of trade, industry and population growth progressively undermined those feudal and religious communities, social distinctions and structures that formerly enabled populations to co-exist, and which had contained, adjudicated and resolved their struggles and opposing interests. The mechanisms and technologies of disciplinary power have gradually replaced or absorbed older structures as the means to social cohesion and functioning (Foucault, 1977a: 216). At the same time, however, power has not given an answer to the general and abstract question 'how are people to live together?', but to more specific ones: namely, 'how are the rest to live with me/us/the bourgeoisie/the modern state?' and 'how are people to be if they are to meet the needs of state and industry?' Power has answered the question of government in ways that favour the needs of capitalism and the state, and of the several professions and institutions it has brought into being (Foucault 1977a: 221; 280). It has therefore been an instrument of class and professional domination, although its role and functioning are not reducible to that, and there have, as Foucault points out, been many opportunities of resistance to such domination (Foucault, 1988i: 12–13).

But even if historically power has favoured the interests of a class, and of various institutional groups, this should not cause us to forget that it is at the same time one answer to the general question about government. Foucault's accounts of the development of the structures and technologies that have sustained power, and their relationship to the development of industrial capitalism, are not ones in which all connections and linkages are necessary. Power has not always and everywhere served the interests of the bourgeoisie, and there is no reason to suppose that it must always do so (Foucault, 1988i: 12–13). Any society that has embarked on industrialisa-tion and modernisation, whether or not it is economically dominated by the bourgeoisie, must have ways of normalising and making efficient use of its population, just to exist.

In addition to what it enables, any social arrangement must deny certain freedoms, both to maintain sustainable cohesion and to protect those freedoms it makes possible. It is a truism in political philosophy that the existence of any freedom always requires the denial and exclusion of others. Therefore, just as teachers, educators, doctors and social workers are the ubiquitous judges of our behaviour (Foucault, 1977a: 304), so also are they enablers and emancipators. A literate population can be enormously useful to state and industry, but a literate society is also one whose members can have new options and possibilities and be free to enjoy pleasures denied to their forebears.

T.H. Green (1956) famously made the case for legal standards of health and safety in factories on the grounds that safe and healthy working conditions extend the freedom of workers by providing them with the material conditions for self-realisation.[7] It would be a naive worker who believes that factory inspectorates are interested in maximising her freedom, but workers and their organisations can make informed judgements about the effectiveness of health and safety legislation and factory inspections in protecting and advancing their interests.[8]

To determine the relationship between power and freedom in particular cases, therefore, it is necessary to ask whether the system of health care, welfare, criminal justice or whatever, frustrates or enables us (and those we care about or identify with) to satisfy our interests and get what we want, and how effectively it does so. We can also then ask, as Foucault suggests (Foucault, 1988i: 12–13), whether and how a network of power that frustrates or obstructs us can be resisted, changed or overthrown by individual or collective action. We can ask of the prison system: is a social technology that perpetuates a delinquent population necessary? And if so, for whom and for what? Does any sufficiently stable set of social arrangements require the maintenance and surveillance of deviant groups? Or is it only capitalism that needs this? Can it be reformed or must it be replaced?[9] And how do the answers to these questions stand in relation to my/your/our/their interests? In other words, it doesn't matter that power has its own large designs: what matters is whether they are compatible with ours.

The modern mechanisms of power that Foucault has analysed are not, of course, the only strategies of normalisation there have been. If we follow the Stoic tradition in linking freedom with virtue and reason, we will be reminded that virtue and reason are not universals but weapons of normalisation in the service of particular strategies, struggles and interests (Dreyfus and Rabinow, 1982: 109). Foucault has also pointed out that the concept of self-mastery was originally understood as a necessary condition for the proper exercise of mastery over one's household and the exercise of superiority over others in society (Foucault, 1986: 94–5).

A further, related, problem is that the philosophical aim of resolving the individual's interests, freedoms and conscience with those of community and State may be unsatisfiable: because the emergence of the modern subject, with her modern conscience, renders impossible the identification of self with social norms, laws and practices, which the Stoics could take for granted. It is a familiar Nietzschean theme that the development of the modern conscience, which is not obliged to defer to any authority, spells the end of universal virtues: even selfishness is legitimised (or anyhow decriminalised).

Again, however, we can allow that concepts such as virtue and reason mask strategies of normalisation, and still ask what freedoms and possibilities for living these strategies render possible, what they prevent, whose interests they serve or hinder, and what they mean for us. Indeed, this is in keeping with the spirit of Foucault's enquiries about ancient-world ethical practices as 'practices of freedom' (Foucault, 1988i). Shorn of universalism, the Stoic tradition's claims about the link between freedom and reason and goodness serves to remind us that individual freedoms are socially dependent, and that individual values and standards of reasonability are not created *ex nihilo* by individuals, even though they may always be open to individual critique. An individual's freedom depends on what she is, and how other things stand in relation to that. And what an individual is is partly constituted by shared (rather than universal) values and standards (Taylor, 1984). The pursuit of individual desires and goals, therefore, and whether the individual is able to pursue them freely, necessarily involves values and standards or ideals of rightness and virtue.

In discussing self-mastery, furthermore, Foucault points out that even in the Hellenic period the concept began to undergo an elaboration and metamorphosis, in which domination over the household and assertion of superiority over others was displaced by obligations and relations of reciprocity within marriage and society (Foucault, 1986: 94–5, 147–9, 173). The idea of self-determination has doubtless undergone further shifts and transformations in the modern age, reflecting changes in social arrangements, rights and obligations, which will have taken it further still from its original hermeneutic linkages with master–slave relations and conquest. Foucault's analyses give us no reason to suppose, therefore, that the idea of self-determination is irredeemably bound up with those strategies of domination and subordination with which it was originally associated.

Foucault has often stressed the ways in which systems and strategies of normalisation close off possibilities and freedoms rather than opening them up. He documents the loss of former freedoms to those categorised and regimented as mad or delinquent under the clinic and the prison, as well as their attempts at resistance. In this, he may be suspected of an unacknowledged identification of freedom with spontaneity and lack of restriction,[10] and certainly it is all too easy to be led to such an identification when reading *Madness and Civilization* and *Discipline and Punish*. The unanalysed madman or the wandering vagabond may have been unburdened by responsibility and unrestricted by power, but were assuredly at the beck and call of unbidden voices and the harsh struggle for existence. Foucault's failure to acknowledge that every freedom requires the curtailing of others, together with his general failure to engage in sustained theorising about freedom, is no doubt owed to his genealogist's awareness of the disjunctures and historical specificity of discourses about freedom and the normalising strategies they embody. But it leaves him, as I suggested at the beginning of the chapter, with no positive recommendation to offer for the liberating practices of making and remaking of self whose possibility he saw his later work as contributing to. At any rate, there is nothing in Foucault's analyses of the development of systems of power and normalisation which should cause us to reject Seneca's claim that the virtuous and wise enjoy a qualitatively higher form of freedom than that denied to the wicked and stupid. The mere fact that talk about virtue, reason and freedom is bound up with normalising strategies does not entail that these concepts should be rejected or permanently held in scare quotes.

Surveillance and Freedom

In his account of the development of the modern prison system, Foucault gives central place to the Panopticon, not as the key historical mechanism by which power has gained its place in our lives, but as an ideal symbol of the way in which it operates (Foucault, 1977a: 205). The Panopticon is a system of surveillance designed for the efficient monitoring of prisoners, but what is more important is that it aims at the efficient control of behaviour by involving the prisoners themselves in their own surveillance. This effect is achieved by leaving prisoners with no means of concealment from the central observation tower and no means of telling whether they are being observed. Never knowing whether he is being watched, the prisoner is compelled to behave as if he is always watched, and in doing so his gaze is constantly turned on himself. The system is an ideal machine for the creation of self-conscious individuals: each under the regulation of an individual conscience that internalises the system of panoptic surveillance (Foucault, 1977a: 200–9).[11]

The method of operation of the Panopticon resonates throughout the many historical systems and techniques of power Foucault describes. Populations were monitored in ever increasing detail by health and welfare authorities;

individuals were required to record and report on details of their families, their health, their actions and their morals.[12] In schools, techniques adapted from military and monastic life were set to work in producing healthy, efficient and self-policing individuals. Health and efficiency were not just to be monitored and recorded by technologies of surveillance, however, but also to be improved by them and by a concomitant barrage of normalising disciplines, rituals and skills (Foucault, 1977a: 210–11). These disciplines and skills were directed at the various parts into which power divided and classified the body,[13] with the effect that individuals were made more attentive and discriminating about their appearances, actions, health, thoughts and desires.

The modern individual is neither self-creating nor self-determining, but an effect and a means of disciplinary and surveillance techniques. The notion that subjects can freely choose to refuse power naively assumes they can exist without it. If there are means of escape, therefore, from the regimented identities and purposes that power allocates to us, they are unlikely to be realised by the tools available to us as subjects (conscience, introspection, self-analysis, self-consciousness and so on). For as long as we think and act as subjects, we replicate and sustain power (Dews, 1987: 161, Dreyfus and Rabinow, 1982: 169). Without forgetting the argument I have already set out, that power in its various forms may be a source of some freedoms while being an obstacle to others, is it true that the subject, in being an effect of power, lacks self-determination? That would be true if the aims to which we can put the self-monitoring habits and skills that constitute subjects are necessarily the aims sought by the technologies and systems that inculcate those habits and skills. But self-monitoring, introspection and other skills and habits of mind that are set in motion by power can all be adapted to purposes other than those of normalisation, control, productive efficiency and so forth. Just as a child's first lie adapts what she has learned to her own unsanctioned ends, so can other disciplines of mind and body and the knowledge acquired by habits of self-scrutiny be put to uses other than those of the disciplinary technologies. Someone who cannot escape the gaze of power can think about how to turn the gaze to her advantage (for example, by learning from the responses her behaviour provokes and by manipulating them). Even soldiers can adapt their skills and the disciplines in which they operate in ways that buck the system. To be sure, the possibilities available to the soldier or the prisoner are heavily constrained, but that is partly because of the *coercive* systems within which they live (rather than their involvement in power as such) and the fact that they are monitored much more closely than the population at large.

As mentioned earlier, in 'The Ethic of Care for the Self as a Practice of Freedom' (Foucault, 1988i),[14] Foucault acknowledges the possibilities that individuals and groups have within relations of power to exercise freedom and pursue their interests, and is at pains to redress the view imputed to him that power as an inescapable system of domination leaves no room for freedom (1988i: 13). He distinguishes between relations of power as such, which are fields or games within which liberty can be exercised, and relations of domination. What needs resisting, and often can be, he thinks, are relations of domination. This is an important corrective to the way in which Foucault's account of the relationship between power, subjectivity and freedom has often been understood. Nevertheless, his replies to the charge that he excludes any possibility of freedom leave important questions unanswered. If there is a distinction to be drawn, for example, between those relations of power that are relations of domination and those that are not, where do the various medical, psychiatric and carceral systems of surveillance and discipline, detailed in *Discipline and Punish* and elsewhere, stand in relation to that distinction? And would he have accepted that the possibilities for acting freely within relations of power are partly founded on those self-directed skills and habits that constitute us as subjects, which in turn are founded on the disciplinary technologies?

An individual subject has skills and capacities for self-awareness and scrutiny which make it possible for her to consider herself in abstraction from her situation and what is expected of her, and to imagine alternatives to what she has been and done hitherto. Being a subject does not guarantee that an individual will see the alternatives, and it is possible of course for an individual to spend her life in vain pursuit of her 'true self'. Nevertheless, the habits and skills that mark us out as self-monitoring subjects do create possibilities for us that would be lacking without them.

A further question to consider, echoing what I have already said about power, is whether the various surveillance technologies detailed in Foucault's genealogy of the subject could be replaced by others. I have mentioned Foucault's observation that certain systems of surveillance and control that were outgrowths of the prison system came to be abandoned when they had outlived their usefulness.[15] And since it is possible to question the usefulness or effectiveness of certain systems, and also to ask for whom and for what they are useful, it follows that power itself is open to the critical gaze of subjects.[16] It is unlikely that power in any conceivable form could co-exist with a population composed entirely of individuals living lives of freewheeling spontaneity (even allowing that such a society could exist at all), but it is conceivable that systems of observation and surveillance can be reformed, abandoned and replaced in ways that make power more enabling and responsive to the needs of disadvantaged and marginalised groups and individuals. And part of what makes this possible is a population of individuals who have acquired (albeit in varying degrees) mental and behavioural habits of questioning, scrutinising, self-awareness and recording that had their genesis in the regimes and surveillance techniques of the monastery, the confessional, the army, the school, the prison and the clinic.

Questions can also be asked about the degree to which we need to be monitored and recorded, given that an effect of creating self-monitoring subjects is supposed to be that being self-monitoring and self-regulating means not requiring constant supervision by external systems and officials. (I assume that the existence of subjects requires the existence of some systems of power, including systems of surveillance and recording: that the habits and skills that are inculcated by power will always need to be sustained by monitoring systems, disciplines (especially in schools) and truth regimes.)

The inculcation of skills and capacities by disciplinary technologies also presents an interesting parallel to the way in which the practices of the Stoics were aimed at inculcating principles and rules of conduct which, in Foucault's words, 'tell you in each situation, and in some way spontaneously, how you should behave' (Foucault, 1988i: 6). The idea of such practices is expressed in a passage from Plutarch:

> You must have learned principles so firmly that when your desires, your appetites or your fears awaken like barking dogs, the *logos* will speak with the voice of a master who silences the dogs by a single command. (Foucault, 1988i: 6)

Commenting on this, Foucault remarks: 'You have there the idea of a *logos* who would operate in some way without your doing anything. You will have become the *logos* or the *logos* will have become you' (1988i: 6). This raises a theme repeated throughout the Stoic tradition, that one's wants and desires must be mastered and modified through training so that they can be brought into line with what is within one's power and what is good for one to have. If freedom can be thwarted by obstacles to our desires, we may remedy this either by overcoming the obstacles or by silencing the desires. Many have regarded this as a recommendation for quietism and acceptance of tyranny. However, while the problem of whether to adjust or to resist has been a source of tension within the Stoic tradition, a quick glance at some of its most well-known members [17] gives the lie to the charge of quietism. The enduring lesson of the Stoic argument is that an untrained and undisciplined individual will be subject to conflicting desires and needs. As already remarked, the flourishing of particular freedoms always depends on the denial of others; and we may add that the development of a free individual can often require the 'training out' of desires whose realisation depends on illicit or unrealisable freedoms. The practice of freedom through reshaping the self, therefore, can be as much a matter of adjustment to power relations and disciplinary technologies as of transgression.

   As before, given that we do exist as self-monitoring subjects, with the skills, habits and awareness that go with that, how are we to be free? How can those skills and habits enable us to evaluate and pursue our goals and interests more effectively? And do they make it possible for us to reappraise and change what we want and what we are? This last question brings me on to whether it is possible to know ourselves in ways that make it possible to determine what we really want, and raises the further Foucauldian problem of the relationship between knowledge and power.

Knowledge and Freedom

According to Foucault, the old Stoic idea that freedom requires self-knowledge has, particularly since the sixteenth century, acquired a cognitivist content it did not originally possess (Foucault, 1988g: 22). From Spinoza to Freud, we have been told that for as long as we fail to understand the motives and hidden passions that animate us, we will be subject to them and frustrated by them. In order to be free and fulfilled we must bring those 'passive emotions' (Spinoza, 1910, pt v, prop. ix–x; Goodman, 1987: 33) and neuroses which obstruct our goals and shatter our equanimity into the light, and gradually weaken their hold on us by doing so. By the same token, we are enjoined to discover, by scientific enquiry and self-analysis, what is essential and healthy in us (Dreyfus and Rabinow, 1982: 175) in order to free it from compulsions and obsolete repressions: we must reveal ourselves to ourselves.

   The capacity for introspective self-analysis is central to the individual subject's supposed abilities to self-determine and to take responsibility for what she does and what she is. It is also a central target of Foucault's genealogy of the modern self. In the first volume of *The History of Sexuality* Foucault identifies the belief that the key to our true selves lies in sexuality – that sexuality is the key which will reveal all (Foucault, 1978: 77) – as a dominating theme of our age. The late nineteenth- and twentieth-century idea that we can be emancipated by recognising our true sexual nature and throwing off the systems of repression built around it overlooks the fact that these supposed systems of repression were actually part of an enormous proliferation of discourses of sexuality which produced and sustained sexuality, and that movements for emancipation from sexual repression are simply a continuation of those discourses. The emancipatory theories of Reich and others sought to speak truth to power. But according to Foucault it is power that bids us to speak the truth, to reveal and to confess: 'The obligation to confess is now relayed through so many different points, is so deeply ingrained in us, that we no longer perceive it as the effect of a power that constrains us' (Foucault, 1978: 60). In seeking to discover her true sexual self, the individual becomes enmeshed in a quest for truth that binds her to particular identities. These identities, however, are products of the discourses of sexuality and are imposed on us by the pursuit of inner truth and authenticity, rather than discovered by it.

Foucault also argues that the emergence of sexuality was bound up with normalising strategies of the medical and psychiatric disciplines (Foucault, 1978: 36–49), which in turn were founded on systems of power that sought to bring the health and behaviour of the population under regular and detailed observation, recording and control (Foucault, 1977a: 191, 295–6, 305). The search for authenticity and sexual liberation, therefore, is not a means of emancipation from some supposed repression of our essential natures, but an outgrowth of systems that have sought to control populations and to turn them into healthy and efficient units. The discourses of sexuality have not been engaged in a disinterested pursuit of truth and emancipation, but in the manufacture of 'régime[s] of truth' (Foucault, 1980f: 133) in the interests of control. The ties between knowledge and power are too numerous and strong for us to assume that the pursuit of knowledge must lead to emancipation (Foucault, 1977a: 27–8).

Peter Dews has pointed to an unresolved tension in the claims made by Foucault about the discourses of sexuality and the human sciences more generally (Dews, 1987: 189–92). Science is (part of) a system of regimes of truth which, rather than straightforwardly observing or discovering it, imposes order on the world: it creates truth. If we adopt such a Nietzschean perspectivist view on science, we must conclude that there is no objective or *a priori* reason to view one regime of truth as better or worse than any other. It follows that the human sciences, in imposing identities and regimes of truth on recalcitrant individuals and populations, cannot be rejected as ideological or illusory on that account: they have simply done what all sciences do. But Foucault has also wished to say that the human sciences have been inept, deficient and inconsistent in various ways. In *Madness and Civilization* Foucault argued that the attempt to understand madness through psychoanalysis is misconceived, because the 'sovereign enterprise of unreason' is obscured or distorted by the psychoanalytic schemas and categories that seek to grasp it (Foucault, 1965: 278; see also Dews, 1987: 181–3). The history of the 'science' of criminology is so littered with theoretical inconsistency and *ad hoc*-ness that its endurance and growth could only plausibly be explained by its having a usefulness to the prison system that was not dependent on any strictly scientific success (Foucault, 1980f: 47).

As Dews points out, however, Foucault is reluctant to brand the human sciences as illusory, on the grounds that this would imply discourse-independent standards of truth and objectivity (Dews, 1987: 190; Foucault, 1980f: 118). But we do not need a discourse-independent standard of truth to distinguish between truth regimes and pseudo-truth regimes. To say that the natural sciences are regimes of truth is to identify them as having certain kinds of structure and objectives, and therefore to distinguish them from other practices and pursuits that do not share those structures and purposes. If the human sciences (or, at any rate, some of them) have been modelled on the natural sciences, but nevertheless lack certain structural features of the natural sciences (such as a tolerable level of coherency and consistency), then they can properly be described as pseudo-truth regimes.

If the modern quest to free our true natures and, more generally, to find authenticity, is not just part and parcel of a set of proliferating practices and technologies of control, but also of truth regimes that fail to produce truth, where does this leave the Stoic tradition (especially its modern continuants), with its identification of a true, essential or deep self and its belief in the importance of self-knowledge as a means to the emancipation of that true self?[18] If we give up the notion of an essential self, we are left with the prospect that freedom consists just in being able to act on our strongest desires (even when such desires are repellent to the individual who has them),[19] or that *freedom* (supposing that it means anything) is just a word for a coincidence between what one is motivated to do and how one feels about that. We are left with this because without some notion of what is essential to us – some deep truth or identity – we have no way of privileging some motives (those that best realise what we are essentially or what we really want) over others, as those that will cause or allow us to act freely (cf. Taylor, 1984: 178).

Foucault's solution to this difficulty would presumably be to privilege those motives that point in the direction of transgression of 'who we are', or which optimise the conditions for such transgression (Foucault, 1984a: 46). As Charles Taylor has pointed out, however, such a move does not offer a way out of the problem (Taylor, 1984: 180–1). Without reference to some form of identity, deep self, or fundamental want, we have no reason for adopting any particular practice of transgression. *Freedom* is a contrastive term and we cannot talk meaningfully of freedom or liberation except in relation to some state of affairs that is unfree. For any state of affairs to be characterised as unfree, however, it must stand in opposition to some want or some feature of one's nature or identity.

Remembering that the Stoic tradition has addressed itself at different times to historically different kinds of individuals, what is valid about the Stoic conception of freedom is its identification of freedom with what we/the individual really wants; where this means not what we most powerfully desire, but which desires we most identify with or most value.[20] There is no doubt a lot more to what we are, individually and collectively, than what it is that we want and value, but inasmuch as freedom is to be sought in what we really are – our true selves – it is because of its connection with what we want and value.

Understood in this way, the Stoic tradition has claimed that we are free to the extent that we are able to know and realise what we really want. Sometimes this is straightforward enough: sometimes there is no complication about what we really want, and no difficulty in getting it. Sometimes we need to reflect on and evaluate competing aims, desires and values, but having done this we can put our reflective judgements into action. In these cases our everyday folk-psychological battery of concepts (*belief, desire, hope, wish, care, hate, resentment* and so on) are all we need to calculate and act on what we really want. But what of those cases where we seem unable to resolve value conflicts, or in which neurotic compulsions prevent us from doing what we want? In such cases, we might, if we have the motivation and the opportunity, turn to counselling and psychotherapy to try and resolve our problems. But if the various forms of psychotherapy are all pseudo-truth regimes, then instead of resolving our problems they will merely trap us within limiting identities and fruitless searches for authenticity (cf. Hutton, 1988: 139).

There have, however, been well documented attempts to develop approaches to counselling and therapy that break with the quasi-medical models of psychiatric 'treatments'. The therapeutic approaches of R.D. Laing and others have sought ways of enabling clients to develop their own understandings of their problems, and to find their own ways of resolving them (Laing, 1960; Woodward, 1988). Such approaches have stressed the importance of being attentive to why individuals seek therapy, what they hope to get out of it, and how they understand their problems, rather than attempting to get them to see themselves in terms of one or other pre-existing set of pathologising categories. These approaches therefore share something of the spirit of the practices of *ars erotica* that Foucault sought to recapture, which often involved guidance by experienced practitioners in techniques and practices that would yield a more fulfilling life.

Anti-psychiatric psychotherapies cannot avoid the need for conceptual frameworks which can obscure as well as reveal, and their therapeutic techniques can be unsuccessful: but at least it is possible for an individual to make reflective judgements about the efficacy of a therapy in assisting a resolution of her problems as she understands them. Determining what we really want and how we really want to be, and making use of psychothera- peutic techniques in order to do so, need not be as forlorn as Foucault's accounts of psychiatry and the discourses of sexuality might otherwise lead us to conclude.[21]

By focusing the search for authenticity on what it is that we really want, we can avoid the problem with which Foucault's account of truth regimes faces us: that they impose identities on us rather than helping us to discover them (Dews, 1987: 168). The individual need only know as much about herself, through the prisms of truth regimes and identities, as will enable her to determine what she really wants and how to go about getting it.

Since we, as individual self-scrutinising subjects, cannot take for granted that answers to questions about what we want are always to be found within well-established practices and norms – that what is good for others is good for us – cognitive self-knowledge assumes greater importance for us. But this kind of knowledge is not all we require in order to get what we really want: we need also to develop certain habits and skills (including, where necessary, more well-developed skills of introspection and self-analysis) that will enable us to acquire that knowledge and put it to use in living well and freely. And there are also limits to how much of this knowledge an individual will want: as I said, whatever is enough for her to determine what she really wants and to enable her to go about getting it. There is no limit on further questions that cognitive self-knowledge might suggest, but there are certainly limits to the point of asking them.

Foucault's retrieval of practices and techniques of aestheticisation and care of the self can be taken as implicitly recommending a replacement of discovery of truth about the self with projects of self-creation (or at least as valuing one over the other (Bernauer and Mahon, 1994: 155)). To adopt such a recommendation, however, would be to forget that the background to both creativity and discovery is what we want, which is to say, what we seek, what we need and how we wish to be. Projects of self-creation do not provide an alternative to the pursuit of truth because they are motivated by many of the same concerns for which we as individual subjects seek to know the truth about ourselves. Self-creation and the pursuit of self-knowledge are overlapping and interdependent enterprises. This is not to say that any act of self-creation must be motivated by an explicit pursuit of truth. We may experiment with self-forming practices or modes of being with the aim of seeing how we might be (Foucault, 1984a: 50) or of conforming to some ethical or aesthetic ideal, but in engaging in such experiments we will inevitably face questions about whether they are what we really want or how we really wish to be, and the answers to such questions will be constrained by truth, identity and integrity.

Neither, therefore, can an 'art of existence' (Foucault, 1986: 43) be considered an alternative, as such, to the various struggles (against and within systems of power) by means of which individuals seek to protect and extend their freedoms and interests collectively. Knowing and discovering what we want, we continually face questions about whether to try and change the world or ourselves. For reasons that will be familiar by now, Foucault's analyses of the omnipresence of relations and systems of power should not lead us to conclude that we cannot ever change the world in ways we would wish to.

It might be objected that to identify freedom with knowing and getting what we really want (which is to say, what we value, or those desires with which we actively identify) is arbitrary, since what each of us wants is socially constructed, contingent and shaped and constrained by systems of power. As I have already argued, however, the fact that values, desires, freedoms, or whatever are created and sustained by power, is in itself no reason for doubting their validity or value.[22] Whether we should be troubled by the relationship between disciplinary power and our values and desires will depend on whether we judge a system of power to be one that enables us and with which we identify.[23] It can happen, of course, that the point at which an individual is satisfied that she knows what she really wants is arrived at in some degree arbitrarily. It is always possible that someone might discover, by considering other options or taking more time to reflect, that she has been mistaken about what she really wants. This is always possible, because for self-knowing and self-critical subjects no value, desire, or putative need is exempt from critique. For example, a professional soldier who seeks fulfilment in pursuit of the military virtues, and to an extent finds it, may, because of his preoccupation with that kind of life, fail to consider alternative ways of living that would have been more fulfilling for him.

Individuals must make decisions about how much time and energy to spend on reflecting about which goals to pursue and how to pursue them. Sometimes such decisions are made because lack of time prevents further reflection. Some individuals decide not to reflect further, because the conclusions they have arrived at just 'feel right'; or because a troubling problem has been solved; or again, to take up a suggestion of Harry Frankfurt's, we sometimes make decisions because we judge that further reflection is unlikely to yield a different result, just as we judge, after having checked and rechecked a calculation, that we can be sure enough of the result not to have to check it again (Frankfurt, 1988: 167–9). To know what one wants, where there is some doubt about it, requires critically examining goals, values and desires and bringing them into correspondence with others. There is no Archimedian point in all of this from which we can uniquely and conclusively determine what we want most: but it does not follow from the fact that our judgements about what we want are always open to potential revision that we cannot arrive at informed judgements about what to do and what to be that will make us freer than we would otherwise be. To say that we can be free and that freedom has to do with getting what we want implies that there are things we want and that we can often know what they are: not that as knowing subjects we have an unquestionable authority in respect of what we want.

Foucault's analyses of the links between knowledge and disciplinary power, therefore, are a salutary caution against quests for authenticity that depend on revealing our deeper selves and motives, and against acceptance of the normalising identities that the discourses of sexuality and psychology attempt to impose on us. His account of the ancient idea of self-knowledge as embedded in techniques and practices of care of the self also serves as a corrective to the one-sided preoccupation with cognitive and discursive knowledge that has characterised epistemology since Descartes (and with it, no doubt, the understanding of the link between self-knowledge and self-determination to be found among the modern inheritors of the Stoic tradition). An important lesson of Foucault's work should therefore be to remind us to ask ourselves why we want self-knowledge and how much we need to know in order to be sure about what we want and how to get it. That the search for the inner-truth about ourselves has its origins in the Christian confession, and more generally that knowledge has myriad links and dependencies with disciplinary power, does not rule out the possibility of emancipation through knowledge. Rather, Foucault's insights may enable us to come to a better understanding of how it is that knowledge can make us freer.

Conclusion

We modern individuals are not the men the Stoics were. We cannot, as they could (within an admittedly narrow and exclusive social framework), straight-forwardly identify ourselves and our freedoms with established norms and practices, or take for granted a shared understanding of rightness and goodness. We must know more. And we must judge for ourselves (Foucault, 1984a: 34–8). For all that, the Stoic belief that freedom, understood as self-determination or self-mastery, can be acquired by learning to think and act in accordance with reason and virtue, thereby realising our better or essential selves, remains valid for us. Self-determination for us means understanding and being able to do and be what we really want, and this involves an idea that there are features of ourselves and our lives that are more fundamental or essential than others. Those features can include inherited and shared values: values that shape our understanding of what is reasonable and good. We can also gain greater insight (when we need to) into what we really want and how to overcome those psychological and external obstacles to getting it, by means of psychotherapeutic methods and knowledges.

In analysing what it means to be free philosophers engage in a dialogue that collapses millennia. Thereby we assume a degree of shared understanding of concepts and terms of art with Socrates, Plato and the Stoics. This is as it should be, but if we are to know what it is to be free, we need also to keep in mind who and what we are; and Foucault's most important contribution to philosophy is, I think, in helping to show us what we are (and can be) and in reminding us of our peculiarity.

If as subjects we cannot escape power (supposing it might make sense to want to), we can adapt the monitoring, scrutinising and self-analysing habits and skills with which power has equipped us, to assess and evaluate how particular systems of power stand in relation to what we want, and we can bring our judgements about that into correspondence with judgements we make about ourselves. The responsibilities and practices that disciplinary power places on the individual can be seen as a source of tyranny and loss when contrasted with some of the unencumbered and 'spontaneous' freedoms it has destroyed. But discipline can create as well as destroy freedoms. The question that Foucault's work poses for the philosophy of freedom is not 'is freedom possible?', but 'how are modern individuals, imbued with and sustained by systems of discipline and surveillance, to be free?'

NOTES

1. In addition to the Stoics, according to Adler, the tradition of 'the acquired freedom of self perfection' encompasses, amongst others, Plato, Augustine, Aquinas, Spinoza, Leibniz, Rousseau, Kant, Hegel, Freud, Whitehead and Russell; and arguably also Comte, Marx, Engels, Nietzsche and Durkheim (Adler, 1958:134).
2. Some members of the tradition, notably Locke and Hegel, treat favourable environmental circumstances as a distinct but lesser freedom.
3. See, for example, Wolf, 1990.
4. For examples of the link between the creation of delinquency, and of disciplinary power more generally, to the economic interests of the bourgeoisie, see Foucault, 1977a: 221 and 280; Dreyfus and Rabinow, 1982: 135.
5. And if it cannot, then so much the worse for freedom, since the only serious alternatives to the Stoic idea of self-mastery are an implausible and increasingly abandoned empiricism, which identifies freedom with the ability to realise one's strongest desires, or a mysterious spontaneity that is not subject to causation.

6. Arguing that discourses are not 'once and for all subservient to power', for example, he comments that whereas discourse 'transmits and produces power; it reinforces it, but also *undermines* and *exposes* it, renders it *fragile* and makes it possible to *thwart* it' (Foucault, 1978: 101, emphasis added).
7. Green's argument challenged the claims of free-traders that any factory legislation necessarily involved a diminution of freedom.
8. Foucault does not, of course, deny that workers and their organisations can exercise liberty in relation to power, but where he mentions this it is apt to be resistance to domination, in the form of strikes, struggles, and so forth, that he has in mind (Foucault, 1988i: 12–13). He does not appear to consider that there are forms of power, such as health and safety legislation, which workers' organisations would not wish to resist, since they advance the liberties and interests of workers.
9. As Foucault points out, aspects of the carceral system of extended observation and control, such as police management of prostitution, having lost their usefulness, have been abandoned (Foucault, 1977a: 306). The system is therefore open to certain sorts of reform.
10. Of the kind expressed in a passage Foucault quotes from *La Phalange*:

    He [a youth who was tried for vagabondage] is well aware that the apprentice, the worker is a slave and that slavery is sad. ... This liberty, this need of movement that possesses him, he is well aware that he would no longer enjoy it in a life of ordinary order. ... He prefers liberty; what does he care if others see it as disorder? It is a liberty, that is to say, the most spontaneous development of his individuality, a wild development and, consequently, brutal and limited, but a natural, instinctive development. (quoted in Foucault, 1977a: 292)

    Foucault – typically non-committal – is careful only to bring this passage to our attention, without identifying himself with any of the sentiments expressed.
11. Dreyfus and Rabinow (1982) treat Foucault's analyses of the Panopticon and the prison system as dealing with the means by which human beings have been constituted as objects, whereas his examination of the discourses of sexuality is taken as tracing the genealogy of the individual subject. This is a handy enough distinction, but should not lead us to forget that panoptic surveillance, and observation more generally, are also understood by Foucault as having subjectivising effects, and as central to the creation of the individual subject. What is distinctive about the contribution of the discourses of sexuality to the emergence of the subject is the spreading of methods and habits of introspection, inwardly directed self-analysis and the need to speak the truth.
12. For example, 'the Christian School must not simply train docile children; it must also make it possible to supervise the parents, to gain information as to their way of life, their resources, their piety, their morals' (Foucault, 1977a: 211).
13. See, for instance, Foucault's description of a set of instructions for good handwriting (Foucault, 1977a: 152).
14. See also Foucault, 1978: 100–2.
15. See note 9 above.
16. Here one thinks of the work of dissident monitoring organisations, watchdog groups, trade unions and professional associations, organisations aimed at

gaining greater information and control over our own health, researchers, investigative journalists and so on.

17. See note 1 above.

18. The Christian ascetic project of exposing the hidden self in order to renounce or transcend it (Foucault, 1988g: 48) jars somewhat with this reading of the Stoic tradition. However, since the purpose of such renunciation is somehow to affirm one's higher spiritual nature or potential, the project is not entirely at odds with that of emancipating one's better or essential self.

19. It has been suggested to me that the essential self might turn out to be a creature of unpleasant desires. In that case, of course, such desires would not be fundamentally repellent to the individual who has them.

20. The strongest desire of a drug addict, for example, may be to get a fix as quickly as possible, but if she does not want to be a drug addict and wishes that she could resist her cravings, her desires for the drug are opposed to what she really wants. Saying what structure of will, desires and values is required in order to provide an adequate theoretical grounding to the distinction between what we merely desire and what we really want is no easy matter (cf. Frankfurt, 1971; Watson, 1982 for seminal discussions of the difficulties involved; Magill, 1996); but the difficulties in providing a theoretical account of the difference between those wants we embrace and those from which we are alienated gives no reason for abandoning what is otherwise a familiar and unremarkable distinction most of us make in respect of our own desires and those of others.

21. Foucault argues that 'people know what they do; they frequently know why they do what they do; but what they don't know is what what they do does' (quoted in Dreyfus and Rabinow, 1982: 187). That lack of knowledge can certainly pose obstacles to individual and collective freedoms, but it is not a necessary lack and Foucault's own work has done much to heighten our awareness of 'what what we do does'.

22. A person might, for example, be well aware that her desire for a thin figure is a product of gendered norms and expectations, and even judge that a society without those norms and expectations would be better, and yet still affirm what she desires as a valid means of self-valorisation in the society in which she must live.

23. I therefore see no reason to accept Foucault's claim that power is tolerable only on condition that it masks a substantial part of itself (Foucault, 1978: 86).

4 Foucault's Ethics and Politics: A Strategy for Feminism?

Moya Lloyd

As Foucault showed us in his last books and in his life, there is a kind of ethical and intellectual integrity which, while vigorously opposing justifications of one's actions in terms of religion, law, science or philosophical grounding, nonetheless seeks to produce a new ethical form of life which foregrounds imagination, lucidity, humour, disciplined thought and practical wisdom. (Dreyfus and Rabinow, 1986: 121)

What are we to make of Foucault's turn to ethics in his later work? Does it signify, as his critics contend, a recognition of the aporia of his genealogical work, a work allegedly suffused by 'empirical insights' but riven with 'normative confusions'? (Fraser, 1989: 17–34). Is his treatment of self-formation tacit acknowledgement of the stultifying passivity (in the face of omnipresent power relations) of those docile bodies whose fate he traced in *Discipline and Punish* (1977a) and *The History of Sexuality: An Introduction* (1978)? Has the autonomous subject 'returned'? My aims in this chapter are threefold: to consider why Foucault turns to ethics in the first instance, and thus, to assess what he hopes to achieve by this shift; to explore some of the linkages between ethics and aesthetics (in Foucault's senses of those terms), and their relation to politics; and, then, to consider the extent to which his work has been used by feminists. I will argue that there are three elements to Foucault's ethical work: a consideration of the conditions of possibility for self-understanding inherent within practices of subjectification; a problematisation of contemporary forms of ethics; and an exploration of strategies of transgression in the face of the increased normalisation of the modern (Western) world. These three facets are reflected (to different degrees) in a number of feminist theories: a non-essentialist enunciative position (Probyn, 1993), an ethics of the body (Diprose, 1994), and a theory of gender performativity (Butler, 1987; 1990a; 1990b; 1991; 1992; 1993a; 1993b).

A Genealogy of Ethics

Foucault's aim in the later volumes of *The History of Sexuality* is to present a genealogy of ethics: an exposition of the ways in which 'we constitute ourselves as moral agents' (1984d: 351). According to him, the term 'morality' normally connotes either a moral code: the values, precepts, rules of action (and the like) which are recommended to individuals, or a series of acts: 'the real behaviour [compliant or transgressive] of individuals in relation to rules and values recommended to them' (1985: 25; 1984d: 352). To this, Foucault adds a third, ethical, dimension: those practices or technologies by which 'one tries to work out, to transform one's self and to attain a certain mode of being' (1986: 2). This formative relation of the self to the self operates in accordance with a code and, clearly, consists in acts; it remains, however, conceptually distinct from the other two senses of morality.[1]

As with his other genealogical studies, Foucault is interested in the differences and discontinuities underpinning apparently similar practices. In this context, his main concerns are Christian and ancient practices of ethical self-formation and self-understanding (here, specifically, sexual ethics).[2] Both of these historically distinct forms of ethical life appear at first glance to share a number of themes, prohibitions and concerns. However, despite their resemblance they do not have the same significance or ethical and cultural valence in antiquity and in Christianity (Foucault, 1985: 14–20; 26). There are a number of practical disjunctures between them in relation to self-formation which Foucault illustrates by recourse to a fourfold schema.

Every ethical relationship to oneself is, he asserts, constituted by the interplay of four aspects (see 1984d: 352–9; 1985: 26–8). These are the ethical substance, the material upon which ethical activity works; the mode of subjectification, the ways in which 'people are invited or incited to recognize their moral obligations' (1984d: 353); practices of the self, the means by which ethical transformation is effected (that is, asceticism and/or ethical work); and teleology: 'the kind of being to which we aspire when we behave in a moral way' (1984d: 355). The actual contents of each of these elements and their interrelations vary according to the mode of ethical behaviour under consideration,[3] as does their relation to the codes, behaviours and modes of subjectification which constitute Greek and Christian morals; for the former is ethics-oriented while the latter is code-oriented.

What appears to impress Foucault most about Greek ethics was its lack of any normalising impulse.[4] This was possible because 'the principal aim, the principal target of this kind of ethics was an aesthetic one'; 'an aesthetics of existence' (1984d: 341, 343, 348; see also 1988c: 49). Instead of attempting to legislate a pattern of behaviour for the entire population – a universal, and normalising morality – Greek ethics was a matter of personal choice.[5] This is not to claim that it was determined by individual whim, however, for Foucault is categoric that all ethical activity is context-dependent and culturally laden to some extent (1985; 1986; 1988i: 11). It was simply an attempt to 'affirm one's liberty and to give one's life a certain form', the form of 'a personal work of art'. For Foucault, ethics represented the outcome of 'a practice, a style of liberty' (1988c: 49). By comparison, Christian morality functioned as a 'unified, coherent, authoritarian moral system that was imposed on everyone in the same manner' (1985: 21). It prescribed a code of behaviour based upon 'very strict obligations of truth, dogma, and canon' (1988g: 40) exemplified in the 'religion of the text' as the word of God (1988c: 49). It was an absolute morality. To be a good Christian was to obey a system of laws or moral precepts; it was to act as the perfect juridical subject, whereas to be an ethical Greek was to practise liberty.[6] Thus, the way in which subjects 'decipher, recognize, and acknowledge themselves as subjects of desire' varies historically (1985: 5).

This differentiation of Greek from Christian morality (or ethics) enables Foucault to point out that sexual ethics have not always been tied to systems of interdiction and prohibition, or even to systems of obligation. Instead of reflecting deep or essential injunctions, themes of sexual austerity and their practices of self-creation and self-understanding can be, and have been, posed in terms of liberty; as practices of self-stylisation (1985: 24). What is the purpose of Foucault's differentiation here? Why is he drawing our attention to such different modes of ethical self-formation? In part, it is in order to expose the manifold ways in which the self has been positioned in relation to, and produced by, alternative ethical discourses and practices. But, it goes further than this.

In 'Nietzsche, Genealogy and History', Foucault observes that an essential trait of 'effective history' (Nietzsche's term for genealogy) is 'its affirmation of knowledge as perspective' (1984b: 90). Genealogy seeks not to erase those traces which situate the historical investigator temporally and locationally, nor to deny the partiality of their excavations. Instead 'it reaches the lingering and poisonous traces in order to prescribe the best antidote' (1984b: 90; see also 1984a: 45–6). How does this bear upon Foucault's genealogy of ethics? In an interview with Alessandro Fontana, Foucault asserts: 'if I was interested in Antiquity it was because ... *the idea of a morality as obedience to a code of rules is now disappearing, has already disappeared. And to this absence of morality corresponds, must correspond, the search for an aesthetics of existence*' (1988c: 49, emphasis added). Foucault's interest in the Greeks bears the trace of his present location as an inhabitant of an age and culture which, he declares, is (becoming) profoundly sceptical of the possibility of code-oriented moralities: 'most of us', he asserts, 'no longer believe that ethics is founded in religion, nor do we want a legal system to intervene in our moral, personal, and private life'. The problem for contemporary liberation movements, he avers, is that they cannot find any grounds for ethics other than science, be that the science of desire, or of the unconscious (1984d: 343). His reflections upon the Greeks should be regarded, therefore, as a moment in an historical ontology of ourselves as subjects of morality: the moment at which the suggestion of another (non-scientific) ethical relation with the self is opened up – one which takes the form of an aesthetic.[7] The purpose of studying the Greeks is to create an aperture through which to expose contemporary certainties as just so many 'events' (Foucault, 1991a: 76–8) or 'historical coagulations' (Dreyfus and Rabinow, in Foucault, 1984d: 350). By exposing the singularity and historicity of various modes of experience, it becomes possible not only to expose the contingency of our moral, economic, social and political arrangements but also to identify strategies of transgression (see Foucault, 1984g: 334–6): '[T]he effort to think one's own history can free thought from what it silently thinks, and so enable it to think differently' (Foucault, 1985: 8–9). Tracing 'lines of fragility' within existing discursive formations enables the genealogist to isolate the 'kinds of virtual fracture' which 'open up the space of freedom understood as a space of concrete freedom, i.e. of possible transformation' (1988b: 36).[8] So it is the presence of virtual fractures which create the conditions of possibility for the kind of interrogative relationship with contemporary reality (which Foucault discerns in Kant's essay 'Was ist Aufklärung?') which can then lead to (political) transgression (see Lloyd, 1996b). Furthermore, it is this interrogative activity (or limit-attitude) which makes possible the formation of a community of action, what Rajchman terms a critical community (Rajchman, 1991: 102).[9] Rejecting the idea of a prior identification of a 'we' to ground and validate political activity – the function of the signifier 'Woman' in feminist theory – Foucault proposes a 'we' as the result ('and the necessary temporary result') of questioning identity (1984f: 385). It is this critical community which 'makes our "subjectivity" an open and endless question, at once individual and collective' (Rajchman, 1991: 102); a process of perpetual change and (re)formation (see Cohen, 1991 in relation to gay identities). Put differently, it is this critical community which prompts ethical activity (in the Foucauldian sense). Contrary to the criticisms of some commentators, Foucault revises, rather than eschews, a notion of community (Haber, 1994: 107–9, but see 89–90).

Ethical activity is about becoming-Other; about stylising one's existence, a process Rajchman calls 'the choice of a mode of being' (Rajchman, 1992: 219).[10] A revived notion, in the present, of ethics as aesthetic practice suggests tactics of resistance, not in the form of mere refusal or blockage[11] then, but in terms of the creation of 'new forms of subjectivity';[12] that is, forms in defiance of an increasingly governmentalised (and individualised) subjectivity (Foucault, 1982: 216). This is why Foucault is interested in ethics as aesthetic activity.[13] Aesthetics represents an (individuated or collective) act of self-creation, an act of liberty which is fundamentally political (1984d:

354, 357; 1986: 6); in Foucault's terms a 'politico-aesthetic choice' (1984d: 357). Centred upon the activation of a critical attitude to the present, ethical self-stylisation acts as the spark to 'fresh acts of [political] inventiveness' (Gordon, 1991: 6). It furnishes direction pointers for a new ordering of political activity. Just as in his essay on Kant (1984a) where he disavows a revivification of the doctrines or concepts of the Enlightenment in favour of the (re)activation of a critical attitude – the attitude of modernity – so in his account of ethics, Foucault refuses the resuscitation of actual Greek practices or ideals in favour of the (re)animation of an aesthetic relation to the self.[14]

In terms of the brief survey of Foucault's later work offered in this chapter, I want to suggest that three factors are of significance: first, Foucault is engaged in rethinking the connection between the subject and sexual ethics in terms of that subject's self-constitution and self-comprehension; second, he is motivated to do so by a genealogical concern with the contingency of current ethical presumptions; and, finally, he suggests a trajectory – albeit sketchy – for an alternative ordering of politics. In the next part of the chapter I will explore some of the ways in which these features have been rearticulated within feminist theory. Before turning to specific instances of Foucauldian-inflected feminist work, a brief word is needed about the relationship of feminism in general to Foucault. Until relatively recently, feminist engagements with the work of Foucault have tended to concentrate upon his genealogical studies and, in particular, upon the (f)utility of his analytic of power for understanding women's position in the world and upon the future of feminist politics in the face of a discursively constituted subject (Diamond and Quinby, 1988; Fraser, 1989; Hartsock, 1990; Phelan, 1990; Sawicki, 1991; and most of the papers in Ramazanoglu, 1993). In this regard, relatively little attention has been paid to his ethics (or, indeed, to his archaeological work – see Cain, 1993 for one rare instance of this). This has some interesting implications. As Haber observes: 'His understanding of the self as the effect of disciplinary and normalizing power regimes forces one to be skeptical about the viability of a Foucauldian politics' (Haber, 1994: 77, see also 98–109). Yet if my earlier interpretation of Foucault is plausible, one of the very possibilities opened up by his later work is precisely a politics – a politics of transgression. By omitting consideration of the aesthetics of existence or the limit-attitude, feminist writing freezes Foucault in genealogical mode. In what follows, therefore, I will explore some of the ways in which Foucault's later work has been taken up by feminists. Given the openness of Foucault's writings, suffice to say that the three theorists I examine all stress different elements of his ethical work. However, one feature which unites them is an interest in the potential politics of a feminist Foucauldian turn. While they may not satisfy those critics who contend that a viable politics can only be based upon the idea of a stable subject, Probyn, Diprose and Butler (to varying degrees) do provide insights into some alternative routes opened up by Foucault. (For more critical accounts, see McNay, 1992, 1994; Grimshaw, 1993; and Soper, 1993).

Elspeth Probyn: Writing the Self

In her book, *Sexing the Self* (1993), Elspeth Probyn explores recent debates in cultural studies around issues of representation, specifically the difficulties of representing the other. She is particularly concerned with a (re)turn to writing autobiography and the resurgence of two trends: first, autobiography as a guarantee of authenticity, the manner in which 'the truth of the self guarantees a special order of reality located in a personal "truth"' (1993: 135); and, second, a return to individuality. Probyn wants to suggest a third alternative, one which draws upon a partially Deleuzean reading of Foucault's last work (Foucault, 1984a; 1985; 1986). Her explicit aim is to produce a mode of speaking/writing which, while recognising gendered specificity, generates non-essentialist feminist theory. It is an attempt to develop autobiographical writing which takes account of the ways in which broader structures both position us in relation to others, and work through us. Probyn's analysis is framed by a concern with the universalism and essentialism endemic to such 'sovereign signifiers' as 'Woman'. Sensitive to the need to listen to women's voices, but fearful of the potentially deleterious effects of a yearning for *the* truth, Probyn deploys Foucault's injunction to think with attitude as a mode of interrogating relations of alterity (Foucault, 1984a; Probyn, 1993: 109).

Thinking with attitude involves two interrelated practices (see above): the construction of an ontology of ourselves as subjects of an historical present, that is, tracing the localised limits of our identities in order to problematise (or denaturalise) them, and, secondly, the transgression of those limits, that is, a going beyond what we are to what we might (in some unspecified sense) be(come). Reflecting upon specific instances of these two elements in Foucault's work – especially his plotting of the bumpy path of sexual ethics as it traverses shifting forms and practices of the self – Probyn concludes that the self is always the effect of a complex, and historically diverse, interpolation of problematisations and practices. Different apparatuses generate the possibility of 'various "subjectivities", of various "truths" about ourselves' (Probyn, 1993: 126). This further implies four things: first, that the self is not a universal guarantee of anything (politics, epistemology, autobiography); second, that the self is a form and not a substance; third, that the self operates on several levels – it combines a multiplicity of practices and a variety of discourses and, as such, it 'cannot condense into a unified

Individual or Subject'; and, fourth, that it is not representable: 'no one aspect ... can be represented metonymically' (1993: 129, 127). The self is the expression of localised power relations, power struggles and resistances, and the figure through which they can be analysed. It is, Probyn contends in a paraphrase of Barthes on texts, a self 'experienced only in an activity of production' (1993: 3).[15]

Moreover, since individuation is always already social or public, it suggests to Probyn certain ways of thinking through relations of alterity. For example, she notes Foucault's account of erotics reveals that the self-forming Greek subject took care of himself by a particular relation to others: he avoided passivity in sexual relations with boys/men; that is, he adopted 'appropriate' sexual behaviour. In taking care of himself, he also took care of others (by mastering his desires and treating other men and boys ethically). Probyn argues that these intimate, although historically and culturally variable, connections between self and others subvert any separation of the self from the social. The self is thought through social relations: 'the care of the self ... can only be conceived of and performed within the exigency of caring for others and for and within our distinct communities' (1993: 169; for quite dissimilar readings see McNay, 1992: 157; Diprose, 1994: 30; Dews, 1989: 40). It is here that Probyn espies the opportunity to reconceive relations of alterity:

> Foucault's care of the self allows me to consider a way of speaking and of theorizing that proceeds from 'me' without reifying me as the subject of my speaking. This opens the way to considering a mode of theory that is *not organized around individuals but that with force offers us a space where we can take seriously how we are individuated.* From this point I can begin to envision ways of thinking that can fold the line between us, and bring together the question of 'who and what is she?' and 'who and what am I?' (Probyn, 1993: 136, emphasis added)

If the self-society boundary is blurred by an understanding of the self both as produced within everyday practices and as a theoretical articulation which can be used to problematise or discomfort the 'real', then, Probyn surmises, any rigid separation of self–others would also appear to be susceptible to problematisation. In the context of feminism, transgressing limits involves rejecting the outside–inside alternative of me or she, replacing it with a mode of thinking the two together. It prompts a way of speaking about experience which is neither exclusionary nor occlusive: 'a motivated set of practices that foreground and hopefully encourage the necessary movement of identities' (1993: 167). It suggests a way of incorporating difference while contesting its limits; of retaining distinctiveness while discovering compatible registers. The question this raises is how?

In part, Probyn's answer relies upon turning the 'self' into a methodological tool; a phenomenon which can be made to work in the creation of a new enunciative position within cultural studies, that is, another way of addressing others. In the context of autobiographical writing, a shift in emphasis would occur: stress would be removed from celebrations of individual selves towards a consideration of how women produce themselves as gendered speaking subjects in a specific cultural landscape. That is, how they make the many lines of analysis (of race, gender, sexuality) work upon themselves. This is a profoundly self-reflective strategy. However, it says little about how we are to understand (if not represent) others, how we can reach beyond our own contexts into the specific contexts of others. In order to resolve this dilemma, Probyn turns her attention to the role of imagination and empathy. Drawing on the work of bell hooks, in particular, she traces the ways in which imagination may be used to think difference differently (Probyn, 1993: 147). Reiterating her Foucauldian impulse towards the disruption of limits, she argues that imagination provides a means for thinking across identity, across the binary logic which positions individuals as mutually exclusive beings. Recognising the impossibility of speaking in another's voice, and profoundly sceptical of liberal calls for meaningful conversation because of its purported blindness to the material inequalities positioning actual speakers in the social world (1993: 146), Probyn contends that imagination opens up new spaces within which difference can be understood. It allows for a reconception of the ways in which relations are structured by race, class and so on. An imaginative enunciative position relies not upon forgetting the self, but upon thinking at the limit of the self, thinking how certain images, representations, may make someone else feel. This is using the imagination with attitude: stretching our-selves to the limit so that we dissolve into other selves, alternative selves, selves who move and touch others, provoking moments of communal transformation, even communal being. As an example of such empathic imagination, Probyn discusses the work of the lesbian photographer, Deborah Bright. Bright 'pastes' her 'constructed butch-girl self-image' on to stills taken from Hollywood films depicting heterosexual narratives in order to suggest certain (unnamed) erotic possibilities (Bright quoted in Probyn, 1993: 162). As Bright puts it: 'I fantasized pursuing, courting and making love with the heroine, while at the same time, I also fantasized *being* (like) her' (Bright quoted in Probyn, 1993: 163, original emphasis). Through this photographic juxtaposition of self and other a moment of empathy is generated.

Probyn's is a close and inventive reading of Foucault's ethical work transported on to the map of cultural studies. Like Foucault, Probyn argues for an understanding of modalities of the self as the outcome of an interplay between practices and problematisations, suggesting that selves (how they are produced, deployed and understood) are fluid, and unstable entities. She turns this observation into a methodological strategy. Not only is this how selves are constituted, but it is also a way in which the self can be consciously mobilised to produce non-essentialist feminist theory: that is, by working at the limits of our identities, continuously unpicking them, unravelling the threads that tie us to them. This seems particularly apposite in the realm of autobiographical composition as a way of contesting the prevalence of the view that it is possible to retrieve from one's past authentic experiences of gender, class and race in which others will recognise themselves and their own experiences. In the place of the idea that any self can be accurately captured or represented in enunciation, Probyn suggests a critical use of the self as a device to 'refract any straight line of equivalence' (1993: 171) between one self and another. Autobiography becomes a mode of transforming the self; a practice of freedom; the articulation of another self. In the act of doing this, Probyn surmises, we also begin to rethink alterity. This is where her argument is most ambiguous, and least persuasive.

The call to use our imaginations to empathise with others has some laudability. It invites us to consider more carefully how we talk or write about others, particularly the abstract ways in which we deploy categories such as race or disability. It has the potential to provoke a more contestatory reading of cultural texts by commending that we imagine how those texts situate or represent others. As an injunction to imagine alternative futures, to think across the boundaries which presently demarcate us, however, it seems utopian. While it may construct a useful methodological approach for theorising representation, it is not clear how the dissolution of the self/other boundary is effected nor what the critical–political purchase of such work might be. The problem is that the idea of empathy often implies an appropriation of the experiences of the other for oneself (as witnessed in the quotation from Bright above and in Probyn's other example, Sandra Bernhard's film *Without You I'm Nothing*. Here Bernhard desires (to be) the unnamed black woman of the film and spends much of the movie appropriating various black, and occasionally, white personae (Probyn, 1993: 150–63). In this way, 'empathy' is evacuated of the notion of 'indignity' so central to Foucault's account of the specific intellectual (Foucault and Deleuze, 1973: 105; Lloyd, 1993). Indignity involves a recognition that 'others' should be able to speak for themselves. What is central, then, is the creation of the conditions necessary to enable others to speak, and not a process of speaking for them – however tenuous the separations between us. Probyn leaves unresolved the issue of how the 'other' (however, spuriously separated from other others including myself) participates in this form of cultural studies: do they remain, as it seems they do, passive subjects of enquiry? Is it not possible, even likely, that using imagination rather than prompting 'us' concretely to address the material inequalities which position us in our relations to others simply allows us to escape, ignore or eroticise them?

Central to Probyn's account is the relation between care of the self and care of others. Even though the relationship is hastily sketched, it remains pivotal to her aims in rethinking autobiographical writing and cultural criticism. In the next section, I want to examine the work of Rosalyn Diprose. Diprose's aim is to develop a theory of ethics which takes sexual difference into account; specifically, one which deals with the issue of female embodiment in ethical contexts (for example, the ethics of pregnancy or surrogacy). In making this claim, Diprose is refusing both traditional (contractarian) ethics and the new feminist ethics arising out of the debate around sexual difference: the former for its privileging of the male body while claiming to favour no body at all and the latter for its failure to account for the generation within a specific social context of sexed or embodied identity (Diprose, 1994: 1–17).[16] She turns to Foucault to see if his work can resolve two specific issues: first, the emergence of sexed/embodied identity; and second, the mechanisms through which changes in this identity are produced. As with Probyn, a central element of Diprose's theory is the role played by others in the care of the self; however, that role is very differently conceived by Diprose.

Rosalyn Diprose: Embodying Ethics

Debates on feminist ethics have tended to fall into one of two camps: the first working within existing theories of justice but making them more sensitive to gender (see Benhabib, 1992; Okin, 1989); the second, attempting to define a distinctive feminist theory of ethics based upon sexual difference. This latter debate has been dominated by the concept of the ethic of care developed by Carol Gilligan (1982; Larrabee, 1993). Without overstating the lines between these two approaches, there are a number of features they share: they are both procedural (rather than content-oriented) accounts (although one is formalistic, the other contextualist); they both stress the role of the moral 'reasoner' (although the processes of reasoning vary: the former stressing cognitive skills, the other empathic skills); and they both believe that justice is ultimately attainable. Given some of the elements of Foucault's ethics sketched above, it would seem that a feminist Foucauldian ethics would be very different in focus and tone. I will explore the work of Rosalyn Diprose in order to assess this claim.

Diprose begins her chapter on Foucault by offering her own definition of ethics. *Ethos* derives from the Greek word for dwelling, understood both as a noun denoting the place which one inhabits, and as a verb signifying the practice of dwelling. Diprose concludes, therefore, that habit and habitat form the twin elements of ethics: *'ethics can be defined as the study and practice of that which constitutes one's habitat,* or as the problematic of the constitution of one's embodied place in the world' (1994: 19, original emphasis). Ethics is primarily a corporeal phenomenon: habits are 'constituted through the repetition of bodily acts' making the body 'the locus of one's ethos' (1994: 19, 22). Foucault's aesthetics of the self, is then read as 'how one's embodied ethos is constituted' (Diprose, 1994: 20). Diprose's definition of ethics is important for a number of reasons: first, because it clearly differs from Foucault's own definition. His account of ethics is explicitly tied to practices of self-(trans)formation which include, but also extend beyond, the body. For instance, Foucault allows very strongly for the possibility of aesthetic work on souls, thoughts, conduct and ways of being (Foucault, 1988g: 18). Further, Diprose's interpretation of ethics permits her to argue that Foucault's *genealogical work* is already *'ethical';* ethical precisely because it is concerned with those factors generative of one's habits and habitat. Thus, Diprose reads *Discipline and Punish* as an account of the subject's 'relation to a disciplinary moral code' and *The History of Sexuality: An Introduction,* somewhat surprisingly, as a narrative of 'our dominant mode of self-forming activity' (1994: 21). 'Discipline' becomes shorthand for a normalising morality; and 'social context' synonymous with 'moral code' (Diprose, 1994: 21). This has some important consequences both because it raises the unresolved question of whether the 'normal' and the 'ethical' are, in fact, equivalent terms; and because of its effect upon Diprose's account of practices of self-formation. The subject, she asserts, is both 'subjected to the actions of others (where the body is the object of disciplinary power) and he or she attains a social identity through self-knowledge (where the body is the object of self-reflection and the subject of confession)'. In both instances, the individual's ethos 'becomes co-extensive with the body politic and they take their roles to heart' (Diprose, 1994: 22).

Foucault's work on the generative nature of power can be usefully applied to ethics (particularly bio-ethics, where it is frequently women's bodies which are the site of ethical debate) and to feminist ethics more generally, for it challenges the whole concept of a moral high ground (or Truth), independent of constraining social codes, from which to make moral judgements. Moreover, it reveals that a universalist ethics can itself be a mechanism of disciplinary power and not a moral position untainted by the carceral society. Foucault's writing is also important because it reveals that there is no truth of the self 'outside of the ethos constituted by productive power' (Diprose, 1994: 23), thereby deflating all possibility of the kind of pre-given moral identity upon which ethical theory often draws (1994: 22–5). This has consequences for any ethics based upon, for instance, 'interactive rationality', for this form of ethical exchange requires the ideas of autonomy and self-identity, properties disputed by a Foucauldian ethics in which the self is actually constituted in the process of dialogue or confession. For Diprose, therefore, Foucault's work upon the social regulation of corporeality is useful insofar as it compels us to rethink the 'ethics of subjection': how we are positioned unequally as subjects. She remains sceptical, however, about the chance of producing an ethics of sexual difference. The question is why? Why should a rethinking of the ethics of subjection be impermeable to questions of sexed identity? It is at this point that Diprose turns her attention to Foucault's ethical work *per se*.

Although able to account for the production of certain differences between subjects, Diprose argues that Foucault's own ethic of difference – 'his aesthetics of self-formation' – is insufficient for an ethics of sexual difference (1994: 28). Diprose identifies a major problem with Foucault's position: that his call to promote new forms of subjectivity implies that there is a space outside of the effects of disciplinary power for agency, for self-transformation and, moreover, that there is a 'locus of difference beyond the kind of difference constituted by and denigrated within the hierarchical spaces of discipline and surveillance' (1994: 29). According to Diprose, Foucault's Nietzschean impulse – using the body as aesthetic material – is of limited use to feminists. Limited, first, because it relies upon a dissolution of any necessary or analytic link connecting techniques of the self to social, economic and political institutions, institutions presently dominated by patriarchal values; that is, it would operate outside of the sphere of disciplinary power. This is problematic, Diprose claims, because it leaves unresolved women's exclusion from the existing body politic. She notes that 'feminism cannot afford to separate the ethical relation to the self from the operation of other social structures' (1994: 35). Limited, secondly, because it assumes a certain (interestingly unspecified) kind of male body as material for aesthetic transformation. Foucault's (re)turn to the Greeks as an instance of non-normalising ethical practices exposes this inherent androcentric bias. For the model which, Diprose problematically implies, Foucault wishes to recuperate is an aesthetic which was elitist, exclusionary and, worse still, virile. It was an aesthetic which could only confer a high value on the male body through a parallel devaluation of the female body; an aesthetic dependent upon a rejection of passivity – a value associated with femininity. Foucault's aesthetic always implies, therefore, an asymmetry of power (Diprose, 1994:

33–4) founded upon the denigration of women. By neglecting this question of gender asymmetry Foucault's ethics are inadequate for feminism: 'even the most flexible communal ethos is reluctant to value or recognise women's embodied modes of being' (Diprose, 1994: 31). Feminist ethics has to be able to account for the production of sexed identity and, particularly, those which reinforce male privilege: only an ethics which addresses the reproduction of sex difference in this way is of use to women. Working on the body in order to produce it as a work of art cannot do this, for this is work which (for Diprose) is already gendered.

There are two problems with Diprose's critique: first, in making her claim it is significant that Diprose maps the traits of masculinity and femininity of antiquity directly on to the *bodily* differences between contemporary men and women (respectively), effacing the fact that, for a Foucauldian, the connections between anatomical sex and gender are historically contingent so that what applied with the Greeks is not necessarily identical to our own arrangements. The assertion that the body amenable to aesthetic transformation is a male body, relies upon interpreting Foucault as if he were recommending a return to Greek ethics and all that this implied about gender relations. This is a misreading of Foucault's position. His stated aim is to demonstrate that our current ethical practices are historically distinct; that ethical practices in the past were different and, importantly, that those of the future can also be different.

Second, the notion that Foucault believes in a strict disjuncture between ethics and social, economic and political realms is dubious. Foucault's observation that there is no 'analytical or necessary link between ethics and other social or economic or political structures' (Foucault, 1984d: 350) can be read as Diprose chooses, as an assertion that techniques of the self operate outside those institutions which disseminate disciplinary power and in isolation from other people (Diprose, 1994: 30–6), or it can be read, as I have already argued, as a claim that the way in which the relation of ethics to other structures is configured is entirely contingent upon the accidents of history. This means that there are other possible relations between ethics and politics, economics and society (which may, of course, be less equally or more normalising) than the one under which we currently operate. This is not to deny that we are produced in a multiplicity of (competing and contradictory) ways by disciplinary institutions, nor that we need to critically address the means by which we have been formed as self-policing or compliant subjects. Both of these assertions are valid, and both of them are accepted by Foucault. Foucault makes clear in 'What Is Enlightenment?' that our resistance to the normalising power of our present society consists both in the construction of a critical history of our present and in the construction of new forms of subjectivity outside of the sway of normalisation (Foucault, 1989a). An aesthetic of the self furnishes one means of so doing. It is not that this transformation takes place outside present social structures, but rather that it occurs in the gaps within those structures; gaps exposed via a critical ontology. This is the 'realm of concrete freedom' resident in the 'virtual fractures' of the present discussed above. If an aesthetic of the self is to be successful in contemporary terms, it has to be an aesthetic of the present; one developed in the interstices between contemporary disciplinary practices.

Where Diprose continues to operate within a binary logic of male/masculine versus female/feminine, the next author, Judith Butler, problematises that very binary by seeking to unfix (rather than fix, as Diprose attempts) gender identity. Both are motivated by a concern to understand the factors which function to reify gender differences. However, Diprose does so by exploring the mechanisms constitutive of gender inequality in a traditional sense (the perpetuation of patriarchy) while Butler takes the more radical route of seeking to destabilise feminist normalising strategies.

Judith Butler: A Transgressive Stylistics of Existence

Christine di Stefano in her article 'Dilemmas of Difference' observes that gender differences 'do more to divide and distinguish men and women from each other than make them parts of some larger, complementary, humanistic whole' (1990: 64). There is no doubt that gender is a necessary component of our identities today. Part of our very cultural intelligibility derives from the ascription and self-recognition of a gendered identity. Without one we do not make sense, either to ourselves or to others. But what exactly is meant by gender? Jane Flax (in a manner resonant of Diprose) suggests the following: 'Through gender relations two types of persons are created: males and females, each posited as an exclusionary category' (Flax, 1990a: 23). According to gender logic, one can only be one gender ('rarely the other or both'). Although historically and culturally variable in content, these are rigid categories of identity and identification: to be female is not to be male. Within feminism, the categories of gender are frequently represented as part of the mechanisms which structure inequality into social life. Understanding the mobilisation of gender is thus vital to feminist enquiry (Bordo, 1990; Di Stefano, 1990; Flax, 1990a, 1990b). The question is: how helpful is it (for feminism) to assume that there are only two mutually exclusive (albeit, socially constructed) genders?

Judith Butler (drawing upon the work of Foucault amongst others) turns a highly critical lens on the concept of gender. Her mode of analysis is to problematise feminist expressive theories of gender and the notion of natural sexes in order to expose the politically phantasmatic nature of identity, in particular the categories 'Woman' and 'lesbian' purportedly so necessary to the coherence of feminist politics.[17] Like Foucault, she questions whether any identity category (normalising or 'liberatory') can operate in a non-regulatory fashion.

An expressive theory of gender is one which assumes the existence of some underlying core or myth of origin (be that a primary identification in object relations theory or a primary repression in post-Lacanian feminist psychoanalysis) which establishes gender specificity (masculinity or femininity) and which subsequently 'informs, organizes, and unifies identity' (Butler, 1990a: 329). Gender signification is thus closed within a binary frame which posits only two legible genders: male/masculine and female/feminine. While neither object relations theory nor post-Lacanian feminist theory relies upon a naturalised or essentialist version of identity – both view gender as socially scripted and thus regard themselves as contributing to the desta-bilisation of masculinist versions of psychoanalysis, such as Freud's – they both produce narratives which presume (inscribe) discrete sexed and gendered subjects with (fairly) fixed identities. They create, therefore, their own ontologies of gender with in-built exclusionary injunctions defining 'what qualifies as intelligible sex' (Butler, 1990b: 148) and what kinds of 'identities' cannot 'exist'.[18] By asserting the existence of a unitary category – femininity – feminist psychoanalysis falls into what Shane Phelan calls the 'trap of counter-reification' (1989: 15). Instead of describing reality, expressive theories of gender establish their own normalising, and thus disciplinary, frameworks.

They do this by relying upon the notion of an 'inside' – here intrapsychic processes – which causes the acquisition of gendered identity – the 'outside'. As Foucault's account of the processes of subjectification makes clear, 'the inside is an operation of the outside' (Deleuze, 1988: 97; Probyn, 1993). It is the outside, folded back upon itself, which produces the effect of interiority. In the context of gender, this means that intrapsychic processes – a gender core – are actually the effect(s) of a 'surface politics of the body'. Gender is the effect of 'corporeal signification' (Butler, 1990a: 336); it is written on the body. In making this claim, Butler adopts Foucault's concept of a 'stylistics of existence' to describe the practice of the (self)-creation of gendered bodies. Gender is achieved only through a 'stylized repetition of acts', the stylisation, that is, of the body (Butler, 1990b: 139, 140, 135; see Foucault, 1977a: 29). It is these various 'styles of the flesh' which constitute the illusion of 'an abiding gendered self' (Butler, 1990b: 139, 140). Gender is not expressive; it is performative: 'it constitutes as an effect the very subject it appears to express' (Butler, 1991: 24). The gendered body has no ontological status apart from the acts which compose it. It is purely fictional; an imitation without an original; an enactment of 'cultural and aesthetic performances' (Deveaux, 1994: 239). This is exemplified, for Butler, in the practice of drag where the connections between sex, gender and performance are exposed as contingent as the (anatomically) male drag artist performs femininity while displacing or muting his own masculinity (his gender) (Butler, 1990b: 137–8).

Gender as an 'active style of living one's body in the world' (Butler, 1987: 131), can be defined in Foucauldian terms as agonistic:[19] a process of 'reciprocal incitation and struggle', a 'permanent provocation' (Foucault, 1982: 221–2). At present, gender defines all of us; it prescribes acceptable behaviour and exacts punishment for unacceptable behaviour. It is currently impossible to evade our interpellation as gendered beings; it demands our respect. However, it is still possible, as the work of Butler suggests, to violate gender. Parody provides the mechanism. Parody can expose the fictionality of gender. Occupying subject positions outside of the hetero-normative framework (that is, that which prescribes compulsory heterosexuality) potentially deprives hegemonic culture of 'its claim to naturalized or essentialist gender identities' (Butler, 1990b: 138; 1991: 23).

The assertion that gender is performative involves a number of claims. First, gender identity can never be achieved; rather it is always in need of continual repetition or reiteration (Butler, 1993a). Second, there are no rigid borders around or between genders, only permeable ones, ones open to resignification and inventive (re)figuration.[20] Via 'identificatory and practical crossings' the discreteness of male/masculine–female/feminine gender categories can be disrupted (Butler, 1991: 17). Lipstick lesbianism, camp and the kinds of playful combinations of the symbols of virgin and whore used by Madonna, can all be regarded as instances in the denaturalisation and radical destabilisation of gender identity (see Butler, 1990a: 337–9; 1990b: 136–8; 1991: 18–25; see also Tyler, 1991: 32–70). Third, gender thus becomes an 'improvisational theatre' where identity is repeatedly deconstructed, redefined (Osborne, in Osborne and Segal, 1994: 33). The more that selves work on themselves, the more they aestheticise themselves, so to speak, and the more indeterminate and less regulatory binary conceptions of gender become. In this regard, Butler, like Foucault, attempts to develop a mode of politics as the 'undoing of ... categories' (Deveaux, 1994: 239); the opening up of practices of subjectification through liminal activity, border crossings.

The impulse underpinning Butler's work, like that of Foucault, is to explore ways in which increases in governmentality can be resisted (see Foucault, 1984a).[21] Both thinkers are engaged in exploring the conditions of possibility for transgressing ever more individualising and totalising narratives and practices. This impulse takes an interesting turn with Butler when critical attention is focused not only upon dominant regimes of truth and discipline but also on feminism, that is, on discourses of the marginalised. Butler's exploration of certain forms of feminist psychoanalysis exposes their essentialising and exclusionary effects. Her response it to argue for the de-determination of identity; that is, for a conception of subjectivity in which identity is always provisional, open, capable of multiple signification. Butler's argument that gender is performative is very compelling. However, it is not immune to criticism.[22] Her emphasis on the constituted nature of corporeality seems to deny the materiality of the body: that is, suggesting that gender is just so many styles of the flesh implies that disciplinary power simply crafts bodies in any way it chooses. But clearly, the body (as a material entity) exists prior to, and indeed may exceed, power relations. Can discourse do anything it likes to bodies?[23] Butler's stress on the body as impressed and etched by power reflects her limited utilisation of Foucault's later work. She borrows the term 'stylistics of existence' without reckoning seriously with some of the other facets of the apparatus within which this notion is embedded: for instance, the notion of an historical ontology of ourselves as a condition of possibility for the production of alternative forms of subjectivity. Gender parody remains fundamentally corporeal; a messing around with styles of the flesh. Understanding gender from the perspective of Foucault's ethics obviously demands consideration of the somatic imperatives of engendering, but it also requires exploration of epistemological factors. It demands that we explore how we come to know ourselves as gendered subjects and, through that knowledge, how it is then possible to transform ourselves, to create new forms of (gender) subjectivity outside of the pantheon of performativity. It compels us to contest the boundaries of engenderedness by, in Deleuzean terms, folding the outside back on itself, bending yet again the relations of power (Deleuze, 1988: 102). A politics of parody may imply such a critical practice, but it does not make it explicit – at least, not in the version offered by Butler.

Conclusion

> The only valid tribute to thought such as Nietzsche's is precisely to use it, deform it, to make it groan and protest. And if commentators then say that I am being faithful or unfaithful to Nietzsche, that is of absolutely no interest. (Foucault, 1980a: 53–4)

What are we to make of these feminist interpretations of Foucault's work? In common with many of the other contributions in this book, feminist work on ethics exposes the textual openness of Foucault's writing. Probyn thus uses the concept of the limit-attitude as a mechanism for asking questions about representations of both the self and the other; Diprose applies Foucauldian insights to the project of developing a feminist ethics able to accommodate sexed or embodied difference; while Butler problematises the whole notion of gendered (and by extension any form of normalising or liberatory) identity by regarding it as a stylistics of existence.

Not only are the goals of the three thinkers disparate but also the extent of their borrowing from Foucault. Butler primarily borrows a vaguely sketched concept of stylistics omitting much of the framework within which Foucault locates it. In this respect, she utilises the substance of the ethical work the least. She is thus faithful in spirit if unfaithful in content. By contrast, Probyn gives a particularly close reading of Foucault, taking on board most of the significant aspects of the later work. In the process of her interpretation, Foucault is made to 'groan and protest', to work in ways he might never have envisaged, as when Probyn turns his account of care of the self into a methodological practice for the composition of feminist cultural studies. Diprose's borrowing is more complicated, for at times she is clearly the least faithful to Foucault. Thus, her idiosyncratic reading of ethics as both habitat and habit allows her to weld together the principal components of both the genealogical and the aesthetic dimension of Foucault's work in a way which Foucault does not. The question of fidelity may not be all that important. As Foucault himself suggests, a partial, even deformed reading is not, in itself, problematic. The difficulty arises when the reading obfuscates features of his account which might be helpful in answering the comments of his critics or in strengthening the case of his advocates. This happens when Diprose presents all aspects of discipline as aspects of ethics. In so doing, she breaches the boundary Foucault endeavours to establish between aspects of domination and aspects of freedom.

For Foucault, ethics is the result of practices of freedom, one becomes ethical by becoming free: 'Liberty is the ontological condition of ethics. But ethics is the deliberate form assumed by liberty' (Foucault, 1988i: 4). There is space for some choice about ways of behaving, of being (or of not-behaving, of not-being). Ethics, understood in Diprose's terms, comes to stand for habituation to disciplinary norms; the embodiment of the roles prescribed by various normalising institutions, including instances of domination where there is no choice about modes of conduct. By running together the genealogies and the ethics, Diprose occludes Foucault's differentiation of technologies of power from technologies of the self. The former objectivise the subject determining their conduct and the ends of that conduct while the latter 'permit individuals to effect by their own means or with the help of others a certain number of operations on their own bodies and souls, thoughts,

conduct, and a way of being' in order to attain some self-determined goal
(Foucault, 1988g: 18). This differentiation is important because it implies
that while subjects may act to transform themselves within a disciplinary matrix
of some kind (within the panopticon, say), the ends of the conduct are what
determine whether their act is free or not. As I have argued elsewhere, the
only real means for making this determination is via critique, a feature
which Diprose implies is absent from Foucault's work (Lloyd, 1996b). It is
this capacity which enables the subject to unpack the specificities of their
historical constitutions (and, therefore, how certain modes of being are
attributed specific status).

Similarly, Butler extends and develops Foucault's account of the history
of sex through her account of the role of feminist expressive theories of gender
in the perpetuation of heterosexual coherence, remaining faithful to the
project of genealogy and, in the process, plotting the trajectory of new forms
of gendered subjectivity, whereas Diprose in her account of 'sex' makes
Foucault groan and protest. Foucault cannot provide the kind of ethics
Diprose wants because his understanding of sexuality undermines the ethics
Diprose is advancing: an ethics of sexual difference. A more faithful
Foucauldian approach would problematise the very elements Diprose takes
for granted: that is, binary sex difference, woman as the necessary other of
man. It would subject them to a critical ontology. The decision not to explore
the historicity of sex means that sex difference appears in Diprose's work
as an irreducible difference. Foucault's genealogy of the 'modern' apparatus
of sexuality (the *scientia sexualis*) in the first volume of *The History of Sexuality*
and his tracing of the notion of desire (the *ars erotica*) in the later volumes
of that same work surely make clear that what we understand by 'sex' is
contingent, not irreducible. Despite the variations amongst these feminist
writers, it is clear from the work of Probyn, Diprose and Butler that Foucault's
ideas have had a significant, if uneven, impact upon a wide range of feminist
'disciplinary' preoccupations: in cultural studies, ethics and political
philosophy. Whether by posing questions to existing ways of thinking, by
hinting at interesting theoretical trajectories, or by discomforting his readers
with his conclusions, Foucault has been an important influence on the way
in which debates over identity, difference and ethics have been conducted.

I suggested at the outset of this chapter that one of the interesting openings
produced by Foucault's later work concerned feminist politics. It has become
a commonplace within certain feminist literature (Tress, 1988; Bordo, 1990;
Di Stefano, 1990; Alcoff, 1988, 1990) to claim that the very idea of a
discursively constituted subject fatally jeopardises that politics by precluding
the possibility of a being who is oppressed and who can act to overcome that
oppression. What becomes apparent from the work of the authors under

discussion is that a Foucauldianesque feminism is not so much apolitical as differently political. Parodying gender is one way of refusing to be categorised and marked irretrievably by an increasingly normalising society; it is a transgression of the boundaries of the currently acceptable. By revealing the artifice of gender, acts like drag may help to expose the constraining pressures bearing upon all gender performativity. This is political activity. In a similar way, the attempt to enunciate a form of cultural studies which endeavours not to subsume the other into some simplistic sovereign category – be that race, disability, sexuality or gender is – also political. It is, again, an attempt to defy definitions which bind us to specific identities. Producing critical ontologies of ourselves enables us to highlight the complex intercalation between practices and problematisations which have (contingently) coalesced to produce us in our historically present forms, and, moreover, empowers these present subjects to move beyond these boundaries into other selves. Similarly, there is a clear political value in an ethical theory which can explain the production of gender/sex-differentiated bodies. However, there is one feature of the work of both Probyn and Butler which causes some concern: is a transgressive politics necessarily individualistic or can it have a collective dimension? Furthermore, if it has a collective dimension, then upon what is this founded, given the impossibility of calling on a shared nature or an identical experience of oppression?

Probyn's concept of thinking the self through, and against the boundaries of, others may enable us to produce more sensitive theory but it never adequately addresses the question of how change in our modes of relating to one another in actual everyday life is to occur, nor how the prospect of developing a new enunciative position could become a collective endeavour. In this regard, her account never satisfactorily gets beyond the self: others never figure in quite the forceful way that she promises they will; they remain someone to think about, not someone to talk or work with. Analytical privilege remains with the speaking/writing self as they attempt to think through their own occlusive and exclusionary practices. It is possible that Probyn's version of care of the self is simply a strategy for writing about others. However, Butler's theory of gender performativity is clearly not. It concerns practices of everyday existence: our movement through the social, political and sexual worlds as gendered beings. A similar problem belies it: emphasis remains with the individuated subject as they parody gender in a fashion comparable to that of drag. Butler's account of the (active) acquisition of gender lacks, therefore, a satisfactory exploration of the mechanisms by which subjects (in a plural sense) might act collectively to dis/figure gender identities. The effect of individualisation is exacerbated by the very concept of performativity itself, which concentrates upon individuated instantiations (or enactments) of gender identity: how subjects assume, and parody, various 'styles of the flesh'. What is absent from this is an 'intersubjective' dimension: the ways in which (connections with) others may modulate, inflect and refract gender performativity. Who we perform our gender with, for, or to, will alter the content, the mode of expression, the style of the flesh adopted, and will refract the political implications of parody. In order to understand fully the performative production of the self as a gendered subject we need to fill out this relational dimension; to incorporate those others with whom gender performativity is enacted and transformed.

One issue remains: does Foucault's understanding of resistance and transgression necessarily produce an atomised politics? I want to argue that it does not. Foucault, arguing in response to Rorty's criticism that he fails to appeal to a 'we' to validate or ground his politics, cautions that the 'we' should be the outcome of the process of problematisation: politics is not found in a collective experience but rather in contestation, in posing questions about, for instance, identity, sexuality or madness. It is this (temporary) 'we' which becomes a 'community of action'. It is this critical or ethical community (to revert to the terms used earlier) which acts to destabilise identity, to render subjectivity open to endless transformation and play. So although Cooper, Laing, Foucault and Basaglia themselves formed no conscious community nor had any corresponding relationship, they (inadvertently) sparked the anti-psychiatry movement: their problematisation of madness generated a community of action (Foucault, 1984f: 385). The absence of a discussion by either Probyn or Butler of a collective political dimension is produced, in part, by their selective use of Foucault for their own ends. After all, neither thinker is engaged in generating nor endorsing a strictly Foucauldian version of feminism. Probyn deploys Foucauldian categories in order to theorise writing about others. This is a different ambition to Foucault's; his concern is to survey the panoply of practices of the self in which ancient peoples were engaged. So for him, writing the self is only one possible technology of the self. Butler, on the other hand, utilises the term 'stylistics of existence' to signify the simulated nature of gendered identity and to propose a politics of parody as one means of undoing the hegemonic hold of a dualistic theory of gender. Although appearing to share with Foucault an interest in resisting normalisation, Butler's goals are firmly pointed in a feminist direction; Foucault's, of course, are not. For him the stylistics is inextricably bound with instances of sexual ethics and with the concern to generate a contemporary form of ethics not premised upon (quasi)-scientific or universalisable grounds. He is, however, more explicit about the mechanisms by which a community of action can be formed. Assuming a prior commonality (of nature, experience, intention) to unite political actors would be anathema to Foucault. Rather, it is in the very process of dissolving normalising identity categories that joint action occurs. It is here that the conditions of possibility are generated for the promotion of alternative forms of subjectivity. It is here, within collective activity, that a process of transforming the self in relation to, and/or with, others can be effected. It is not enough to say that a Foucauldian politics is antipathetic to feminist goals. Feminist writers still need to explore in terms of viability and effectiveness the implications for feminist politics of critical communities based in strategies of identity destabilisation and self-transformation. So far, this remains to be done.

NOTES

1. McNay mistakenly describes 'ethics' as 'real behaviour' and the degree of compliance/non-compliance (1994: 135; see also 1992: 51–2), whereas Foucault perceives this as one facet of morality with the term ethics (or, occasionally, ascetics) reserved for techniques of the self (1985: 29).

2. On the problems of collapsing the many differentiations in the development of morals from the Greeks onwards, see Rochlitz (1992).

3. For a comparison of the details of the differences between Greek and Christian morals in respect of these four elements, see Foucault (1984d: 353–7; 1985: 13, 26–8).

4. Foucault does acknowledge, however, both that some versions of Greek morality were more rule-governed – he draws attention to Plato's *Laws* and his *Republic* – and that certain forms of Christianity were more ethics-oriented (1985: 30).

5. The 'demands of austerity' in classical thought were, Foucault contends, akin to a 'supplement, a "luxury"', an adjunct to popular morality (1985: 21). This means that there was no expectation of their strict observance.

6. Although there is latitude for the exercise of a certain degree of personal liberty (in ascetic practices, especially – see 1988g: 41–3; 1985: 21) within Christianity, the opportunities are much more restricted than in antiquity.

7. On the ambiguities of Foucault's use of the term 'aesthetic' see Dews (1989); Thacker (1993). On the question of whether Foucault is simply reiterating an appeal to art as a privileged realm of freedom, see Simons (1995). On his debt to Nietzsche in this context see Thiele (1990).

8. Or, as Foucault puts it: that which has 'made possible the transformations of the difficulties and obstacles of a practice into a general problem for which one proposes diverse practical solutions' (1984f: 389; see also 1985: 11). This is the method he sometimes calls 'problematization' (1985) and at others 'eventalization' (1991a: 76–8); what John Rajchman titles 'nominalist critique' (Rajchman, 1992: 220).

9. To be distinguished from the two other categories he identifies: namely, given community and a tacit community (Rajchman, 1991: 101–2).

10. For an example of this, see Foucault's treatment of Baudelaire (Foucault, 1984a).

11. Arguably, this is also an element of Foucault's overall politics (1982: 216; 1984f: 383–5; 1988f: 323–30; 1984a: 45–6). It forms part of what elsewhere I have labelled 'politics as critique'. To view it, however, as the sole mode of political practice made possible by a turn to Foucault would be a mistake. His later work clearly indicates that reflection on who/what we (individually or collectively) are is the condition of possibility for making ourselves other (Lloyd, 1996b; see also Lloyd, 1993, 1996a).

12. Interestingly, Haber, in *Beyond Postmodern Politics*, claims that Foucault precisely denies to oppositional groups the capacity to 'remake the future' in terms of new subjectivities (Haber, 1994: 107). This is because she pays almost no attention to Foucault's ethical work.

13. In reading Foucault in this way, I am expressly taking issue with those commentators who can perceive no link between Foucault's ethical work and his writings on bio-power. See, for example, Dews, (1989); Rochlitz (1992); McNay (1992, 1994). For an interesting account of the connections between objectification and subjectification see Goldstein (1994b: 108–10).

14. Foucault notes, on a number of occasions, the inappropriateness of Greek practices for the contemporary world. For instance, he is explicitly critical of the 'virile' – misogynistic – nature of their ethics, of its foundations upon slavery, and of its exclusionary or elitist nature (1984d: 344–6; 1985: 22–3; 1988i; 1988g).

15. As an example of this see Probyn's (1993) account of Pierre Riviere and Herculine Barbin. Both were the worked upon by normalising power but, through their 'confessions' also made power work upon themselves in a transformative way. They produced a versions of themselves through the act of writing: 'The self is not simply put forward, but rather it is reworked in its enunciation' (Probyn, 1993: 2). Probyn re-reads their autobiographies as practices of the self. For a more critical view, see Haber (1994).

16. In terms of these two alternative ethics, Diprose clearly favours the feminist ethic of care for its consideration of the relational factors central to mature moral reasoning. The problem with it is that it has no explanation of the origins (or perpetuation) of those relations.

17. The presumption being that feminism requires the notion of Woman (as a unitary and relatively stable category) as the agent and subject of liberation.

18. Butler takes issue with Foucault with relation to processes of exclusion, arguing that since Foucault makes all subjectification contingent on discourse then he is unable to explain the 'ruse of erasure' which produces 'abjects' – unviable (un)subjects – without naming them (Butler, 1991: 20, n.11).

19. Foucault's notion of agonism relies on a particular configuration of the power–freedom relation. He asserts that power can only be exercised over free subjects: it requires (rather than annuls) the capacity to act (Gordon, 1991: 5). This account poses a challenge to those who present disciplinary power as omnipotent rather than omnipresent (McNay, 1992: 40–7; Hartsock, 1990: 168–70, for instance). On the interrelations between power, domination and freedom, see Foucault (1986: 19); Gordon (1991).

20. Here Butler's work echoes some of her other influences, namely Derrida and Zizek.

21. This term 'government' has several meanings, the most important (and general) of which is the idea of 'the conduct of conduct', which Colin Gordon defines as 'a form of activity aiming to shape, guide or affect the conduct of some person or persons' (Gordon, 1991: 2). To govern is, therefore, 'to structure the possible field of action of others': 'it incites, it induces, it seduces, it makes easier or more difficult; in the extreme it constrains or forbids absolutely' (Foucault, 1982: 221, 220; see also Foucault, 1986: 19–20).

22. For other critical readings of Butler, see Benhabib (1992, 1995); Bordo (1993); Cohen (1991); Deveaux (1994); Fraser (1995a, 1995b).

23. In *Bodies That Matter* (Butler, 1993a), Butler goes some way towards answering this by exploring Lacanian and post-Lacanian psychoanalysis.

5 Foucault and International Relations Theory
Kimberly Hutchings

By scrutinizing how proto-diplomacy was exercised at multiple sites, we can better understand how diplomacy emerged from unfamiliar relationships of force and truth at the infra- and supra-state levels. In short, a genealogical approach to diplomatic theory allows us to challenge its traditional state-centricity without denying the centrality of power politics in international relations. (Der Derian, 1987: 83)

Introduction

The traditional concerns of international relations theory (war, interstate relations, foreign policy, diplomacy, security) seem a long way from Foucault's preoccupation with the micro-politics of power relations and the construction and limits of subjectivity. In the different incarnations of his work, as archaeologist, genealogist and ethicist,[1] Foucault rarely makes explicit reference to the terrain of what, after 1945, has come to be defined as the social science of international relations. There are two notable exceptions to this: the first is the significance for Foucault of the Westphalia settlement of 1648; the second is Foucault's use of the vocabulary of war in many of his accounts of the workings of power and its relation to knowledge and truth.[2] On examination, however, the implications of these two areas of coincident interest are very different for international relations theorists and Foucault respectively. For traditional international relations theory, the Peace of Westphalia is significant because it confirms the emergence of a modern state system (Bartelson, 1995: 86; 137).[3] For Foucault, the significance of the Peace of Westphalia is that it provides one point of origin for what he calls 'the governmentalization of the state' (Foucault, 1991b: 104). Instead of reading Westphalia and *raison d'état* as the culmination of sovereign state power (and the confirmation of a 'juridical' conception of power), Foucault reads it as the beginning of a different kind of power at work in the internal art of government. Where the international relations theorist looks out at the relation between states and takes the category of the state as sovereign actor for granted, separating sovereignty from questions of government, Foucault is interested in external relations between states only in so far as they impinge upon governmentality within the state (Foucault, 1991b: 94; 98–104). This brings us back to the second way in which the concerns of international relations and of Foucault appear to overlap: the use Foucault makes of a military vocabulary and his suggestion that perhaps Clausewitz's famous aphorism should be inverted and that power (politics) should be understood as war continued by other means (Foucault, 1978: 93; 1980f: 90–1). Here again, however, the meanings attached to concepts of war and strategy in international relations theory and in Foucault's work turn out to be distinct. The prevailing conceptions in mainstream international relations theory are premised on the assumption of states as self-interested agents operating under the structural constraints of *realpolitik*. Whereas Foucault conceives of war, strategy and tactics in the context of a very different, much more flexible, understanding of the nature of agency and interest (Foucault, 1978: 94; 1982: 224–5). One has only to contrast standard accounts of deterrence within the international relations literature with Foucault's conception of war as dynamic, ever shifting relations of forces to note the difference (Trachtenberg, 1985: 355–66; Foucault, 1980f: 90–1).

On the basis of this it would seem unlikely that Foucault's work could become a point of reference for contemporary scholars working in the field of international relations. However, as this chapter demonstrates, Foucault's work is being appropriated by international relations theorists critical of the traditional theoretical options for both understanding and judgement in their field. The first section of this chapter will be an exposition of the aspects of Foucault's work most drawn upon by critical international relations theorists. In the second section, a brief account of orthodox international relations theory and current alternatives to it, including those using Foucault, will be given, along with a rehearsal of some of the objections within the international relations literature to the use of Foucauldian ideas. In the third section, I will look in more detail at two attempts at a Foucauldian-type genealogy in the work of Der Derian (1987) and Bartelson (1995) and at two other attempts to use Foucault to illuminate problems in regime theory (Keeley, 1990) and to rethink normative theory (Forbes, 1987) respectively. In conclusion, I assess the implications of uses of Foucault in international relations theory and judge whether these implications derive from the ways in which international relations theorists adapt Foucault for their own purposes or are traceable directly to Foucault's own work.

Genealogy: Power, Knowledge, Truth, Critique

The following exposition is based on the significance that certain aspects of Foucault's work have for the international relations theorists discussed below. Within international relations it is Foucault's conception of genealogy and its complex relation of power, knowledge and truth which is most often cited and used. In addition, the notion of critique as 'critical ontology' or transgressive critique (Foucault, 1984a: 50), and the ways in which this is linked to the practice of genealogy, have also acquired considerable importance for some international relations theorists (Ashley and Walker, 1990; Walker, 1993: 190–1). I will therefore focus my exposition on Foucault's concepts of genealogy, power, knowledge, truth and critique.

Foucault discusses the nature of genealogy in several different contexts in his work, from the point at which he turns away from archaeology as a methodological technique, to his late writings (for example, Foucault: 1980f: 82–5; 1980g: 71–3; 1984b: 76–100; 1985: 3–13; 1988f: 264–7).[4] There are two characteristics of genealogy which differentiate it from more conventional historical enquiry. First, genealogy is not the search for truth (either as origin or scientific explanation) but rather explores both the discursive conditions which make regimes of truth possible and the effects of power inseparable from those discursive conditions (Foucault, 1980f: 83–4; 131–3).[5] Second, genealogy is history which sets out not to make the past familiar, but to make the present strange; this is exemplified most clearly in Foucault's *History of Sexuality, Volume 1,* and his challenge to the 'repressive hypothesis' (Foucault, 1978: 8–13). Foucault's histories are always geared to questions about how and why 'we' in the present come to take the limits of 'our' existence for granted (Foucault, 1977a: 31; 1988f: 262). These two characteristics suggest that there are two dimensions to the critical implications of genealogy. The first dimension challenges claims to truth which presume the separability of power, knowledge and truth through demonstrating their perpetual entanglement. The second dimension, in drawing attention to the constructed, contingent and political nature of regimes of truth, opens up the possibility of alternative regimes, whether in the sense of subjugated knowledges (Foucault, 1980f: 81–7) or radically new constructions. When he describes the idea of transgressive critique in his essay 'What Is Enlightenment?', Foucault says:

> And this critique will be genealogical in the sense that it will not deduce from the form of what we are what it is impossible for us to do and to know; but it will separate out, from the contingency that has made us what we are, the possibility of no longer being, doing, or thinking what we are, do or think. (Foucault. 1984a: 46)

If a social scientific theorist is to take on board Foucault's conception of genealogy, then it is clear that they must also reckon with the conceptions of power, knowledge and truth which accompany it. It is in the texts *Discipline and Punish* (1977a), *The History of Sexuality, Volume 1* (1978) and

Power/Knowledge (1980f) that Foucault's most explicit discussions of the relationship between power and knowledge are found. The argument of *Discipline and Punish* makes a series of claims about the nature of power as 'disciplinary' that are set against what Foucault terms traditional 'juridical' conceptions of power (Foucault, 1977a: 194). The difference between the two conceptions of power is exemplified in the famous contrast Foucault draws between the public and spectacular punishment of Damiens, the regicide as opposed to the treatment of prisoners within the panopticon (Foucault, 1977a: 3-6; 200–2). Juridical power belongs to and is exercized by a sovereign body to repress and control its subjects.[6] Disciplinary power, on the other hand, belongs to nobody and is productive rather than repressive in its effects: 'Discipline "makes" individuals; it is the specific technique of a power that regards individuals both as objects and as instruments of its exercise' (Foucault, 1977a: 170). According to *Discipline and Punish*, the construction of the sovereign individual, which is both the premise and the accomplishment of the panopticon, is inseparable from the development of the human sciences. The discourses of human behaviour which helped inspire and account for changes in the penal system in the nineteenth century are most frequently presented as effects and channels of disciplinary power (Foucault, 1977a: 194; 204; 305). Thus, Foucault's argument appears to be that power produces discourses of knowledge, which in turn produce regimes of truth, criteria through which to discriminate between true and false or normal and deviant. This argument is carried through into *The History of Sexuality, Volume 1* where Foucault again stresses the necessary relation of power to knowledge and the ways in which psychiatric and psychological sciences carry through effects of power (Foucault, 1978: 98–100). However, in this text it is clear that the relationship of power to knowledge and, therefore, to truth is more complex than that suggested in *Discipline and Punish*. Although Foucault continues to claim that there is no *exteriority* between *techniques* of knowledge and *strategies* of power (Foucault, 1978: 98), this does not mean that discourses of knowledge and truth regimes are always in some sense secondary or subordinate to power: 'Discourse transmits and produces power; it reinforces it, but also undermines and exposes it, renders it fragile and makes it possible to thwart it' (Foucault, 1978: 100–1).

One of the most frequent complaints made about Foucault's account of disciplinary power is that it seems to leave nothing outside of power for the purposes of explanation or normative judgement. If Foucault is read in this way then the traditional Enlightenment opposition of knowledge and truth to power appears to be rendered meaningless.[7] This is a reading encouraged by aspects of *Discipline and Punish* and the first volume of *The History of Sexuality*. Both texts debunk the pretensions of nineteenth-century penal reformers and twentieth-century psychiatrists to be involved in a project of the liberation of the true/genuine subject from repressive power or the power of repression. However, as the quotation above suggests and as Foucault himself repeatedly asserts, this reading rests on a misunderstanding (Foucault, 1991c: 148). In commenting on his conception of power, Foucault stresses that 'power' always stands as a shorthand for 'power relations' in his work and that relations of power are inherently immanent, tactical and strategic rather than in any sense transcendent (Foucault, 1978: 94–6; 1982: 217; 1988f: 103–6). In contrast to physical determination, Foucault argues, power involves the possibility of resistance, and although it is inseparable from knowledge, truth and freedom, the latter are not simply reducible to power (Foucault, 1978: 98; 1982: 217–18; 1988f: 106). For Foucault, to pose the conceptual choice as that between defining power in opposition to knowledge, truth and freedom, and defining power as sovereign over knowledge, truth and freedom is to succumb to the 'intellectual blackmail' of being for or against the Enlightenment (Foucault, 1984a: 45). Instead, Foucault requires that the genealogist recognise, first, that relations of power presuppose freedom (Foucault, 1982: 221); and, second, that discourses of knowledge and regimes of truth are in perpetual interplay with, but not simply identical to, relations of power (Foucault, 1980f: 81–5; 131–3; 1988f: 106–7).

What does it mean to claim that relations of power presuppose freedom? Foucault's meaning is most clearly expressed in 'The Ethic of Care for the Self as a Practice of Freedom' (1988i) and 'The Subject and Power' (1982). Here Foucault contrasts power relations with relations of violence and domination (Foucault, 1982: 220; 1988i: 3–4). The latter are marked by a kind of totally unilateral freezing of possibilities, in which one party has absolute control over a passive subject:

> On the other hand a power relationship can only be articulated on the basis of two elements which are each indispensable if it is really to be a power relationship: that 'the other' (the one over whom power is exercised) be thoroughly recognized and maintained to the very end as a person who acts; and that, faced with a relationship of power, a whole field of responses, reactions, results, and possible inventions may open up. (Foucault, 1982: 220)

This dependence of power on freedom which returns us to the metaphors of relations of war which mark all of Foucault's writings on power from *The History of Sexuality, Volume 1,* onwards. Foucault's choice of a military vocabulary expresses the meaning of power relations as being a reflection of the inherent dynamism of battle, in which it is a constant strategic challenge to hold your ground, let alone advance or retreat (Foucault, 1978: 92–3). The necessary and perpetual tension between relations of power and strategies of resistance described in 'The Subject and Power' (Foucault, 1982: 221; 225) raises the question of how the distinction between power and freedom can be drawn. Foucault clearly rejects the idea that there can be any universal criteria of judgement which would settle this question. Relations of power and strategies of resistance are always specifically located and the recognition of what counts as either power or freedom depends on the particular context. However, the question still remains for actors in specific contexts as to what would count for them as practices of liberation. Discussing some specific examples of resistant practice in 'The Subject and Power', Foucault concludes that central to these struggles (for example, the women's movement and the anti-psychiatry movement) is the attack on the form of power which makes individuals subject (1982: 211–12). This form of power encompasses both external control of individuals and their internal self-governance (Foucault, 1982: 212). Participants in these resistances ask the question of who they are and refuse the definitions and relations through which the question has previously been answered. Later in the same essay, Foucault contrasts two kinds of philosophy: the universalist philosophy of Descartes, which asks about the nature of the 'I' as an unhistorical subject; and the specific analysis of ourselves and our present which he ascribes to Kant's reflections on Enlightenment (Foucault, 1982: 216). In parallel with the political movements of resistance he has already discussed, Foucault maps out the practice of critical philosophy:

> Maybe the target nowadays is not to discover what we are, but to refuse what we are. We have to imagine and to build up what we could be to get rid of this kind of political 'double bind', which is the simultaneous individualization and totalization of modern power structures. (Foucault, 1982: 216)

The account of the relation between power and freedom as one of mutual dependence has implications for Foucault's other claim, that is, that discourses of knowledge and regimes of truth are in perpetual interplay with relations of power, although not reducible to them. What Foucault's account of critical philosophy suggests is that knowledge and truth may well be complicit with power, but that they may also be part of the strategic forces of resistance, opening up new possibilities for thought and being. This helps make sense of one account Foucault gives of genealogy as a practice of local criticism which is involved in the *'insurrection of subjugated knowledges'* (Foucault, 1980f: 81, original emphasis). According to this account, genealogy, through painstaking research, recovers not only the discursive conditions of dominant regimes of truth, thereby displaying the fragility of globalising theory

(1980f: 83), but also reveals knowledge and truth which has been suppressed and which provides a ground for critique of dominant theory:

> Concretely, it is not a semiology of the life of the asylum, it is not even a sociology of delinquency, that has made it possible to produce an effective criticism of the asylum and likewise of the prison, but rather the immediate emergence of historical contents. And this is simply because only the historical contents allow us to rediscover the ruptural effects of conflict and struggle that the order imposed by functionalist or systemizing thought is designed to mask. Subjugated knowledges are thus those blocs of historical knowledge which were present but disguised within the body of functionalist and systematizing theory and which criticism – which obviously draws upon scholarship – has been able to reveal. (Foucault, 1980f: 82)

This quotation shows the two dimensions of genealogy identified earlier. Through exposing the essentially political nature of claims to truth, particularly within the human sciences (Foucault, 1988f: 106), genealogy traces the interrelations of power, knowledge and truth. By revealing power relations as tactical struggles in which dominant discourses are sustained through an encounter and subjugation of alternative discourses, genealogy opens up the way to thinking differently about those dominant discourses (Foucault, 1980f: 81–2; 1982: 216). As with power and freedom, however, it is clear that what counts as a subjugating as opposed to a subjugated discourse is dependent on context. As a theoretical practice, genealogy is slippery and its effects are undecidable in advance. The genealogist is no more immune to relations of power than any other kind of theorist and there can be no guarantee that the genealogist speaks on behalf of the oppressed: 'I carefully guard against making the law. Rather, I concern myself with determining problems, unleashing them, revealing them within the framework of such complexity as to shut the mouths of prophets and legislators: all of those who speak *for* others and *above* others' (Foucault, 1991c: 159, original emphasis). As is made increasingly clear in Foucault's late work on ethics and the care of the self and his account of his critical work as 'critical ontology' (Foucault, 1984a: 50; 1988f: 95), it is not possible to assess genealogy in terms of a set of criteria of truth or method in a traditional sense. In Foucault's terms, claims to have uncovered truth or advanced knowledge, such as those of the nineteenth-century human sciences, derive from a mode of critique which assumes necessary and stable limits to the conditions of knowledge and therefore to what can be known. In opposition to this, Foucault identifies his own theoretical practice as 'a practical critique that takes the form of a possible transgression' (Foucault, 1984a: 45).

There are two significant implications of Foucault's work for social scientific understanding and normative judgement. The first has to do with the ways in which the object of study is conceived. The second involves a rethinking of the relationship between the discourses of social scientific analysis or normative judgement and that which they are attempting to explain and/or judge. As far as the former implication is concerned, taking Foucault seriously entails a conception of socio-political structures and relations in dynamic terms as the outcomes of the play of relations of power and resistance, which can be traced at the micro level of the formation of subjectivities. This has encouraged a range of work focusing on the practices which produce and support understandings of subjective identity, normality and deviance which in turn help to keep power relations in place or, alternatively, which may be potentially subversive of those relations.[8]

The second implication of taking Foucault seriously has more radical consequences for orthodox conceptions of the social sciences. Traditionally, the goal of social scientific work has been to produce accounts of social reality which can be independently validated and are, to the extent that this is possible, value free. Traditionally also, normative theory has operated on the assumption that there are standards of moral judgement, however derived, which are not reducible to the state of affairs to which they are being applied. Even those critical traditions which accept the impossibility of detaching social scientific accounts and normative standards from the conditions which they claim to describe, explain and judge, operate with assumptions about the adequacy of descriptions, explanations and judgements which relate to standards which exist in detachment from existing power relations.[9] It is this assumption of the possibility of separating discourses of knowledge and truth from relations of power which is fundamentally problematised by Foucault: 'It is not a matter of emancipating truth from every system of power (which would be a chimera, for truth is already power), but of detaching the power of truth from the forms of hegemony, social, economic, and cultural, within which it operates at the present time' (Foucault, 1980f: 133).

As was evident in the above discussion, Foucault's claim that 'truth is already power' is not a straightforward dismissal of the power of truth to disrupt dominant relations of power. However, the claim that 'truth is already power' does imply that the social scientist must understand not only the discursive conditions of the realities they are examining but also their own discourse in strategic terms, identifying it with either subjugating or subjugated knowledges: power or resistance. This is an identification which cannot hold in any transcendental or universal sense, since what counts as relations of power or strategies of resistance depends on the dynamics at work in a specific context. On the one hand, the bracketing together of power, knowledge and truth encourages the deconstruction of all theoretical perspectives which lay claim to a standpoint beyond power. On the other hand, the bracketing together of power, knowledge and truth appears to render the status of the claims of the Foucauldian critic perpetually open to question. Foucault himself implies that at best the Foucauldian social scientist aspires to the goal of transgressive critique. The transgressive critic challenges the limits put in place through power relations by pointing to the subjugating practices on which those limits depend and unsettling the presumption of their necessity. Exemplary transgressive criticism includes both questioning the self-evidence of theoretical boundaries as they are drawn by key concepts within social science and putting into question the assumptions which organise socio-political existence.[10] There is, however, a stronger, ethico-political sense in which transgressive critique can be considered exemplary. The trangressive critic echoes at the level of theory and research the strategies of resistance exemplified at the level of practice by those who 'refuse what they are' (Foucault, 1982: 211–12; 216). The work of the transgressive critic is inevitably political, and its politics is in principle the politics of the struggle against established modes of subjection, although in practice the effects of transgressive theorising are always undecidable in advance.

International Relations Theory: Orthodoxy and Critique

In the post-World War Two period, the study of international relations has been most powerfully influenced by the idea of the distinctive nature of the international arena as opposed to the domestic state. It has been assumed that international politics are of a specific kind and that the way to understand and judge them must reflect that specificity. The result of this has been that the study of international relations has developed in a way semi-detached from its close relatives of political science and normative political theory.[11] The most obvious evidence for this is found in the significance of the theoretical paradigms of realism and neo-realism within the international relations literature.[12] The governing assumption of realism is that states operate as unitary self-interested actors within an international context which is one of systemic insecurity. Realism makes a clear distinction between domestic politics, in which post-contractual standards of legitimacy and justice may operate, and international politics, in which there is no authoritative ground of right. Key explanatory concepts within realism are the *state* and *power*. Like the rational actor in the Hobbesian state of nature, states pursue power in order to guarantee security insofar as they are able. However, unlike the Hobbesian individual, states are unable ever to transcend the terms of *realpolitik* through contractual relations. Thus the third crucial explanatory concept within realism is that of the *interstate system,* the context within which states act.

Critics of realism point out that its understanding of the international sphere has significant epistemic and normative implications which are open to challenge. The realist theorist is effectively blind to questions about the nature of states and the relevance of the domestic to the international as well as to the significance of transnational, non-state actors in international politics. According to realists the international is constituted by a system of states which relate to one another in a context of anarchy. The international is understood through the detailed examination of certain state agencies, governments, diplomats, the military and so on. The nature of actual states and the existence of non-state actors (for example, multinational corporations and non-governmental organisations) must, therefore, either be essentially marginal to the understanding of the international or have to be read back into the vocabulary of interstate relations. On the normative side, the effect of the isolation of the international as a realm of anarchy is to raise power politics to the level of an absolute end of history. In closing off the possibility of change, realists close off the possibility of criticism and present their own judgement as a simple reflection of the way things are. Critics such as Rothstein point out the ways in which realism reflects the Cold War context in which it came to theoretical prominence, but also argue that it helped construct a kind of fatalism about international relations which has had significant policy implications (Rothstein, 1991: 409–18). What underlies these problematic implications of realism are assumptions both about international politics and about the nature of theoretical practice. Both these sets of assumptions rely on an understanding of power and truth as entirely separable concepts. The realist theorist seeks to demonstrate the truth about power, the task of demonstrating that truth is not conceived as a political task, but as a task of neutral reflection.

The claims of realism have been and continue to be challenged, and in the last twenty years a variety of alternative theoretical paradigms have been formulated within the discipline of international relations. These alternatives include liberal-pluralist, Marxist, critical theory (Frankfurt School), feminist and postmodernist perspectives.[13] Although these perspectives differ greatly from each other, one thing they all have in common is the claim that the focus on the state, its power and the interstate system as the sole ultimate reference points for the explanation and judgement of international politics, is inadequate. In this section I concentrate on the postmodernist alternative strand of theorising in international relations insofar as it draws upon the work of Foucault.

The postmodernist turn in international relations theory is highly eclectic in the sources upon which it draws.[14] Perhaps the best single example of the claims implicit in postmodernist international relations theory is to be found in an article co-written by Ashley and Walker which concluded an edition of *International Studies Quarterly* devoted to critical or 'dissident' essays. Ashley and Walker refer in their paper to a disciplinary crisis:

> Whether one speaks of the 'discipline of international studies,' the 'discipline of international relations,' the 'discipline of international politics,' or the 'discipline of world [or maybe 'global'] politics,' the words manifestly fail, even as they promise, to discipline meaning. The words but broadly connote (they cannot denote) a boundless nontime and non-place – a deterritorialized, extraterrestrial zone of discourse – where the work of producing the subjects, the objects, and the interpretation of an institutional order and its limits visibly eludes the certain control of that order's supposedly reigning categories. (Ashley and Walker, 1990: 376)

Ashley and Walker's claim is that the conceptual ordering of international relations theory, rather than reproducing reality in accordance with the timeless truths of the centrality of state sovereignty and power politics, increasingly reproduces accounts of international relations which subvert those (supposedly) timeless truths. They also claim that the critical work which is effecting this disciplinary crisis 'resonates' with dissident movements in the practice of international politics (for example, feminist, ecological and peace movements) (1990: 377). Thus the theoretical transgressions of a conceptual order in international relations theory are being mirrored by practical transgressions of the global political order in international politics, and vice versa.

Ashley and Walker centre their critique of orthodox approaches to international relations theory on the concept of 'sovereignty', understood in a dual sense as both the assertion of the unquestionable primacy of state sovereignty in international politics and the assertion of sovereign claims to truth in theoretical practice (1990: 367–8; 376; 381–3). However, it is sovereignty in the latter sense with which they are most deeply concerned, and their critique here targets Marxism and critical theory as well as more mainstream theoretical approaches. Ashley and Walker argue that theorising in response to disciplinary crisis is possible in either a register of desire (religious) or a register of freedom (celebratory) (1990: 379–81). The register of desire encompasses any theoretical approach which lays claim to have fixed the boundaries of explanation and judgement. The register of freedom, in contrast, celebrates the instability of these boundaries:

It does not try to hold on to some imagined totalizing standpoint. ...
Instead ... it celebrates a space of freedom – freedom for thought, for political
action in reply to hazards and dangers, for the exploration of new modes
of ethical conduct detached from the presumption of a transcendental
standpoint – that opens up when, in crisis, this ideal is deprived of practical
force. (Ashley and Walker, 1990: 381)

It is clear from the above account that the postmodernist theorist of
international relations wants to take up an argument about the relationship
of power, knowledge and truth. To what extent does this argument rely on
Foucault's work? There is evidence to suggest that Foucault is a significant,
though by no means the only significant, source for Ashley and Walker.[15]
They make use of Foucauldian concepts such as 'countermemory', 'genealogy'
and 'power/resistance' (Ashley and Walker, 1990: 384; 392) and cite Foucault
as an example of a thinker theorising in a register of freedom (1990: 389–90).
Even without these explicit hints, however, the dual direction of Ashley and
Walker's critique recalls the two critical dimensions of genealogy discussed
above. On the one hand, Ashley and Walker are concerned to make explicit
the inseparability of power, knowledge and truth in orthodox and critical theory
which makes sovereign claims to truth. On the other hand, they define their
preferred theoretical practice in strategic and transgressive terms, linking it
to projects of self-making in a manner reminiscent of the parallels Foucault
draws between political movements of resistance and critique as 'critical
ontology' (Ashley and Walker, 1990: 391–2; Foucault, 1982: 211–12; 216).
In an earlier work Ashley quotes from Foucault's 'What Is Enlightenment?'
to express the nature of critical practice (Ashley, 1989: 283–4). In a more
recent work, Walker explicitly acknowledges the importance of Foucault for
his theorising (Walker, 1993: 23), and also quotes from 'What Is
Enlightenment?' to explain critical theoretical practice (Walker, 1993:
190–1). In both cases the quotations confirm the idea of postmodernist
international relations theory as a Foucauldian challenging and transcending
of existing limitation.

Ashley and Walker are writing at the broadest theoretical level and it is
difficult to be sure quite what purchase their reflection on different modes
of theorising may have when it comes to addressing problems formulated
within traditional approaches to the understanding of international relations.
Classically, these are the problems of explaining interstate conflict and cooperation and the normative assessment of international intervention, from
war to arguments over humanitarian aid and distributive justice. However,
certain implications of their arguments are clear and suggest the likely
consequences of a Foucauldian approach to international relations theory.

A Foucauldian theorist of international relations cannot take for granted the object of study reproduced by realism, which is defined by the idea of the centrality of sovereign states and, in Foucault's terms, a 'juridical' conception of power as owned and exercised by states over against other states in a context of anarchy. This means that the boundary between domestic and international politics is terminally blurred by a Foucauldian approach, entailing wholesale rethinking of what is relevant to both the definition and explanation of international politics. It seems likely, therefore, that the Foucauldian international relations scholar will pay more attention to the sub-state and trans-state strategic relations of power through which the state is enabled to effect its appearance as a unitary actor in the international context. A Foucauldian approach to international relations will also disturb and unsettle any fixed boundaries for explanation and judgement within the international realm, on the basis that theorising cannot itself be separated from the strategic relations of power which traditional theory would locate solely in its object. Relatedly, a Foucauldian approach to international relations invokes a connection between the practice of postmodernist theory and the political struggles of marginalised international actors; as a theoretical practice, it embraces a politics of transgression.

The postmodernist turn in international relations theory and its debt to Foucault have not gone undebated within the discipline. Broadly speaking, there are two directions of criticism within the international relations literature. The first comes from mainstream theory of both the realist and liberal-pluralist kind and usually involves an attack both on the abandonment of the idea of the specificity of the international sphere in relation to domestic politics and on the abandonment of traditional conceptions of social science as an attempt to represent the truth (or, in the case of normative theory, the good) in contradistinction to power (Hockaday, 1987; Keohane, 1988; Rosenau, 1990). The second direction of criticism is best represented by critical theory, but is also common to Marxist, some feminist and some liberal-normative theory. According to this line of criticism, the Foucauldian assertion as to the inseparability of knowledge, truth and power ensures that the Foucauldian theorists' claim to identify their theoretical practice with a project of freedom (the political struggles of the oppressed) is unsustainable (Hoffman, 1988; Krishna, 1993). The latter critique echoes a general line of criticism of Foucault's work (Taylor, 1984; Walzer, 1989; Habermas, 1987a; Fraser, 1989; McNay, 1992). At the heart of this critique is the argument that 'truth' and 'freedom' lose their meaning as a point of reference for progress if they are always implicated in relations of power. For these critics, the inescapability of power relations in Foucault's theory, renders any state of affairs in the world the same. Within international relations theory this has led to postmodernist theory in general, and Foucauldian theory in particular, being accused of an implicit return to realism, in which the truth that the international is always already power is simply reflected and reasserted in more complex and sophisticated ways. In the third section I will look more closely at examples of work in international relations theory which are heavily indebted to Foucault. Then I will return specifically to consider the second of these arguments against the idea of a Foucauldian international relations theory.

Genealogy, Power and Morality

Both Der Derian's *On Diplomacy* (subtitled 'A Genealogy of Western Estrangement') (1987) and Bartelson's *A Genealogy of Sovereignty* (1995) are genealogies in a Foucauldian sense of histories of the present and both aim to offer a rethinking of received international relations wisdom about the concepts of diplomacy and sovereignty respectively (Der Derian, 1987: 69–70; Bartelson, 1995: 7–8).

The Der Derian text is not a consistently Foucauldian one, since it gives central place to a conception of alienation drawn from a reading of Hegel and Marx (1987: 8–29). However, *On Diplomacy* displays the classic features of a Foucauldian genealogy insofar as it takes as its primary purpose the effect of unsettling 'common-sense' assumptions about diplomacy by displaying the ways in which different discourses of diplomatic culture have been constituted historically through strategic relations of power (1987: 70). Der Derian uses an historical and textual examination of pre-modern discourses of diplomacy to challenge the accepted assumption in diplomatic theory of the irrelevance of pre-modern international political practices of mediation to the comprehension of diplomacy. This is an assumption which itself rests on the grounding premise of contemporary orthodox international relations theory which makes states central to all aspects of international politics, and which sees the Treaty of Westphalia as marking the origin of the modern state system and therefore of diplomacy proper (Bartelson, 1995: 137). Der Derian signals two reasons why the exploration of what he terms 'proto-diplomacy' might be illuminating: first, because it disrupts a narrative of seamless progress characteristic of the 'common-sense' school, in which discontinuities in history and the 'violent and uncertain periods in which early diplomacy is formed' (1987: 81) are ignored; and, second, because proto-diplomacy exemplifies the range of 'disorderly and unconscious forces' (1987: 80) which form and transform diplomacy at any given time. Der Derian traces discourses of diplomacy up until the present time, always emphasising diversity, discontinuity and the dynamic relations between subjugating and subjugated discourses of diplomacy in the production and reproduction of modern diplomatic relations:

> The value, then, of this analysis of diplomacy's origins should be weighed by its ability to *devalue* the accepted truth or theory that diplomacy has an essence of common sense, and an origin that can be chronologically and geographically fixed. The method of devaluation has been ... to flood the market place of the diplomatic discourse with multifarious interpretations which have at one time or another been implied or imposed by power relations. (Der Derian, 1987: 200, original emphasis)

Der Derian's argument clearly demonstrates two of the aspects of Foucauldian international relations theorising identified in the previous section. First, Der Derian explicitly challenges traditional state-centric accounts of the international arena, bringing in not only sub- and trans-state economic and political factors but also texts, religious and cultural practices as having effects of power and explanatory significance in the understanding of diplomacy. Secondly, Der Derian's account works with the idea of the inseparability of theoretical discourse and relations of power to disturb traditionally fixed boundaries of explanation and judgement in the understanding of diplomacy. What is less clear is the relation of Der Derian's work to the third feature of Foucauldian theory, the connection between theoretical practice and political resistance. In the final section of the book Der Derian sketches out the future of diplomacy as 'techno-diplomacy' and its manifold dangers (1987: 199–209), concluding with two references to Foucault. First, a parallel is drawn between techno-diplomacy and Bentham's panopticon as 'the perfect design for a technology of power' (1987: 208). The implication is highly pessimistic and reinforces an emphasis on '*Realpolitik* struggles of power' (1987: 70) which runs through all of Der Derian's analysis. The second reference to Foucault arises in relation to the question of what can be done to address present dangers of alienated international relations (1987: 209). Der Derian agrees with Foucault that one cannot assume solutions to problems which will themselves avoid danger, but that this is not an invitation to political passivity, since, 'if everything is dangerous, then we always have something to do', and in the light of this, 'the ethico-political choice we have to make every day is to determine what is the main danger' (1987: 209). This double reliance on Foucault in the closing passages of Der Derian's book presents the reader with an intriguing ambiguity. On the one hand, the possibility of change appears to be closed off by 'the *telos* of omniscience and omnipotence which is implicit in techno-diplomacy' (1987: 208) (a reading which would be grist to the mill of the second line of critique of Foucault and Foucauldian theory mentioned earlier). On the other hand, the closing reference to Foucault returns us to the necessity of ethico-political choice, the challenge to transgress and transcend the boundaries of thought and being which Foucault identifies with 'critical ontology' and Ashley and Walker with an ethic of freedom. This challenge, however, appears to be for a realm beyond Der Derian's text; it is not clear how the challenge relates to the genealogical analysis within the text. There are definite parallels between Bartelson's genealogy of sovereignty and Der Derian's genealogy of diplomacy. In both cases the genealogies disrupt common-sense assumptions within international relations theory through exposing the discursive struggles and discontinuities which condition key concepts at different times. In Bartelson's case, however, there is a much more thorough engagement with Foucault's work and a greater degree of methodological self-reflection (Bartelson, 1995: 7–8; 53–87). Bartelson also takes care to spell out his conception of genealogy and to indicate both his debt to Foucault and some of the problems he sees in Foucault's work (1995: 69–84). In particular, he notes that the claim that there is no exteriority in the relations between knowledge, truth and power has given rise to an ongoing debate about the critical and normative implications of genealogy (1995: 73). Bartelson argues that Foucault's own later accounts of power relations can be read as implying an 'outside' of the logical limits of discourse (1995: 81–2). Setting aside whether Bartelson's claim is right, he argues against it and claims that any notion of an 'outside' renders genealogy self-refuting or hypocritical. Genealogical critique must therefore be both immanent and modest (1995: 82–3). However, Bartelson also stresses that this does not mean that participants in discourse are passive victims of discursive conditions, since these are open to reinterpretation (1995: 78).

Bartelson identifies three hypotheses in international theory about the origins of sovereignty and international relations: the Renaissance hypothesis; the Westphalia hypothesis; and the modernity hypothesis (Bartelson, 1995: 85–6). The first argues that the origins of the modern state system are in the politics of the city-states of Renaissance Italy. The second suggests that the modern state system originates with the Peace of Westphalia. The third corresponds to the argument that it is with the emergence in the nineteenth century of the modern nation-state that international relations as such originates.[16] Bartelson then examines the interplay of power, knowledge and truth in the discourses of outside/inside which mark Renaissance, classical and modern eras. As might be expected, Bartelson's analysis both challenges and accounts for the persuasiveness of prevailing hypotheses about the origins and nature of sovereignty. Although opposing a history of sovereignty reliant on the notion of seamless development, he explains the appeal of such accounts in terms of the discursive conditions of the modern episteme (1995: 186). The centrality of the modern conception of sovereignty for political knowledge lies, Bartelson argues, in its *parergonality,* the way in which it frames both inside and outside, domestic and international as the fundamental ordering of modern political reality (1995: 247). The origins of this ordering, however, are not essential; they cannot be tied to a notion of historical truth or progress. Instead the concept of sovereignty and its effects emerge 'as the unintended consequence of the clash between the core concepts and forces of modern knowledge' (1995: 247). For Bartelson, in good Foucauldian fashion, the career of a concept cannot be disentangled from effects of power. He therefore takes very seriously the arguments of critical theory of international relations which criticise the centrality of sovereignty for explanation and judgement in international relations theory, and suggests in the concluding passages of his argument that conceptually and effectively sovereignty is becoming increasingly fragile:

> *So where do we go from here?* I began this book by stating that knowledge is political, and that politics is based on knowledge. I should end it by observing that if epistemic change is essentially political, it also involves the political responsibility of deciding upon sovereignty, a decision which we for the moment seem unfit to make. (Bartelson, 1995: 248)

In Bartelson's case, as with Der Derian, the use of Foucault in international relations theorising involves rethinking the object of theory and challenging other theorisations which neglect the inseparability of knowledge, truth and power. As with Der Derian also, however, there is an ambiguity in relation to the politics of genealogical practice itself. In many ways, Bartelson's argument reflects what he himself terms a 'positivist' approach of neutral and detailed description in which the presence of the theorist is effaced and the inescapability of discursive relations of power/knowledge is confirmed (1995: 82). On the other hand, Bartelson also stresses an attitude of responsibility on the part of participants in the discourses of sovereignty and (like Der Derian) gestures at the end of the book to the necessity of ethico-political choice. Again, however, the political challenge is located in a realm beyond the boundaries of the text, and the relation between the genealogical analysis we have been given and ethical and political choices remains unclear.

Both Der Derian's and Bartelson's arguments represent attempts at full-scale Foucauldian genealogies. I will now examine further the implications of using Foucault in international relations theory by looking at two much more modest and exploratory attempts drawing on his work: Keeley's 'Toward a Foucauldian Analysis of International Regimes' (1990); and Forbes's 'Warfare Without War: Intervention in the International System' (1987).

International regimes are constituted by state and non-state actors and exemplify a co-ordination of interests in the international system, the most common examples are economic although the idea of a regime can be extended to a variety of international organisations (Keohane, 1984; 1989; Krasner, 1983). Keeley himself takes the case of nuclear non-proliferation to exemplify a regime (Keeley, 1990: 100–5). As Keeley points out, there are both realist and liberal variants of the concept of a regime. Whereas the former would stress the idea that regimes embody the hegemonic power of states in the international order, the latter take a more consensual view, suggesting a community of international actors bound together by implicit and explicit principles, rules, norms and decision making-procedures (Keeley, 1990: 83). As Keeley sees it, the standard liberal conception of a regime has two weaknesses: first, it overstates consensus within international regimes, making them appear more harmonious than they are; and, second, because it overstates consensus, it implicitly legitimates the power of the dominant actors within regimes (1990: 84). Keeley suggests that a turn to Foucault's work might be helpful in addressing these weaknesses. Specifically, Keeley draws on Foucault's concept of power/knowledge, his notion of discourse as discipline, and the idea of subjugating and subjugated knowledges (Keeley, 1990: 84–5). Keeley argues that the apparent consensus which is presented as the organising principle of a regime is always the more or less unstable outcome of struggles between subjugating and subjugated knowledges. The definition of a regime is the result of battles between the actors within the regime and their competing accounts of what constitutes a legitimate order. Regimes are therefore always the 'loci of greater or lesser, but inevitable, tension' (Keeley, 1990: 98). According to Keeley, rethinking the concept of 'consensus' in terms of the interplay of power, knowledge and truth enables the regime theorist to differentiate between groups of actors within regimes in terms of their relation to the subjugating/subjugated knowledges on which the regime's existence is premised (1990: 97–8). However, Keeley argues that this is not the only advantage that follows from using Foucault: 'What this sort of analysis does not do, especially by its attitude, is encourage particularly regime-supporting perspectives or prescriptions; if anything, its bias is in favour of resistance' (Keeley, 1990: 99). The above claim is an interesting one since it implies a direct connection between Foucauldian-inspired theorising and the interests of resistance. The apparent acceptance of the relation between theory and a particular kind of political practice is reminiscent of both Foucault and Ashley and Walker, and also echoes the gesture towards an ethic of responsibility in Der Derian's and Bartelson's work. However, it soon becomes apparent that Keeley does not make any direct connection between the theoretical discourse he is using and political action or judgement:

> Any policy prescriptions that might follow from it would be largely strategic and tactical, available equally to supporters of and resisters to regimes, and useful for blocking, altering, or destroying as well as creating or maintaining an order. It does not suggest that we should or should not want any specific regime or regimes as such. It leaves such debates to particular theories or ideologies in and for regimes. (Keeley, 1990: 99)

Although Keeley recognises significant distinctions between his Foucauldian analysis and the key explanatory assumptions of realism, he nevertheless concludes by claiming Foucault as a potential ally for realism, offering 'enrichment rather than opposition' to realism in the analysis of actual regimes (1990: 99–100). As Keeley sees it, because a Foucauldian analysis 'accepts power and conflict as basic' (1990: 99) it captures the central insight of realism without committing the mistake of restricting power to interstate relations in which states are presupposed as asocial actors. The theoretical tools offered by Foucault therefore enhance an essentially realist understanding of politics as strategic relations of power, and the idea of social scientific explanation as a fundamentally disinterested enterprise. Paradoxically, the understanding of political life and the distinction between theory and politics which appeared to be challenged by Foucault's thought is reinstated in Keeley's use of Foucault.

It is Foucault's conception of the interrelation between power, knowledge and truth which Forbes (like Keeley) appropriates for his own purposes in assessing normative theorising about the interventionary practices of states (Forbes, 1987: 58). In an article in which he critically reviews a number of theoretical approaches to the question of the rights and wrongs of state intervention, Forbes points to a perpetual tension in normative international relations theory between a realist and a liberal/moral vocabulary. Whereas the former assesses the actions of states in purely strategic terms, the latter invokes principles of judgement which transcend state interest (Forbes, 1987: 52–3). Forbes' principal concern is with the discourse of liberal morality and its claim to universal standards of moral judgement (1987: 53). Forbes traces various attempts to ground universal standards and norms for conduct in the context of international intervention and finds they run into a variety of both conceptual and pragmatic problems (1987: 56–8) centring on the difficulties of grounding conceptions of state and individual rights and on the tensions between the two. It seems as if one is obliged either to prioritise the rights of collectivities, in which case there is always a *prima facie* ethical case for non-intervention, or to prioritise individual rights, in which case intervention becomes more likely to be morally sanctioned. The first approach implies a return to realism and the essential irrelevance of morality to the international sphere; the second raises problems of ethnocentrism and the question of how judgements in favour of intervention are to be grounded (1987: 56–8). Forbes argues that liberal normative theory of international intervention becomes caught in a series of impasses, and he suggests that Foucault's work on the relation between power and knowledge provides a way out:

> Power is not caught in the alternative: *warfare* or *morality*. In fact every point in the *activity* of *warfare* is at the same time a site where *moral* knowledge is formed. And conversely every established piece of *moral* knowledge permits and assures the *activity* of *warfare*. (Forbes, 1987: 61, original emphasis)

Forbes argues that liberal normative theory pretends to a distinction between morality and warfare which does not exist and claims that the moral vocabulary surrounding state intervention is an example of Western subjugating knowledges which have come to dominate global relations in theory and practice (1987: 64). The implication of Forbes' argument is that the competing claims of normative moral theory should give way to a genealogical approach, tracing the ways in which ideas like 'human rights' or 'self-determination' are deployed strategically to further the interests of certain international actors (1987: 65). In conclusion, however, Forbes voices a concern about the kind of theorising of international intervention he has been recommending. This concern reflects a dissatisfaction with the idea of theoretical work as the reflection or exposure of dominant relations of power rather than the resistance of those relations:

> It is to the subjects of intervention, therefore, that I look, not with compassion, but with hope for resistances to those exercises of power which lock us into a system of domination and its power/knowledge discourse. A large reservation remains, however. This kind of conclusion may end up as quietism. Although admittedly likely, this is not essential. With this view of international relations, it is still possible to proceed by empowering the subjects of intervention, or by reversing the habits of the interveners themselves. (Forbes, 1987: 66)

Although Keeley's and Forbes' concerns are very different, there are some obvious parallels both between the ways in which they both use Foucault's conception of the interrelation of power, knowledge and truth, and the kinds of conclusions they draw from that use. In both, the immediate target of the argument is liberal theory and, as with the work of Der Derian and Bartelson, we find a legitimising vocabulary revealed as a guise for strategic power relations, and a distinction between theorising and the object of theory is shown to be unsustainable. In both cases also, the theoretical approach being argued for is presented as being more 'realistic', both in the common-sense use of the word and in the way in which it is understood in international relations. This is particularly marked when Keeley links Foucault and realism as allies in their conception of the centrality of power and the neutral stance of the traditional social scientific investigator. However, even in Forbes' case, the line drawn between theory and practice following the substitution of genealogy for normative theory suggests a traditional demarcation between the nature of the world and the nature of theoretical practice. The suggestion made at the end of Forbes' article as to the possible political effects of his discourse is accompanied by a kind of dismay at its quietist implications.

In the light of the above examination of some examples of international relations theory which draw upon Foucault's work, it is clear that the implications of Foucault's own account of his theorising, and the Foucauldian elements in Ashley and Walker's work identified above, are to a large extent confirmed. In relation to the ways in which the object of international relations theory is conceived, the use of Foucault poses a fundamental challenge to realist theory by revealing the fragility of realism's founding concepts, something which is the major concern of Der Derian and Bartelson. It also does this by problematising the relations between conceptual and actual orders so that the range of explanatory factors in international relations theory extends beyond states and the interstate system not only to other non-state actors but also to textual and cultural practices, including those of international relations theory itself. For both Der Derian and Bartelson the relationship between power, knowledge and truth means that the history of concepts like 'diplomacy' and 'sovereignty' is not an abstract exercise since the theory and practice of international relations cannot be disentangled. It is also clear that all four writers confirm that the Foucauldian-inspired theorist unsettles fixed boundaries of explanation and judgement within theory by pointing to the ways in which they are constructed through discursive struggles and strategic relations of power. A primary effect of Foucauldian theorising is to upset claims to given explanatory reference points, whether these are taken to be eternal truths about the international system, or stories of historical origins or, on the normative side, transcendent standards of judgement. Genealogy, as Bartelson puts it, cuts the present down to size within history (Bartelson, 1995: 83). This element is clearly evident in Keeley and Forbes, who take the pretensions of different kinds of liberal theory as their target. There is, however, a sense in which the implications of

Foucauldian theorising in international relations do not unambiguously follow the path suggested by both Foucault's own account and the appropriations of it by Ashley and Walker.

As was evident in the first two sections of this chapter, Foucauldian theorising is a transgressive criticism which, like all theorising, is political, but which distinguishes itself by making analogies between trangressive critique and movements of resistance. Foucault draws parallels between his own practice and feminist and anti-psychiatry movements; Ashley and Walker draw parallels between their practice and dissident movements in international politics. What, then, is the politics implicit in the work of the theorists who have just been considered? This is a question which is difficult to answer given that, in Foucauldian terms, there are no general criteria through which power and resistance can be judged. What counts as subjugating or subjugated discourse, domination or freedom, depends on context, but also on effects, which are undecidable in advance. In the case of international relations theory the criterion of judgement must therefore be drawn from the strategic situation of competing discourses within that discipline, and the effects of Foucauldian theoretical interventions. Theoretically, the agenda of the discipline has traditionally been set by realist and neo-realist assumptions, with liberal-pluralist paradigms providing a mainstream alternative approach. At first sight, then, there is no question that Foucauldian international relations theory constitutes resistance, since it is set against the dominant voices of both realism and liberal-pluralism. However, as was demonstrated in the discussion of Der Derian, Bartelson, Keeley and Forbes, Foucauldian theorising appears to be much more unambiguously against liberal-pluralism in its outcomes than against realism. Although all thinkers reject the state-centricity of traditional realist accounts, as the quotation from Der Derian opening this chapter suggests, they also read Foucault as confirming the realist insight into the centrality of power politics in the explanation of international politics. When it comes to an account of their own practice, however, the acceptance of inescapable relations between theory and politics has a tendency to give way to the acceptance of a line between theory and practice and a tone of disinterest and neutrality. Political commitment is consigned to a realm beyond analysis in a manner worthy of Weber.

In the concluding section of this chapter I consider whether the ambiguous relationship of Foucauldian international relations theory to realism bears out the criticism mentioned at the end of the last section, that is, that Foucauldian approaches simply represent a sophistication of realism. And whether this in turn means that rather than resisting dominant relations of power, Foucauldian theory is in fact fatalistically complicit with them, much as realism can be accused of being complicit with the hopelessness of Cold

War. If this is the case, then Foucauldian theory appears self-defeating, in that it fails to live up to its own account of itself.

Conclusion

Foucauldian theories of international relations are not simply sophistications of realist theory and neither is it the case that Foucauldian theory implies political fatalism. Nevertheless, there are reasons stemming both from the traditional assumptions of international relations and from Foucault's own work as to why the blurring of the lines between realist and Foucauldian analysis remains an everpresent possibility. We have seen how work already done indicates just how enriching Foucault can be to international relations analysis, but that same work indicates this is a legacy which must be handled with care.

The claim that Foucauldian international relations theory is a sophistication of realism rests on the assertion that Foucauldian theory repeats two central claims of realism: first, that power is central to political understanding; and, second, that although power marks the limits of political understanding as an explanatory reference point, the claims of knowledge and truth reflect the realities of power but are distinct from those realities. Although there is an apparent overlap between Foucault and realism on the first claim, as the discussion of Foucault in the first section demonstrated, this is more apparent than real. There is a great difference between the concept of power as something struggled for and possessed by sovereign actors in realist theory and Foucault's concept of power relations. Paradoxically, Foucault's all-pervasive conception of power is much more open to the possibility of change and transcendence than the realist one. Whereas the vocabulary of war for the realist confirms eternal truths about interstate relations, that same vocabulary for Foucault is used to stress both the fragility and dynamism inherent in what may appear as the most rigid systems of domination. With regard to the second claim, again, Foucault's theory is radically different from realism. For Foucault, theory is always an irreducibly political practice, whether it confirms or challenges existing relations of power. On the basis of Foucault's conceptions of power and theory, therefore, there appears no reason why Foucauldian international relations theory should lapse into a repetition of the eternal verities of *realpolitik*. Why, then, is it the case that the relation of Foucauldian international relations theory to realism is ambiguous and that Der Derian and Keeley can identify Foucault as an ally of realism?

The first reason for this is the centrality of a vocabulary of battle for both realism and Foucault. Although the significance of this vocabulary is very different for the two parties, it is very difficult for a theorist of international relations to appropriate Foucault's work without being affected by meanings of terms such as power, strategy, tactics and struggle which have traditionally defined the discipline in terms of *realpolitik*. This is most evident in Keeley's argument, in which Foucault's work confirms both that strategic self-interest and the struggle for power provide the key to understanding international politics, and that the nature of social scientific analysis is to reflect neutrally the strategic relations of power which are defined as the object of theory.

If Keeley's reading is taken as exemplary then the Foucauldian theorist, like the realist, always knows in advance what he or she is going to find. This brings us to the second reason why the terms of realism tend to haunt the Foucauldian international relations theorist. There is a paradox at the heart of Foucauldian theory, which is that the only fixed general assumption for theoretical practice is that everything in both theory and practice is contingent, in the sense that, in principle, there are no limits which may not be transgressed. In contrast to theories which assume given limits to their object and to explanation and judgement, Foucauldian theories emphasise the fluidity and fragility of limits. The vocabulary of power, strategy, tactics and struggle is used by Foucault to express the perpetual openness which underlies apparently fixed and solid realities and it is central to Foucault's critique of alternative modes of theory. Having said this, however, the assertion of fundamental contingency which all Foucauldian theory reflects as its basis should not be confused with the truth which Foucauldian theory aims to discover. Instead, the basis of contingency works as the general condition of possibility for the production of truth in Foucauldian theory: never *the* truth, but *a* truth. When international relations theorists identify Foucault as an ally of realism they are confusing the conditions of possibility of genealogy and transgressive theory with its product, a confusion compounded by the overlap in the realist and Foucauldian vocabularies. There is a genuine problem here, which is not simply constructed by misreadings of Foucault, but raises a central philosophical question about the relation between the conditions of possibility of theory and the ways in which it constructs its object. We may be able to acquit Foucault of realism, but doesn't he, like the realist, always know in advance what he is going to find? In one sense, clearly the answer to this question is 'yes', we know that Foucault and Foucauldian theory will always find the contingency of limits which are given to us as fixed and absolute. However, in another sense the answer to the question must be 'no', since the specific meaning of any transgression of the limits of theory or its object cannot be understood in advance of genealogy. Whereas the realist always already knows that consensus masks competition and morality masks strategy in the interrelation of states, the Foucauldian theorist knows nothing specific in advance.

At present the impact of Foucault on the theorising of international relations is at too early a stage for any definitive assessment. It is clear, however, that like Marxist, critical theory, feminist and other postmodernist approaches, Foucauldian international relations theory fundamentally challenges the conceptual armoury of traditional international relations theory and with it an image of world politics essentially restricted to interstate relations. In addition, what the analysis of this chapter suggests is that Foucauldian theory is likely to enhance a grasp of international politics which subverts the epistemic and normative implications of realism and of any theoretical framework which makes sovereign claims to criteria of understanding or judgement. Nevertheless, it is also clear that international relations theorists need to be careful not to read Foucault's vocabulary in realist terms, and thus lay themselves open to the charge of once more reducing international political life to the terms of *realpolitik*, whilst neglecting the necessarily political nature of their own theoretical practice.

NOTES

1. I am not suggesting that the theoretical shifts in Foucault's work amount to epistemological breaks – there are clearly continuities between them, and in later work Foucault sometimes refers to them as complementary dimensions of analysis (Foucault, 1984a: 46; see also Foucault, 1982: 4–6; Davidson, 1986).
2. Foucault's use of a vocabulary of battle to express relations of power and resistance is central to his genealogical work (Foucault, 1978: 93–6; 1980f: 90–1; 123; 1982: 224–5).
3. The Peace of Westphalia, according to traditional accounts in international relations, established principles of territorial integrity of states, non-intervention by states in the domestic affairs of other states and mutual recognition of sovereign equality as the basis of relations between states (Bull, 1977: 10; Nardin, 1983: 57). Bartelson argues against the idea that Westphalia established the equivalent of a modern state system (Bartelson, 1995: 137–85).
4. For a thorough account of the nature of genealogy, see the chapter by Thacker in this volume; see also Visker (1995: 30–73).
5. This is not the same as a claim that there is no such thing as truth. Foucault's point is simply that claims to truth, whether in the natural or social sciences, cannot be disentangled from power relations (Foucault, 1988f: 106–7).
6. It is this juridical conception of power which Foucault argues has been central to mainstream political theory (1980f: 121). The focus of this kind of political theory has been on distinguishing between legitimate and illegitimate power.

The idea that legitimate power is confined within the bounds of the sovereign state has rendered international political theory virtually oxymoronic and helps to account for the dominance of *realpolitik* accounts of interstate relations, as discussed below.

7. For a discussion of criticisms of this kind by Walzer and Taylor, see Simons (1995: 59–67). Similar objections are made by critics such as Habermas and Fraser, who argue that Foucault's account of power undercuts his claims to be a critical theorist (Habermas, 1987a: 266–93; Fraser, 1989: 35–53). For a discussion of Foucault in relation to Enlightenment thinking, see Habermas (1986) and Dreyfus and Rabinow (1986).

8. For a range of examples of applications of Foucault in the social sciences, see the collections of essays in Burchell et al. (1991) and Gane and Johnson (1993).

9. Amongst such 'critical' traditions I would include Marxism and critical theory as well as non-postmodernist feminisms. The most well known contemporary example of such critical social theory is the work of Habermas (1984; 1987b).

10. For discussions of Foucault as an exemplary trangressive critic, see Owen (1994: 210–13; Simons (1995: 81–4).

11. For a brief account of international relations as a discipline, see 'The Growth of a Discipline' (Hollis and Smith, 1991: 16–44).

12. Morgenthau's work exemplifies classical realist thinking in international relations (Morgenthau, 1948); Waltz is the paradigmatic representative of neo-realism (Waltz, 1959; 1979). Neo-realism places more emphasis on the systemic constraints of inter-state relations which remain in place regardless of the specific intentions of states.

13. For examples of critical responses to realism in recent years, see Keohane (1986); Der Derian and Shapiro (1989); Linklater (1990); Sylvester (1994).

14. Sources of postmodernist international relations theory include Nietzsche, Heidegger, Derrida, Bakhtin, Barthes and Baudrillard, amongst others, as well as Foucault (see Krishna, 1993). Important examples of postmodernist international relations theory include Der Derian (1987); Ashley (1988; 1989); Der Derian and Shapiro (1989); Walker (1993). The international relations journals *Millennium* and *Alternatives* have provided the most consistent forum for work of this kind. See Brown (1994: 60–2).

15. Derrida is the other most crucial source for the paper under consideration here, although Baudrillard, Irigaray, Kristeva and Lyotard also appear in the bibliography.

16. Bartelson links these arguments to three texts: Wight (1977), Bull (1977) and Hinsley (1973) respectively.

6 Rejecting Truthful Identities: Foucault, 'Race' and Politics

Bob Carter

> Our society is one not of spectacle, but of surveillance; under the surface of images one invests bodies in depth; behind the great abstraction of exchange, there continues the meticulous, concrete training of useful forces; the circuits of communication are the supports of an accumulation and a centralization of knowledge; the play of signs defines the anchorages of power; it is not that the beautiful totality of the individual is amputated, repressed, altered by our social order, it is rather that the individual is carefully fabricated in it, according to a whole technique of forces and bodies.
> (Foucault, 1977a: 217)

This chapter will seek to do three things. First, it will explore the rich, but ambiguous, legacy of Foucault's ideas for sociological understandings of racisms (Foucault, 1977a, 1978, 1980f, 1988f). My chief contention here will be that the ambiguities in Foucault's legacy arise from his commitment to a well established tradition of philosophical idealism, in which our knowledge of the world does not refer to real objects in the world but is a construction of mere ideas, interpretations, discourses or whatever.

Secondly, the chapter will assess the usefulness of these ideas for an understanding of contemporary forms of racialised political identities, that is, those versions of self in which we make sense of who we are primarily through exclusionary notions of 'race'. The study of racisms provides a crucial testing ground for a critical social science since any explanation of racisms entails that we critically evaluate them. Specifically, I shall apply Foucauldian concepts to an analysis of Cabinet responses in the 1950s to the migration of black British subjects to the UK. This example illustrates the importance of critical evaluation. Unless we can decide, for example, whether Cabinet ministers were factually correct in their beliefs about the unassimilability of black people to a 'British way of life', we cannot adjudicate between different explanations of events. That is, we cannot discriminate between politicians' own versions of the need for immigration controls and other interpretations of racialised social relations.

The final section of the chapter suggests, then, that the difficulties associated with Foucault's analysis and its application to the study of racisms stem from his unwillingness, or inability, to identify an evaluative position. This, in turn, leaves his notion of resistance empty.

Foucault, 'Race' and Racisms

A central theme in Foucault's writings is his emphasis on the ways in which human beings are made into social actors, or, more formally, his concern with the construction of human subjectivities (Foucault, 1982: 208). Foucault's stance here is strongly anti-essentialist: he rejects not only the notion that the social world can be made intelligible by starting from the standpoint of individual consciousness, but also the idea that there is some essential self, some real 'me'. Instead his concern is with how social beings come to be made into certain types of subject – a consumer, a conservative, a parent, a heterosexual – through the various modes of seeing, knowing and talking about the world that are made available to them by society.

Foucault refers to such ways of seeing, knowing and talking as discourses; human subjectivities are thus discursively formed and *profoundly* historical. Rather than expressing the inner essence of an individual, subjectivities are the creation of specific discursive practices (Foucault, 1980f: 151). Systems of etiquette produce the 'well brought up' person, just as medical knowledges and practices produce the 'sane' person. Such a strategy renders problematic any politics based on transhistorical notions such as 'race', or indeed any concept resting on claims about putatively essential human characteristics – hence Foucault's coolness towards those forms of feminism resting on some essential notion of 'woman-ness' (Hoy, 1986: 195).

Discourses may come to congeal in specific ways, more or less loosely, often adventitiously, and in these cases they may constitute a regime of truth; that is, they come to mutually sustain, support and validate a particular way of knowing about the world. There are several aspects of this notion of a regime of truth that are pertinent to our enquiry.

First, regimes of truth come to be powerful, even dominant, ways of seeing and knowing and, at the same time, the sources of their social and historical production are obscured: they become common-sense, taken-for-granted, axiomatic, traditional, normal. Secondly, regimes of truth become the means whereby what is to be regarded as true can be distinguished from what is to be regarded as false. For Foucault, to be able to name something is also to be able to position it within particular discursive arrangements, to literally 'put something in its place' and thereby determine what is to constitute adequate or proper knowledge of it. This is what Foucault means by power as creative: it brings objects into the realm of acceptable knowledge but does so in ways that render them knowable only in terms of that knowledge. In this sense, too, knowledge and power become inextricably intertwined; to know something is also to be able to objectify it, to say definitively what it is. (See Foucault's discussion of the school examination as a 'normalizing gaze' for an illustrative account of this (Foucault, 1977a: 184–94). Indeed, for Foucault, this is one of the most pernicious consequences of the human sciences, their panoptic laying claim to the knowing of more and more areas of social life, a knowing that controls through objectification (Foucault, 1977a). This is a particularly rich idea when applied to racism, where, as we shall see in the case of post-war Britain, Cabinet ministers discussed immigration control of black British citizens in terms of specific forms of 'race-ial' knowledge.

Regimes of truth do not only have consequences at the level of knowledge or epistemology. They carry with them a whole range of practices issuing from their claims and assumptions. These practices Foucault identifies as moral technologies, an unusual coupling of terms whose meaning is perhaps best captured in Rose's phrase 'governance of the soul' (Rose, 1989). Moral technologies are simultaneously means through which social subjects come to be fabricated and individuated – how we come to see ourselves as students or parents or consumers and how we express these subjectivities in everyday social life – and modes of surveillance – the social recognition of ourselves as students or parents or consumers is gained through our complicity with the various calibrating measures of government. To be a student means, amongst other things, registering with a recognised institution, appearing on mark sheets and official forms; to be a parent means, amongst other things, registering a birth, attending a clinic, changing tax arrangements; to be a consumer means, amongst other things, purchasing something, having access to money.

It is important to recognise that when Foucault talks of modes of subjectification, how we come to see and understand ourselves as particular kinds of human subject, he is not merely describing the shaping of our mental selves, the ways in which we consciously come to understand what we are or assemble for ourselves some relatively coherent narrative of self; he is also insisting that moral technologies inscribe themselves upon the body. How we present ourselves physically, and how our physical, corporeal self is interpreted by others, is, to a greater or lesser extent, a product of the ways in which our subjectivities are determined by various moral technologies; as Oscar Wilde noted, only the superficial refuse to judge by appearances. Moral technologies are also techniques of the body, disciplinary regimes for correct training. Being taught the right way to eat with a knife and fork, to sit up straight, to raise your hand to ask a question, to queue properly, are all instances of moral technologies traversing the body and shaping it in specific ways.[1] Foucault points, then, towards a semiotics of the body, seeing bodies as texts bearing, and baring, the inscriptions of a thousand tiny techniques of subjectification. 'A disciplined body,' he pithily notes, 'is the prerequisite of an efficient gesture' (Foucault, 1977a: 152).

These complementary processes of individuation and surveillance in which the regulation of bodies and the formation of self go hand in hand, are designated by Foucault as governmentality (Foucault, 1982: 219). Through governmental practices the self-regulating individual is produced, a subject with historically definite orientations and capacities; a person, in Nietzsche's phrase, 'able to make a promise'. This profoundly historical approach to an 'analytics of self' (Dreyfus and Rabinow, 1982) was accompanied by Foucault's averral that governmentality and regimes of truth were to be studied 'genealogically'. This notion radically uncouples the practice of doing history from any teleological or transcendental purpose, through its insistence on the irreducible and inescapable contingency of history itself. History, in the big sense of evolution or progress, is going nowhere, has no final purpose or ultimate unity. In its place Foucault proposes an 'effective history' (Dean, 1994), the uncovering or laying bare of the internal relations of particular regimes of truth and their associated practices of governmentality and self. This, for Foucault, is the appropriate method for the making of historical sense in the contemporary world (Foucault, 1984b).

What might a genealogical approach to 'race' look like? To begin with, it aims at evaluative neutrality. Once notions of transcendental truth (a truth good for all times and all places) are abandoned then it would appear that with them disappears the point of critique: the site outside the objects of study from which such objects can be criticised as inadequate, false, irrational, unscientific, unjust and so on[2]. A genealogical procedure would thus differ markedly from many conventional accounts of 'race' and racism which do not problematise the site from which they judge – to regard a 'truth' as unscientific or irrational implies a notion of science or rationality. So, rather than begin from the assumption that racism is pathological and aberrant, and that the purpose of social science is to vacuum it away like so much dust on a carpet, genealogy instead examines the ways in which discourses and practices generate an experience of 'race' and make 'race' a truth for us, an experientially valid means of interpreting social relations and negotiating the everyday social world.

By contrast, genealogy restores an important measure of hermeneutic credibility to 'race thinking', including racism, by posing the question of how social actors have come to understand who they are in 'race' terms. There is, though, a danger here of giving too much credibility to racism by implying that racist and non-racist discourses are both just regimes of truth which, in the scrupulous pursuit of evaluative neutrality, one has no means of adjudicating between. Again, Foucault's unwillingness to abandon an epistemology which implicitly denies that knowledge can be assessed in terms of its relationship to its objects leads him to a conservative politics.

The persistent relativism that such an epistemology entails is also expressed in Foucault's account of power. This has been noted elsewhere (see, for example, Owen, 1994; Layder, 1994; Dews, 1987; Ramazanoglu, 1993; Dreyfus and Rabinow, 1982) but some central features of it are relevant to the present discussion. Foucault's main challenge is to what he describes as 'juridical–sovereign' notions of power. This is an orthodox conception of power which views power as *held by* somebody and therefore denied to others. Foucault also refers to this as the repressive view of power, a model in which some have power and use it to repress those who don't (Foucault, 1980f: 156). Against this view, Foucault urges a model of power which regards it in the following ways: as diffusely distributed throughout social relations, as indeed, constitutive of such relations (Foucault explicitly rejects as contradictory a social world where power is absent)[3]; as productive, that is, as generative of knowledges and the distinctions between what is to count as true and what false; and as generally available – the power to resist is an unavoidable implication of power being exercised at all, since the exercise of power, for Foucault, is only necessary where resistance has to be overcome (Foucault, 1980f: 119; see also Foucault, 1984b). Locked into this symbiotic relationship, power and resistance, like wrestlers vying for an advantage, goad each other into renewed effort (power and resistance thus have what Foucault terms an agonistic relationship). Power operates to overcome resistance whilst resistance prompts a more intense exercise of power (Foucault, 1982: 221). In place of power as the struggle between those who have it and those who do not, Foucault offers an interpretation of power as strategy 'spread throughout society in a capillary fashion' (Hoy, 1986:134).

Since power is not something possessed by a sovereign or a class, it is not manifested globally, nor is it concentrated at nodal points. Power, for Foucault, is omnipresent (Foucault 1978: 93), it is a 'machinery that no one owns' (Foucault 1982: 156). This is, as Layder (1994) has observed, a 'flat' view of power, one which sees it as permeating social relations at all levels and which characteristically expresses itself at local points as 'micro powers'.

There are benefits to be gained from broadening our approach to power from a sole emphasis on the state and government to a concern with the diffuse ways in which social relations and social spaces, such as the school and the prison, are permeated by power. However, this may prove frustrating for those interested in practical politics, for whom the identification of points of greater and lesser strategic political significance is of paramount importance. If, for example, you believe that poverty is a bad thing and ought to be abolished, it helps, in reviewing possible political strategies, to be able to distinguish key factors in the reproduction of poverty – such as the maldistribution of wealth – from the less essential ones – such as the amount of money the poor allegedly spend on cigarettes, alcohol or videos. This is not necessarily incompatible with a concern for the micro politics, of course, but it introduces a tension in Foucault's work, noted by others (the chapters by Smart and Said in Hoy, 1986, for instance, as well as Habermas, 1987a; Dews, 1987; Soper, 1993), between the critical cast of his own outlook and the need for effective politics.

In summary, Foucault provides us with a distinctive procedure for analysing historical forms of truth, their moral technologies, forms of subjectification and practices of governmentality. The critical pull of these 'social analytics' (Dreyfus and Rabinow, 1982) is to dislodge embedded truths by exposing their historical determinations, relocating them as discursive products of contingent processes. Foucault, in other words, reaffirms the social and historical character of knowledge.

Insofar as this is taken to mean a rejection of the idea that knowledge, including racist knowledge, can have indubitable, universal foundations, it is sociologically unexceptionable. If, however, it is taken to mean that knowledge, including non-racist or anti-racist knowledge, is *merely* the product of the social conditions from which it arises, then the possibility of a critical social science vanishes, since knowledge claims must necessarily be incommensurable. To assess the implications of this latter position I want to turn to a consideration of government responses to black immigration to Britain after 1945.

Government Responses to Black Immigration to Britain after 1945

The political responses to black immigration to Britain after 1945 have been well covered in the literature of recent years (see, for example, Miles and Phizacklea, 1984; Solomos, 1993; Saggar, 1992; Holmes, 1988; Carter et al., 1993; Layton-Henry, 1984) and my intention here is not to go over familiar ground. Instead my purpose is twofold: to assess the utility of Foucauldian ideas to the interpretation of a specific historical conjuncture and to see whether they have anything to offer over conventional accounts of the period. I have chosen a limited temporal frame, 1945 to 1955, partly for practical reasons of length but partly too because this period sees the emergence of what Hall et al. (1978) have termed 'indigenous racism'. In other words, this period provides an opportunity to examine the development of novel discursive forms about the prospect of a black presence settled in Britain.

In Britain in 1945, following the end of the Second World War, the newly elected Labour government of Clement Attlee found itself facing, amongst many other difficulties, a labour shortage (see Harris, 1987 for a fuller discussion of this term). This was partly an inescapable by-product of military mobilisation, but it was also sharply aggravated by the policies pursued by the Attlee government, especially the retention of conscription as a means of policing a huge overseas empire. Compelled to find labour from elsewhere, the government turned to the recruitment of workers from outside the boundaries of the nation-state, and from 1946 onwards set up a number of schemes, known collectively as European Voluntary Worker (EVW) schemes, to bring foreign workers to Britain. By 1950, approximately 74000 workers had been brought to Britain under the EVW schemes (Kay and Miles, 1992: 43).

The recognition that jobs were available in Britain also proved attractive to many British subjects – that is, individuals born in territories governed by the British Crown – especially in the Caribbean where imperial policies had resulted in high levels of unemployment. Many Caribbean British subjects had served in the armed forces during the war, had experience, skills and contacts and, furthermore, as British subjects, were fully entitled to enter Britain without restriction, a right that had been reaffirmed by the Attlee government's 1948 Nationality Act. This Act abolished the category of British subject, replacing it with Citizenship of the United Kingdom and Colonies. Citizens of the United Kingdom and Colonies retained the rights of entry and settlement that formerly had belonged to them as British subjects.

However, the response of the Attlee government to the arrival, in insignificant numbers, of black British subjects was one of unease (Joshi and Carter, 1984; Carter et al., 1993). It adopted a number of administrative devices – instructing steamship companies to give misleading information about berths available from Caribbean ports, instructing Colonial Governors to be dilatory about the issue of passports, imposing burdensome conditions such as proof of accommodation or the deposit of a sum of money to cover the costs of repatriation – to discourage the migration of British subjects from the Caribbean (and from British colonies in Africa). How are we to account for these contrasting responses?

Clearly, the colour of the respective migrants plays a key role in what we might term, following Foucault, the racialisation of governmentality. The anxieties of Cabinet ministers about the prospect of black immigration partly derives from its insertion into a particular regime of truth, one in which skin colour was held to signify negatively evaluated 'race-ial' difference. In Foucauldian terms, racism literally inscribes the body in a particularly blunt form of bio-power, allowing a seemingly transparent reading of the self. Black

resources supplied by that particular regime of truth that signified 'race' through colour and, of course, in so doing revivified it, endowing it with the spurious scientificity of the survey method.

Thus, the Ministry of Labour circulated Labour Exchanges in 1954 with a questionnaire which asked, among other things, whether it was 'true that coloured people, or certain classes of coloured people, are workshy, that they are poor workmen, or are unsuited by temperament to the kind of work available?' (Carter et al., 1987: 338–9). Similar claims about the alleged unsuitability of black workers also appeared in the report of the Cabinet Working Party on 'Coloured People Seeking Employment in the United Kingdom', presented to the Cabinet in December 1953. The report noted that unskilled workers were difficult to place 'because they are on the whole physically unsuited for heavy manual work, particularly outdoors in winter or in hot conditions underground and appear to be generally lacking in stamina'. Moreover, there was some indication that 'they are more volatile in temperament than white workers and more easily provoked', though the evidence for this was not conclusive. 'Coloured women', on the other hand, 'are said to be slow mentally, and the speed of work in modern factories is said to be quite beyond their capacity' (Carter et al., 1987: 339).

Cabinet discussion rested on an extensive range of such reports: from Assistance Boards on black people's 'racial' proclivity for 'scrounging'; from the Ministry of Transport on the number of 'undesirables' who had managed to enter the country; from the police and the Home Office on the potential 'law 'n' order' problem lurking beneath the skin of the black population in Britain; from the Ministry of Health on the incidence of TB and venereal disease amongst immigrant populations.

Thus, the 'unsuitability' of black workers for employment was held to be the reason for controlling their entry into Britain, just as it was their 'racial character' that created the 'new Harlems' which ministers claimed to find in inner-city areas (Carter et al., 1993). The Cabinet continued its efforts throughout the 1950s to justify legislative restriction on the rights of black UK and Colonies citizens to settle in Britain, deliberating in committees, drafting secret reports, keeping a weather-eye on debates in Parliament. In all these spheres it is possible to discern the labour that went into the production of 'colour' as a regime of visibility, literally a 'learning to see' colour, both as a signifier of taken-for-granted characteristics and assumptions and as a perceptually manifest somatic feature.

However, the practical effects of the 'regime of truth' about colour and 'race', and the creation of a discursive frame within which certain statements and claims about these categories came to be held to be true, were far reaching. The most immediate and significant one was the passing of successively restrictionist and colour discriminatory immigration control legislation. By 1971, with the passing of the Commonwealth Immigration Act of that year, British governments had erected a formidable and draconian system of controls that denied black UK and Colonies citizens their rights of free entry to, and settlement in, the UK. Moreover, by distinguishing between patrial passport holders – those who had a parent or grandparent born in the UK – and non-patrial passport holders – those who did not – the Act made entry and settlement dependent on a notion of 'belonging' identified by kinship and ancestry. The concept of citizenship in UK law thus no longer necessarily carried with it the right to freedom from immigration control; it was, as Juss (1993) notes, no longer the type of one's passport but the citizenship one held that determined immigration status. This amounted to a far-reaching shift in the practical meaning of citizenship, severely restricting the rights available to certain categories of citizen and doing so on the basis of their colour or, more accurately, what that colour was held to signify.

The Dance of Difference: Foucault, Racisms and Politics

Why did colour become such a powerful signifier of belonging for key sectors of the political elite, of determining 'us' and 'them', 'British' and 'not-British', in post-war Britain? Why was it that discourses of colour and 'race' became a central motif in the reconstitution of 'Britishness', re-presenting colour as a mode of civic signification of the individual body? (This is not to suggest that discourses of racism about colour were insignificant before 1945: the 1919 'riots' and the 1925 Coloured (Alien) Seamen's Act amply demonstrate that this was not the case. See especially Holmes, 1988; Fryer, 1984). Do our answers to these questions imply a point of critique, a position from which a social science critical of its object can be developed?

Although there are few references to racisms in Foucault's writings, his work has proved a ready source for authors wishing to investigate the contemporary construction of identities. Foucault's uncompromising hostility towards essentialist and reductionist notions of the subject have prompted several writers to explore racisms as discourses of representation (Goldberg, 1990, 1993, for example), and would appear to terminally undermine the ontological status of 'race'.

Nevertheless, there are difficulties in applying Foucault's ideas to the study of racisms, some of which derive from his more general philosophical position, others of which have to do with drawing a politics from Foucault's work. I identify three here.

To begin with, there is Foucault's claim that power relations are 'intentional and non-subjective' (1978: 94). Of course, he does not mean by this that power relations do not affect individuals, nor that they operate independently of specific social actors. Indeed he argues that power relations are the 'possibility of action upon the action of others', and are 'rooted in the system of social networks' (1982: 224). What Foucault means by 'intentional and non-subjective' is that power has no teleological source, no purpose 'above' society. So, for Foucault, as we have seen, power is not a thing, nor is it merely a product of class relations, a capacity held by the ruling class and deployed against the labouring class. 'A society without power relations can only be an abstraction', claims Foucault (1982: 222–3) and it is in this sense that it has a subject-less intentionality. Power does not belong to anybody and does not serve any transcendental purpose; it necessarily emerges where social relations are antagonistic.

Although Foucault is careful to insist that such a view of power 'makes it all the more politically necessary' to analyse 'power relations in a given society, their historical formation, the source of their strength or fragility, the conditions which are necessary to transform some or to abolish others' (1982: 223), it is also clear that this approach presents significant obstacles to such an analysis. In particular, in developing a view of power 'no longer bound to the competencies of acting and judging subjects' (Habermas, 1987a: 274), Foucault makes it difficult not only to identify those political conditions favourable to the transformation of particular power relations but also to recognise the stratified nature of social relations; the fact that social actors, individually or collectively, do not contribute equally to the construction of social life.

The neglect of social hierarchies of power that this involves has some damaging political effects, making the identification of strategic locations, of nodal points of power, a barren process (Layder, 1994). Instead, Foucault directs us towards a politics based around those groups that have somehow evaded the unblinking panoptic gaze of Enlightenment surveillance – the criminal, the insane, the marginalised, the outcast: the draft dodgers of Western rationality offering an embattled resistance to the inexorable growth of disciplinary power. Leaving aside the difficulties of political organisation involved in such a strategy, it does not escape the familiar bugbear of voluntarist politics: why bother at all? Why resist the growth of disciplinary power? On what basis could those of us thoroughly subjectified by contemporary regimes of truth unite with those who are less thoroughly subjectified? How are we to identify common interests? Although Foucault sometimes dismissed such questions as 'Enlightenment blackmail' (Miller, 1993: 337), preferring to emphasise local struggles and the 'micro politics' of self, they still retain some pertinence.

Secondly, Foucault's distaste for, and lack of faith in, the great emancipatory narratives of the Enlightenment left him little to say about nationalism, either within Europe or outside it. This has two direct implications. One is that for Foucault's work the 'imperial experience' – an experience that had deeply involved an earlier generation of French intellectuals such as Sartre, Camus and de Beauvoir – is 'quite irrelevant' (Said, 1993: 47). A genealogical history of Foucault's own writings might yet reveal some complex filiations between French intellectual life in the 1960s and 1970s and the history of colonial subjugation (see Bhabha, 1990: 243–4 for a discussion of the 'Eurocentricity of Foucault's theory of cultural difference', for example). Also, it makes it difficult to apply Foucault's ideas to the exploration of contemporary nationalisms and their ambiguous relations with historically specific modes of racism such as ethnic cleansing. It is hard not to see Foucault's eschewal of critique here, in Said's words, as 'a swerve away from politics' (Said, 1993: 336).

Thirdly, there are the vexed, and related, issues in Foucault's work of agency and relativism. Baldly put, in the context of racism and anti-racist politics: why, and to whom, should an anti-racist politics matter? And to what purposes and ends should an anti-racist politics be directed? Answers to these, I would argue, presuppose some evaluative purpose, since we would need to identify those political agents or constituencies with an interest in anti-racism as well as those with an interest in resisting it. And evaluative purpose requires a critical social scientific practice able to assess the relative adequacy of different accounts of the world, of different regimes of truth, a practice Foucault is prevented from specifying by his idealist separation of knowledge from its object. Thus, although Foucault, by implication if not explicitly, relativises racist knowledges, he cannot interrogate the object of such knowledges and identify them as misrepresentations of social phenomena that have structures and properties which exist independently of our individual understandings of them.

This suggests then a renewed concern with structured relations of domination, and their connections with the real, material experience of inequality and difference characteristic of class societies, in accounting for what we might term the impulse of differentiation. In other words, racisms, as discourses that naturalise difference, both sanction inequality of practices and resource allocation and create practical hierarchies of exclusion and acceptability. Recognising this, though, presupposes mechanisms and structures generating and reproducing material inequalities, scarcity and differentiation. While the ways in which racisms interact with, as well as form part of, these mechanisms and structures remains a matter for empirical and theoretical investigation, it is still the case that an account of such mechanisms and structures and of the specific ways in which material inequalities are produced and reproduced occupies a central place in any analysis of racisms.[5]

This is because without an account of structured social relations which recognises their obdurate resistance to cognitive modification and their persistent asymmetries of power, our theories remain unconstrained by any reference to an extra discursive reality and float ineluctably towards the dizzying dead-ends of voluntarism and identity politics. Without a means of adjudicating between competing explanations of racisms (and this is not to suggest such adjudication is either simple or straightforward) it becomes impossible, as Geras (1995) has recently observed, to speak of truth and injustice; rather there are merely different (and incommensurable) versions of truth and injustice.

In summary, then, the application of Foucauldian concepts to the interpretation of this concrete historical episode in the (re)production of racist discourses in post-war Britain can be illuminating. In particular, a genealogical approach points to the (often contingent) connections between different discourses about, amongst other things, 'race', colour, difference, national identities, belonging, community, home, England, Great Britain, colonial empire. This facilitates analyses that can bring together social features and phenomena that are often overlooked (the work of Said, 1983, 1993 and Young, 1990 provide good examples) as well as drawing attention to the disconti-nuities of what were previously considered seamless, monolithic narratives, in, for instance, the insistence on novel forms of racisms in post-war Britain (Hall et al., 1978).

Furthermore, the notion of racism as a moral technology with an accompanying array of disciplinary techniques, can also throw new light on the relations between government deliberations, legislative action and everyday life. The regulation of notions of self and other, such a characteristic consequence of racist discourses, can thus be extended to an exploration of the forms of racialised subjectivities. Foucauldian approaches have much to say on how we become subjects for whom 'race thinking' is 'normal', for whom certain sets of cultural practices and ways of seeing come to seem naturally occurring qualities rooted in the psychic and physical 'truth' of the human subject (see, for example, Goldberg, 1993; Rose, 1989; Walkerdine, 1990).

In turn, the 'truths' of racist knowledges can be seen to constitute an element in the normative, disciplinary regimes of 'bio-power' (Foucault, 1972; 1988h). 'Bio-power', the governance of human populations through the production of 'docile bodies' – in prisons, schools, asylums – whose conduct can be guided by the state in the direction of its own administrative purposes, is central to modern political regimes. It is also a further instance of what Foucault refers to as the 'double bind' of humanism: the very knowledges that individuate 'us' are also the very means by which our subjectivities are locked more securely into modern forms of power relations. While we continue to understand ourselves in terms of essentialised, racialised identities, themselves the product of racist knowledges, we simultaneously subjugate ourselves to the state's own political projects. Instead, Foucault insists that we do not

> try to liberate the individual from the state, and for the state's institutions, but to liberate us both from the state and from the the type of individual-ization that is linked to the state. We have to promote new forms of subjectivity through the refusal of the this kind of individuality which has been imposed on us for centuries. (Foucault, 1982: 214)

Leaving aside the suppressed yearnings for the humanist subject that appear to me clearly present here, it does indicate again Foucault's lack of sympathy with forms of transcendental politics rooted in 'shared meanings'. He offers instead an enquiry into the historical practices that have generated those modes of individuation – white, Aryan, black, Jewish, Croat – that recognise themselves in different types of shared meanings, again radically historicising the question of how we come to believe some things to be real and not others. Immigration and nationality legislation in Britain may be regarded as just such an historical practice, playing a crucial role in reaffirming the facticity of 'race', reproducing racialised meanings of self and inserting these within discourses of nationhood and belonging, profoundly connecting relations of domination with the meanings of everyday life. Of course, this discursive reconstitution of national identities will always find itself confronted with contradictions precisely because those structures generating material inequalities will ceaselessly reproduce the differences that the homogenising project of nationhood seeks to overcome.

Conclusion

In this account I have tried to evaluate the usefulness of Foucault's work for an anti-racist politics. In doing so, I have identified a number of tensions within this work and the question remains now as to whether these tensions can be considered productive or whether they should be regarded as vitiating Foucauldian approaches as sources of oppositional, anti-racist politics. In offering some answers to this I have made the following arguments.

First, Foucault has provided a rich legacy of terms and ideas which have directed attention to the ways in which discourses are temporally and spatially relative; embedded in, and reproduced by, ranges of practices or technologies; and are the product of particular, historically contingent 'regimes of truth'. The anti-essentialist thrust of these notions is blunted, though, by Foucault's idealist insistence that all identities – and this must also include non-racialised ones – are merely products of regimes of truth. The basis for a critique of actually existing, racialised identities, on the grounds that they misrepresent social relations and that therefore non-racialised identities are to be preferred, is lost.[6]

Secondly, and this is more problematic from the point of a practical politics, this 'no boundaries' approach to identities leaves one with the difficulty of explaining why we have the sort of identities we have. Either we go with the now unfashionable notion that identities are in crucial, yet broad, ways structurally shaped – so that the actual content of being black in post-war Britain did imply a common experience of a second-class citizenship – or we go with the more fashionable, constructivist idea that we create our identities in some Nietzschean act of overcoming. This latter idea makes the political task of creating common struggles around the distribution of social goods much more formidable since the notion of commonality is rendered practically indeterminate.

This raises a third point – the issue of power. For Foucault, the key political struggle of modernity is the struggle against the hegemony of humanist discourses and 'the simultaneous individualization and totalization of modern power structures' (Foucault, 1982: 216). These regimes of truth and their associated moral technologies possess the capacity to make individuals subjects. Indeed their power rests precisely in their ability to determine identities within specific, historically contingent knowledges, so that the more we reveal our identities, 'tell the truth' about who we are, within such knowledges, the deeper our attachment to them becomes. The more we construct truthful identities for ourselves within such knowledges – as mad, as criminal, as immigrant – the more intensely they come to hold the key to who we are. We thus become implicated, says Foucault, in an ethics of authenticity, an ethics based on notions of who we *really* are.

The problem with such ethics, for Foucault, is that they constrain our ability to transform ourselves by subjecting us to expert knowledges embedded in particular regimes of truth (such as psychoanalysis, criminology, medicine, racisms). Placed in the seductive grip of such confessional technologies, we are always about to disclose the truth about our self and always under the subjugation of the expert. We are thus willing collaborators in shrinking the circle of autonomy and freedom, swirling centripetally towards the acme of Foucauldian discipline, the docile body.

Against this, Foucault sets the anti-humanist claim that there are no essential truths of what we are.[7] This means that the truthful identities of expert knowledge can be resisted, since they can be revealed, through genealogy, to be aesthetic constructs, imaginative narratives, 'armies of metaphors' in Nietzsche's phrase, whose truths are necessarily partial. Instead, then, of an ethics of authenticity, characteristic of humanism and the human sciences and based on some notion of *the truth* about ourselves, we have an ethics of creativity. This entails a styling of the self, a styling which, in order to strive towards autonomy, must be transgressive of social practices based on humanist discourses and their attendant practices. We must, urges Foucault, reject 'truthful identities' such as homosexual, black, woman, heterosexual, Hutu, Serb, Jew, British. This politics of transgression is not merely a matter of thinking about ourselves differently, since it must entail confronting not only the discourses reproducing, or making available, 'truthful identities' but also the practices that flow from those discourses and also sustain them. Immigration controls, amongst other things, authenticated some notions of what it meant to be British; to transgress these requires not simply a refusal to accept their authenticity, it requires opposition to the discourses and practices of immigration control.

We arrive, then, at a politics aimed at resisting those discourses and practices that constrain or foreclose the possibilities for self-transformation, whilst encouraging those that heighten or extend our capacities for self-transformation and autonomy. For Foucault, 'Human dignity is our capacity to be otherwise than we are' (Owen, 1994: 207). Insofar as racism profoundly denies this capacity, it is a legitimate site of resistance and opposition for Foucault. It is inaccurate, therefore, to claim that Foucault does not offer grounds for a politics of resistance. However, this resistance must itself be a discursive social production, not one based upon, or derived from, what things *are* – unequal and exploitative social relations for example – or from what they are inherently capable of. Thus, the Foucauldian stance remains frustratingly abstract in its failure to specify how and on what basis this resistance is to take place.

I have suggested here that this is not accidental, but is a consequence of Foucault's 'inadvertent idealist foundationalism' (Sayer, 1995, private correspondence) which leaves him not only unable to provide a critique of racialised identities but also failing to identify any transformative social agency other than the self-styling subject. Foucault's fastidiousness with regard to the historical and discursive nature of what we can know, his insistence that reality is undecidable and ordered through contingent truth regimes, leaves him in a poor position to offer insights about the analysis of structural relations of domination. Without such insights an adequate account of racisms in post-war Britain, and an adequate sociology, remain critically incomplete.

ARCHIVAL COLLECTIONS

Public Records Office, Kew, London. PRO documents are given by Department (Colonial Office, Dominions Office, Home Office), box and file number.

ACKNOWLEDGEMENTS

I would like to thank Sue Clegg, Alan How, Marci Green, Ian Grosvenor, Kevin Magill, Mike O'Donnell, Alison Sealey and Leslie Spiers for their helpful comments on earlier drafts of this chapter. I am especially grateful to Derek Layder and Andrew Sayer, whose detailed suggestions helped me to clarify some of the ideas which appear here.

NOTES

1. But see Goffman for a more upbeat interpretation of 'limb control' and the civilising of bodily discipline. Crossley (1995) discusses Goffman's contribution in more detail.
2. The extent to which, in Habermas's phrase, Foucault's genealogical method is 'criticism without critique' is a matter of some debate. Recently Owen has argued that 'the immanent relation of genealogy to resistance entails a principle of critique in terms of which forms of constraint may be evaluated' (Owen, 1994 : 162). In other words a genealogical approach, in seeking answers to the question of how we came to be what we are, implicitly identifies not only other possible versions of what we might be but also identifies those social factors that have inhibited the development of autonomous, alternative modes of self. Whether this convinces depends on how far one buys the (Nietzschean) notion of freedom as the continuous accomplishment of personal autonomy. See Dean (1994) for another defence of genealogy as critique, whilst Dews (1987) and Soper (1993) take a less sympathetic view.
3. The implicit targets of Foucault's capillary view of power are, of course, Marx and Weber, who both held to the proprietorial notion of power. More particularly, Foucault is deeply sceptical of what he regards as a key Marxist claim that a world without power is possible (Foucault 1982: 221).
4. Minute J. Goldberg to MacMullan 24.10.48 LAB 13/42.

5. See Sayer (1994), Layder (1990) and Pawson (1989) for a fuller discussion of structured social relations and their implications for sociological analysis.
6. I am indebted to Andrew Sayer for his trenchant comments on the limitations of Foucault's critique of anti-essentialism.
7. Foucault's anti-essentialism needs some refinement here. To claim that there are no 'essential truths' about who we are, in the sense that human subjectivities are not the product of some transhistorical human essence, is one thing (and sociologically unexceptionable). However, to claim that human subjects, as social beings, have no properties whatsoever is another thing entirely (and sociologically unacceptable).

7 Strategies of Power: Legislating Worship and Religious Education[1]

Davina Cooper

> It is on the way that [religious education] achieves that jump from the statute book to schools that this Act of Parliament will be judged. (Coombs MP, Commons, 23 March 1988, col. 403)

Introduction

Christianity has long been an ambivalent partner within British education. Under the 1944 Education Act, religious education and a daily act of collective worship were prescribed elements within the school day. However, both requirements and their assumed Christian ethos were flouted with impunity in many schools, particularly as the 1970s and 1980s wore on. Religious education, to the extent it remained, became in many instances multi-faith; taught from an implicitly secular standpoint, it stood alone or was incorporated within humanities or ethics-based courses (see Hart, 1993). Worship reconstituted itself into assemblies of stories, poetry and song. While some retained a Christian character, many were multi-faith, broadly spiritual, or indeed secular.

In 1988, this trend away from mono-faith instruction was punctured by the arrival of the Education Reform Act. Through a series of amendments,[2] conservative Christian peers attempted to resurrect what they believed had become 'subjugated knowledges'[3] – traditional beliefs about education and religion stifled by modern, hegemonic, liberal discourses of secularism and multi-culturalism. Through the Education Reform Act 1988, they made explicit what they believed remained implicit within the earlier 1944 Act – the special place of Christianity. Under the 1988 provisions, school prayer was to be 'wholly or mainly of a broadly Christian character', while religious education syllabuses were to 'reflect the fact that the religious traditions in Great Britain are in the main Christian'.

In examining the effects and implications of these religious provisions, it is tempting to characterise the situation as one of state power reasserting dominant cultural meanings, marginalising minority ethnic communities. Within a fixed sum paradigm, power might be said to be transferred from the beneficiaries of multi-culturalism to those with a stake in Christian hegemony. Yet while such a characterisation identifies one aspect of the legislation's impact, alone it provides too static a description. It assumes what needs to be demonstrated, and ignores the complexity and fluidity of legal or legislative interventions.

Not only has the 1988 Act generated a range of responses but it has also, paradoxically, empowered those who would seem most under attack. One of the most significant aspects of the changes between 1988 and 1994 has been the coalescing of forces hostile to the government's religious educational agenda. As traditionally elite actors attempted to entrench past epistemological certainties, local actors resisted, refusing to allow their micro-disciplinary, educational practices to become co-opted. While such resistance from edu-cationalists and community activists proved only partially successful, it nevertheless problematises the notion that government can simply appropriate local power mechanisms without difficulty.[4]

Foucault's methodology of power
To explore the impact of the government's religious education agenda between 1988 and 1994, I wish to utilise a conception of power that draws on Foucault's methods and analysis, while maintaining some distance from it (Cooper, 1994b, 1995a). My objective is not therefore to engage in a close and detailed examination of Foucault's work, pitting one text against another, but to draw on his methodological approach and that of others influenced by his work. Foucault's work is useful in providing a more fluid, relational and productive notion of power that extends the analytical focus beyond static forms of domination.[5] He characterises power in several overlapping ways: as a productive network (1980f: 119); 'as something which circulates' (1980f: 98); as a 'multiplicity of force relations' (1978: 92); and as 'the name that one attributes to a complex strategical situation in a particular society' (1978: 93).

Central to this understanding of power is a shift from juridical power framed as 'thou shalt not' to the modern power of disciplinary societies which operates through the constitution and normalisation of specific desires, truths and behaviours:

> In defining the effects of power as repression, one adopts a purely juridical conception of such power, one identifies power with a law which says no, power is taken above all as carrying the force of a prohibition. ... If power were never anything but repressive, if it never did anything but to say no, do you really think one would be brought to obey it? What makes power hold good ... is simply the fact that ... it traverses and produces things, it induces pleasure, forms of knowledge, produces discourse. It needs to be

considered as a productive network which runs through the whole social body. (Foucault, 1980f: 119)

In order to analyse the historical shift towards a more productive form of power, Foucault identifies several key methodological elements.[6] First, analysis should be concerned with power at its extremities rather than with the 'regulated and legitimate forms of power in their central locations' (1980f: 96). Power is not concentrated within a sovereign or state; thus, a critical examination must focus on those other, 'capillary' forms of power. Second, rather than focusing on *why* people wish to dominate, analysis should concentrate on the processes of subjection (1980f: 97) – the 'how'. Third, power is not something that can be owned, acquired or exchanged, but a chain in which people are embedded as both power's effect and vehicle (1980f: 98). Fourth, analysis should be ascending, to explore the ways in which the most infinitesimal mechanisms are 'invested, colonised, utilised, involuted, transformed, displaced, extended etc., by ever more general mechanisms and by forms of global domination' (1980f: 99).

While Foucault's approach is helpful in challenging some conventional assumptions about power, it is not unproblematic. Many theorists have analysed and critiqued Foucault's approach (for example, Hartsock, 1990; Smart, 1989). Let me briefly mention three difficulties relevant to this chapter. First (and foremost), what power actually means remains unclear in much of Foucault's work. The metaphor of a chain or web may be appealing, but what interior relationships exist between its nodal points? Similarly, Foucault describes power as 'a cluster of relations' (1980f: 199), but fails to clarify the actual character of these relations. While they may, in both instances, be diverse, for power to have any specificity, some indication of the character or parameters of its internal relations is required. A more concrete definition of power is offered by Foucault in 'The Subject and Power' (1982), where he links power with governing – 'to structure the possible field of action of others' (221). This comes closer to the approach used here, although I adopt a wider notion of the terrain upon which power operates.

The second problem concerns Foucault's methodological emphasis on bottom-up analysis, and his suggestion that state or government bodies co-opt, colonise or displace micro-techniques of power. While this argument and approach may be useful for certain analyses, in the case explored here, a bottom-up analysis might miss the centralised nature of the initiative to reform religion in schools. Clearly, government policy has to draw on micro-educational disciplinary forms for effectiveness, but these too are forms that have been in part shaped and constructed through state policy. Thus, in recognising the methodological (and ontological) importance of relations, practices and forces 'beyond' the state, these should not be granted primacy.

In addition, Foucault's justification for an ascending analysis may assume what needs to be proven, namely the extent of government forces' success in utilising or transforming micro-power relations. As I discuss in relation to schools' response to government policy, there is no reason to assume these localised practices will be sympathetic to government agendas or amenable to co-option.

Finally, Foucault's set of equivalences between juridical, law and repressive power is too constraining (for example, Smart, 1989; Hunt and Wickham, 1994). Taken literally, equating law with juridical power reduces the former to sovereign power and interdiction. This ignores the powerful, educative function of law, its operation at a micro-level in terms of civilian daily interactions, and its interconnected relationship to other 'normalising' discourses.

Techniques of power

In this chapter, I draw on a framework of power influenced by Foucault, but which attempts to avoid the problems identified. In particular, my concern is to explore the ways in which law can function as a *generative* form of power. It may say 'no', but it also says a lot of other things as well. While sanctions exist within law as a last resort, British educational law lacks the punitive character Foucault identifies with legal forms (1978: 144). Indeed, the severest penalties may have little to do with legal breach – for instance, the financial disadvantage facing schools unable to compete effectively for pupils within the new educational 'market place'.

In refusing to reduce law to repression, I also decentre its relationship to rights. Religious education provisions in the Education Reform Act 1988 did bestow formal rights, principally on parents and teachers who objected to multi-faith teaching. However, one of the primary effects of the legislation, as I discuss below, has been its processes of cultural normalisation.[7] In other words it rearticulated a chain of equivalences between Christianity, nation, school and family.

In exploring power, my starting point is a productive paradigm which identifies power as the process of generating effects through particular social mechanisms (Cooper, 1995a). These effects can take a range of different forms. In this chapter, I am particularly concerned with those at the level of political activism, changing social meanings, cultural norms, bodily discipline and institutional scrutiny.[8] Conceptualising power as the generation of effects moves away from those Foucauldian analyses which identify power as inherently concerned with (localised forms of) inequality or asymmetry

(McNay, 1992: 110; Sawicki, 1991: 25). Foucault himself appears ambiguous on this point. However, his depiction of resistance as an integral aspect of power (1978: pt 4, 1980f: 142) implies the centrality of conflict (or at least objection) and, hence, that power's exercise entails practices contrary to the interests or desires of particular groupings.

The approach I adopt, by contrast, defines power more broadly, to *include* instances of conflict while not requiring it. Indeed, the most interesting processes concern the ways in which conflict is organised out, fails to emerge, or is produced in particular ways rather than others through the construction of desires, interests and social meanings. I also use resistance in a more limited sense than many Foucauldians to refer to opposition motivated out of a desire to halt change and particular power technology practices (Cooper, 1995a). In the context of religious education, resistance provided just one aspect of an ongoing counter-offensive. In many instances, schools simply continued to develop progressive discursive practices paying only minimal attention to the religious provisions of the 1988 Act. Those they felt they could work with were incorporated, the rest ignored.

In considering the disparate ways religious education legislation generates effects, four broad technologies appear key. Foucauldians tend to focus on two – discourse and discipline. The first concerns the production of knowledge; the second, the production of compliant, trained individuals. I wish to extend this typology to include two other productive mechanisms – coercion and resources. Identifying these latter as techniques of power may be contentious from a Foucauldian perspective. Foucauldians make it clear that force cannot be power since it does not act to structure choice but rather to negate its possibility (for example, see Phelan, 1990: 425). Similarly, in the case of resources, Foucauldians emphasise the fact that power is not a resource. However, given the productive formulation of power I am adopting, both coercion and resources can be seen as ways of generating effects. Let me briefly set out these four mechanisms.[9]

In exploring the production of meaning, Foucauldians tend to deploy the concept of discourse rather than ideology, arguing that the latter suggests (1) false consciousness; (2) a countervailing reality to which ideology stands in a secondary position; and (3) the possibility of true knowledge, such as 'science' (Foucault, 1980f: 118; Barrett, 1991). However, while ideology *can* be given such a restrictive interpretation, it can also be used more broadly to identify frameworks or patterns of meaning (see Cooper, 1994a where I have developed this approach further). Ideology is neither a pejorative characterisation, nor restricted to identifying political belief systems. Its use recognises that social relations and life can only be understood through social concepts articulated together in different ways. These may take the form of dominant ideologies which act (successfully) to naturalise, affirm and entrench the status quo, or as oppositional ideologies which contest taken for granted truths and assumptions, and privilege alternative norms, perspectives and understandings.[10]

In contrast, I use discourse to refer to the specific production of knowledge. Foucault describes discourse as the place where 'power and knowledge are joined together ... a series of discontinuous segments whose tactical function is neither uniform nor stable ... blocks operating in the field of force relations' (1978: 100–1). Discourse, I argue, is the process by which ideology becomes 'textualised' as knowledge or truth. Thus, its external normative agenda is interiorised and self-validated. It identifies the interactive process between institutional settings and social actors, and reveals the ways in which some perspectives are epistemologically invalidated and certain voices excluded, while others are centred and presented as legitimate. Specifically, discourse works by condensing, formulating and converting ideological abstractions into knotty clumps, such as, in law, the 'reasonable man', 'foreseeability' or 'burden of proof'. A second mechanism of power is that of discipline: training through observation, normalising judgements, and rewards (or micro-penalties) (Hunt and Wickham, 1994: 20). 'Analytically it identifies the existence of a whole complex of techniques of power that do not rely on force or coercion' (Hunt and Wickham, 1994: 20). Foucauldian work emphasises the asymmetrical, relatively anonymous aspect of discipline (Dews, 1987: 161). Writers, for instance, have explored the ways in which particular architectural and organisational forms shape and contain people's practices (Fraser, 1989: 22), without explicit action on the part of a discipliner.[11] Where discipliners do act – for instance, the parent or teacher – they are not identified as the source of the discipline but rather as nodal points within a wider system (Foucault, 1980f: 56). By drawing us all into its processes, discipline provides one of the most effective mechanisms of power of modern society. At its height, no external agents are required; for, drawing on the paradigm of the panopticon, Foucauldians argue that people internalise the dominant gaze, and thus censor, police or reinvent themselves (Bartky, 1988). Foucauldians also use the concept of discipline to highlight the ways in which those subject to power are open to scrutiny. Discipline therefore suggests a lack of privacy and invisibility. Silence and concealment consequently become constructed as ways of avoiding discipline.

For many Foucauldians, discipline takes on an inherently negative character. The approach I take, in contrast, defines discipline more neutrally as the spatial, temporal and organisational mechanisms through which social interactions, institutions and bodies become structured or ordered. Discipline is inherent to any society; the important question is the nature of the discipline: symmetrical or asymmetrical?

The third form of power I wish to explore is coercion. This is distinguishable from processes of normalisation since a key aspect of coercion is the *knowledge* that a lack of choice exists.[12] For instance, mono-faith religious practices in schools are only coercive when students, teachers or others know that alternative practices are potentially possible. Thus, paradoxically, coercion entails a higher level of consciousness of alternatives (albeit unattainable) than discipline, where the body internalises particular styles of behaviour. In coercion, the *potential* for resistance always exists. Consequently, *identifying* practices as coercive can be an important discursive strategy. At the same time, the notion of coercion is an unstable one, since *awareness* of lack of choice is likely to generate pressure for change. This highlights a further problem: at what point do we say choice does or does not exist? For instance, under the 1988 Education Reform Act, school students do not have a *formal* choice whether to attend collective worship. Yet, despite its compulsory character, students can choose to physically disobey the interdiction. Does this lack of formal choice constitute coercion, or does coercion require the lack of any kind of choice?

Difficulties in identifying coercion return us to the original problematic: power's productivity. If coercion is conceptualised as a mechanism for generating effects, it is perhaps most usefully characterised as a practice whereby the subject knowingly produces effects for which they cannot be held responsible as agent. In other words they function (unwillingly) as a conduit for the agency of others.

Resources provide the final mechanism through which effects can be generated that I wish to explore. It differs from the other three identified above in that it centres the actor as agent rather than simply the subject of power. In analysing the struggles over religious education, the diverse resources different actors can call upon are key. These include political legitimacy, funding, legal rights and time. Resources can be divided into those which work through transaction, for example, money; those which improve the position of the actor, for example, time and status; and those which simply offer a means or route to achieving desired outcomes, for example, a complaints system.

As with ideology, discipline and coercion, resources also function as the effects of power. Thus the relative value, meaning and efficacy of different resources will depend on a range of criteria. For instance, parental support as a position-improving, political resource for schools has become more significant in recent years as a result of government legislation placing parents on governing bodies, the introduction of market systems for school admissions, and the development of parental complaints systems.

Exploring the effects generated by different technologies of power emphasises the contradictory, fragmented and unpredictable impact of religious education legislation. At the same time, it also raises questions of co-ordination and coherent governance, despite the conflicting objectives of government actors themselves. In examining this practice of management or hegemony, I focus on the ways in which the law has become concerned with the administration of the self, the nation, and its differentiation from the 'other'.

The Legislative Framework for Religious Education

Before applying the framework set out above, I wish to outline key aspects of the 1988 Education Reform Act's religious provisions, as well as some of the ways in which the Act has been extended by subsequent enactments and circulars. As I said at the beginning, the 1944 Education Act required a daily act of collective worship and compulsory religious instruction in all primary and secondary schools; this was developed and broadened by the 1988 Act in several respects.

To begin with, religious education is required as part of the basic curriculum for all students within maintained schools (S. 2(1) Education Reform Act (ERA) 1988).[13] The key development here is the prescription that religious education syllabuses drawn up by LEAs (local education authorities) 'reflect the fact that the religious traditions in Great Britain are in the main Christian whilst taking account of the teaching and practices of the other principal religions represented in Great Britain' (S. 8(3) ERA 1988). They must also be non-denominational, although '[t]eaching about a particular catechism or formulary ... is not prohibited' (Circular 1/94, para. 32).

Initially, the content requirements only applied to new syllabuses. Although S. 11 Education Reform Act 1988 enabled LEAs to convene a conference for the purpose of reviewing the local syllabus, it did not require them to. This provided a loophole, allowing LEAs to retain old syllabuses which contravened the 1988 requirements, for instance, through giving insufficient priority to Christianity. This loophole was closed in the Education Act 1993 which compelled authorities that had not done so, to convene a syllabus conference by 1 April 1995 (S. 256).

Central government has also used other methods to restrict local curricular discretion, including producing, in 1994, model syllabuses. Although these are not statutory documents, they set out the preferred way for fulfilling the legislative requirements. Although the model syllabuses incorporate what are deemed to be the key religions within Britain, at the same time, they assert the privileged position and significance of Christianity (see below).

The second key element of the provisions concerns school assemblies. All pupils are to take part in a daily act of collective worship (S. 6(1) ERA 1988). The responsibility for arranging this lies with the head teacher. Thus, if they do not wish to lead the assembly themselves, they are required to arrange for someone else to carry it out. As with religious education worship is to be of a 'broadly Christian', albeit non-denominational, character (S. 7 ERA1988). Not every act of religious veneration has to be broadly Christian providing the majority of acts are over a term (S. 7(3)).[14] What 'Christian' means in this context has been made more explicit by Circular 1/94 which states collective worship must 'contain some elements which relate specifically to the traditions of Christian belief and which *accord a special status to the person of Jesus Christ*' (para. 63, emphasis added).

Neither the 1988 Education Reform Act nor the 1993 Education Act abrogate the right of individual withdrawal established in the 1944 legislation. Schools must give effect to any parental request that their child be excused from attendance or from participation in collective worship. Schools must also comply with any parental request for a child to be excused from religious education. In neither instance are parents obliged to give reasons for their request.

Where schools have a large number of pupils for whom broadly Christian worship would be inappropriate, it is possible to apply for an exemption. The 1988 Act lays down a procedure for obtaining what is called a 'determination' for all or some students so that they can either attend a common multi-faith assembly or worship within mono-religious groupings. The decision about whether or not to grant a determination is made by the local Standing Advisory Council on Religious Education (SACRE).

The mandatory requirement on local authorities to establish a SACRE appears one of the most innovative aspects of the 1988 legislation. Composed of four groupings, each with a single vote, SACRE plays a role in monitoring religious education, determining when the syllabus might need reviewing, considering applications for a determination, and, in many instances, participating within the complaints process. Its composition has, however, proven a source of contention. The legislation lays down that it comprise four groups: (A) Christian and other religious denominations broadly reflecting the religious or denominational character of the area; (B) the Church of England; (C) representative teachers associations; and (D) the local education authority.[15]

Tensions have arisen over several issues. First, given the broad character of group A, should membership simply extend to all religious groupings in an area or should it reflect the proportionate membership of non-Church of England religious faiths? This can be important since the vote exercised by the group on the SACRE depends on a majority decision. The 1993 Act has clarified the position by stating representation should be in proportion to the localities' religious make-up (S. 255). This will tend to work in favour of Christian representation and against membership by small, minority faiths.

Other concerns have been expressed regarding the definition of denomination or religion against which membership is determined. The Humanist Association who were denied membership of Coventry SACRE appealed unsuccessfully to the Secretary of State to be allowed to come within group A. This matter was clarified in Circular 1/94, para. 104 which states that 'belief systems such as humanism, which do not amount to a religion or religious denomination' cannot be members of group A. It is, however, possible for other people to be co-opted on to the SACRE, although such co-optees do not have a vote.

The Power of Religious Education Law

Ideology/discourse
The Education Reform Act 1988 conveys a series of linked meanings and assumptions not only about religion and Christianity, but also about education, nation and heritage. At the most basic level, the Act inscribes the importance of religion to young people's spiritual, moral and cultural development, and identifies religious education and collective worship as a way of achieving this aim. While the dominant position accorded to Christianity has generated considerable hostility, the more basic centrality granted to religion has been less contested. Similarly, although many academics and educationalists have questioned the appropriateness of prayer within the school curriculum, most have approved of religious education (albeit with differing opinions as to its role and content):

> There is some need for the schools to take on educational grounds the part that RE can play in promoting spiritual and moral development in pupils ... and I think that RE can well provide that support if it's well resourced, and well staffed by qualified people. ... [We] teach Christianity as a world religion and not from a faith perspective or from a nurturing point of view. [LEA inspector, West Yorkshire]

Whether and how the re-entrenchment of religious education and prayer will impact on school students' perception of the world remains uncertain. Any simple model which suggests more RE will lead to more religious students seems flawed, particularly given a wider, secular environment.

However, while the ideological efficacy of RE in relation to students may be minimal, the centring of spiritual, educational objectives works discursively to construct a problem of lack.[16] According to Circular 1/94, '[T]he government is concerned that insufficient attention has been paid explicitly to the spiritual, moral and cultural aspects of pupils' development' (para. 1).

Such a lack functions to explain a range of social problems: vandalism, joy-riding, theft, drugs, under-age sex and violence. Through a series of articulations, prayer becomes the solution or omission that explains the Bulger case (the murder of a toddler by two young boys) and the alienation and delinquency of single-parent families, deflecting attention away from socio-economic explanations or responses.[17] The violence of young children becomes constructed as the unexplainable horror of our age. Religion and the re-emergence of traditional values offer a solution to what appears to be a fast changing or disintegrating youth:

> We want more Christianity; we want children taught right and wrong. Those are brilliantly coded messages which appeal to ordinary people. ... It's good for our children ... and they'll grow up not to rob banks and kill people. And anybody opposing that is actually opposing what's good for our children. Therefore you can't be a good person, can you? [London Labour councillor]

Clearly, not any religion can play this role. A significant facet of right-wing populism has been the damage that 'other' religions might inflict, particularly upon Christian children. At the centre of the religious imperative within the 1988 Act is Christianity's value at both a normative and explanatory level. Although the first is not explicitly developed,[18] the importance of Christianity to making sense of and perpetuating Britain's heritage is crucial (Hull, 1993, 1994). Christianity is discursively framed as 'the predominant religion in Great Britain' (Circular 1/94, para. 16); 'religious traditions in Great Britain are *in the main* Christian' (S. 8(3) ERA 1988, emphasis added).[19] In this way, the law is used not only to assert, but also to produce, truth. Ideological positions are factualised within legal discourse in ways that pre-empt the possibility of opposition; ideological disagreements become legal transgressions.[20]

The explicit Christian emphasis contained within the 1988 Act functions as a counter-offensive – the re-emergence of 'traditional' knowledges, now subjugated, against the new, multi-faith teaching 'establishment'.[21] The pluralist approach developed by a number of LEAs during the 1970s and 1980s attempted to treat all religions as equally valid, highlighting their similarities and differences. While a heritage discourse was largely adopted, it was articulated differently to focus on the heritage of Britain's *present* multi-cultural communities rather than the romanticisation of a historic, mono-cultural past. Indeed, even this latter was discursively problematised, as progressive curricula highlighted the ways in which Britain's past wove together disparate racial and cultural strands.

The revised conception of heritage entrenched within the 1988 legislation highlights a confusion within this new religious settlement regarding the purpose of RE.[22] The inability to obtain exemptions from the Christian religious education requirements is predicated on the distinction between education and faith affirmation. Since religious education is the former, it does not matter whether children are Sikh, Muslim, Jewish or Christian, they all live equally in a country whose Christian heritage and history they must understand:

> In the Government's view, it is of the utmost importance that all children, whatever their ethnic and religious background, should be introduced at school to those Christian beliefs and values which permeate our traditions and culture. [Arran, Lords, 26 February 1988, col. 1486]

At the same time, not only is educational relevance construed narrowly, as Britain's religious traditions (S. 8(3) ERA 1988) – thereby excluding other criteria of educational relevance or a more international perspective – but, as well, Circular 1/94 states 'the precise balance between Christianity and other religions should take account both of the national and the *local* position ... account should be taken of the local school population and the wishes of local parents' (para. 35 emphasis added). Implicit in this statement is the suggestion that the character of religious education is premised, at least in part, in faith affirmation rather than learning about the unknown.[23] This was certainly the wish of many peers who referred in House of Lords debates to the legitimate wishes of Christian parents to have their children socialised into the faith.[24]

Grounding religious education in belief highlights the way in which the subject is not intended simply as a historical discourse – making sense of the past – but also, more normatively, to affirm and reproduce specific, Christian traditions (Hull, 1993).[25] This form of nurturing, to produce a coherent, national Christian identity, is even more apparent in relation to collective worship. While religious education syllabuses are expected to take into account 'the teaching and practices of the other principal religions represented in Great Britain' (S. 8(3) ERA 1988), worship can be 'wholly ... of a broadly Christian character' (Education Reform Act 1988 s. 7). Thus, while the Christian subject at the centre of the legislation should know a small amount about other faiths practised in Britain, it is deemed inappropriate for them to attend their worship.[26]

Management of the self

The discursive focus on the needs of Christian children running through the 1988 provisions and their introduction reveals interesting analogies with Foucault's analysis of the development of a middle-class sexuality:

> the most rigorous techniques were formed and, more particularly, applied first, with the greatest intensity, in the economically privileged and politically dominant classes. ... [I]t was in the 'bourgeois' or 'aristocratic' family that the sexuality of children and adolescents was first problematised. ... [I]t was the first to be alerted to the potential pathology of sex, the urgent need to keep it under close watch. (Foucault, 1980f: 120)

Foucault argues that the middle classes developed these techniques in relation to their own rather than other's sexuality as a strategy of self-affirmation (1980f: 123). A similar argument can be made in relation to religious education. As parliamentary debates made clear, the main function of the legislation was not 'the enslavement of another' (1980f: 123), but the re-creation of a sense of belonging and national identity among white Christians whose ties to blood, history and the land appeared under attack.[27] Thus, the legislation refers repeatedly to Christianity while the names of other faiths remain unspecified; they are simply the forbidding, foreign other, against which Christians define themselves. For despite the focus being on the needs of Christian families, their identity cannot be constructed without the depiction of a non-Christian alternative.

Yet the alternative identity demonised is not Islam, Judaism or Hinduism so much as the 'mish-mash', 'hotch-potch' or 'mixing bowl',[28] a multi-faith approach which emphasises the commonality between faiths from a position of equal respect. For in the mish-mash of different faiths children may lose the ability to identify the boundaries of their own.[29]

Right-wing discourse on multi-faith education is not only based on a functional understanding of RE – the reproduction of differentiated, and in particular, Christian, identities – but is also predicated on, and in turn reinforces, particular notions of religion. Faiths are seen as discrete phenomena that (should) remain pure, simple and relatively unchanging. The idea of faiths as emerging, historical products that people control and shape is entirely anathema to conservative Christians in its implication that people rather than God are in control.

Religious discourse is also articulated to conservative educational perspectives, framed through the concept of simplicity.[30] As several parliamentarians stated, a multi-faith approach that explores in a comparative manner a range of different faiths can only confuse young children.[31] What children need are simple, basic truths – stories from the Book – not the intellectual questions that concern agnostic theologians engaging with a range of faiths.[32] This conservative discourse has manifested itself in the provision that RE syllabuses set out the content of teaching in each faith (see Circular 1/94, paras 33–4).[33] By obliging syllabuses to demonstrate how at each key stage the 'relative content devoted to Christianity ... predominates' (para. 35), it becomes much harder for syllabuses to integrate different faiths on a thematic basis. To protect themselves from criticism or challenge, LEAs are encouraged to establish how many weeks will be spent on each individual religion.

Discipline

Through the contesting of progressive educational discourses, proponents of religious education reform sought to discipline schools, teachers, LEA and pupils. Their objective: to produce compliant members within faith-based, nation-oriented communities. A key mechanism for achieving this was intensified scrutiny – a chain of surveillance (Foucault, 1980f: 158) that included teachers, self-disciplining through internalisation of the Christian parent's gaze:

> There is no need for arms, physical violence, material constraints. Just a gaze. An inspecting gaze, a gaze which each individual under its weight will end by interiorising to the point that he is his [sic] own overseer, each individual thus exercising this surveillance over, and against, himself. (Foucault, 1980f: 155)

In an educational context where funding follows pupils, and competition exists to attract requisite student numbers, parental perceptions become increasingly important. Many head teachers attempted to provide what they felt parents wanted, to avoid being depicted in the local press or by local communities as unchristian or unlawful. As a result, internalisation[34] led some schools to be more responsive to the legislation than they otherwise might have been:

> Five years ago it was not unusual for Christmas in some schools to be very unchristian. It was about yuletide logs and Father Christmas. Now I think the content of nativity is probably higher on the agenda for schools, especially schools that may have a Christian body of parents who are looking at the school with a view to see what the content is ... where the Head feels spied on by parents who are looking for where the schools haven't done the Christian bit properly. [London Labour councillor]

The anxiety of teachers and heads has been exacerbated by two particular developments. First, there have been a handful of well-publicised parental complaints backed by right-wing, Christian organisations.[35] Although they have had minimal direct impact on religious education, the spectacle of intense media, LEA and government interest is enough to intimidate many heads and governing bodies. The Department for Education's (DFE) 1/94 Circular even warns schools to be litigation adverse, to keep detailed records in case of queries.

Cautioning schools about the ever-present risk of challenge needs also to be seen in the context of statutory demands that schools increase the level of information provided to parents. The RE syllabus must be readily available for any parent wishing to see it (1/94, para. 122). The annual prospectus for parents must also contain information on the RE and collective worship provided, including, in particular, *whether any non-Christian elements are included within it* (1/94, paras 123–4).[36] Thus, the 'right to know', by undermining any semblance of school privacy, functions both to scare schools into complying and to provide parents with specific resources they can deploy in their selection of school or in taking out a complaint.

The second means of scrutinising and policing implementation of RE provisions, however, was seen by most people I interviewed as the more serious:

> The point at which we'll be absolutely blown to bits is when OFSTED come round. ... Touch wood not at least for twelve months. But when they come I mean they'll just go spare at us. ... You see the [LEA] advisers ... basically they're on our side ... they would have told us that we were not complying ... and then maybe help us to try and find a way in which to do it. ... Now OFSTED has no such way of operation. I mean they're just going to come and shout at us. [West Midlands primary school teacher]

From September 1993, a new system of four-yearly inspections of schools commenced (Education (Schools) Act 1992), carried out by the Office for Standards in Education (OFSTED). More extensive and rigorous than the previous HMI (Her Majesty's Inspectorate) system, many teachers and LEA officers I interviewed perceived an OFSTED inspection as a key disciplinary mechanism pressurising them to abide by the legislation.[37] First, the length of such an inspection visit made it difficult to avoid the requirement for daily Christian worship. Hidden areas of non-practice, it was felt, would come to light under the scrutiny of a week-long observation. Second, the subsequent report, identifying problems and areas of non-implementation, required a responding action plan by the governing body stating how criticisms would be resolved.

Although a mechanism for disciplining teacher behaviour, these inspections also operate discursively. The interpretation by the inspectors of whether the law is being adhered to in turn creates new forms of knowledge regarding what is within or outside of Christian worship and education.[38] Schools and LEAs discipline themselves trying to predict the interpretation inspectors will lay down. Yet, while this in itself may produce forms of religious knowledge, the extent to which it is possible to predict inspectoral opinion is uncertain. On the one hand, inspectoral teams come from all over the country. Thus, in theory, an urban authority could be inspected by a rural team if they won the tender. On the other hand, the specifications with which teams work are extremely detailed. Thus the margin of discretion may prove very narrow. Inspectors function as disciplinary agents, but, like the panopticon guard, they are neither the origin nor locus of power.

As well as being disciplined through inspections and the threat, fear or actuality of parental opposition and complaint, the processes undergone by schools to obtain exemptions also force them to make their practices and 'consumers' public.[39] While conformity with the Christian worship mandate requires little self-reflection, obtaining an exemption or determination necessitates a school demanding, scrutinising and then evaluating the background of its pupils. The process also forces parents to define or categorise themselves in particular ways since only certain aspects of the family background are deemed relevant. For instance, parents who define themselves as non-religious do not count towards an exemption which can only be on the basis of 'other' faith membership. Likewise, atheist/humanist Jews, for instance, have to classify themselves as Jewish rather than non-religious to assist in obtaining a determination.[40] While this illustrates one of the ways in which the legislation renders secularism invisible, it also highlights the identity-affirming aspects of the law. Secular Christians 'belong', whether they wish to or not. Here power does not structure their field of action so much as deny them a choice altogether. Unable to reject 'their' heritage and traditions, the disciplinary power of the law generates not their activity but rather their non-action. Alternately, if Christian heritage parents attempt to obtain a determination, the law renders their choice non-existent. By law, their refusal of Christian prayer is a non-event that must remain unrecognised.

Thus, Christianity maintains its private, normative status. At the same time, other religions are obliged to declare themselves in order to win consideration. Interestingly, they are also forced to confront Christian hegemony if they wish to be taken into account and to make possible a shift away from mono-cultural, Christian worship. Parents, for instance, who do not complain and who do not withdraw their children from assemblies do not provide the evidence required for an exemption to be granted (Circular 1/94, para. 71).

It is not only the *process* for obtaining dispensation which generates disciplinary techniques of classification, scrutiny and visibility. Dividing children for separate assemblies also produces their categorisation according to faith, and normalises particular identifications. The atheist child or the one from the minority faith is most clearly pathologised. Children become trained to perform mono-cultural forms of worship, whether it is kneeling, standing head bowed, or sitting cross-legged on the floor. Irrespective of young people's own belief structures, most will conform to the postures of submission which enable a single teacher to manage a hall full of children. As they pass each other on the way to their separate prayers, children's bodies become disciplined to follow their facilitator, and to recognise the direction other children take as 'not theirs'.

Coercion
Within this area of education law, coercion plays a relatively insignificant role.[41] While many of the educationalists I interviewed presented themselves as having little choice other than to comply, when actually questioned about the consequences of not fulfilling religious statutory requirements, their response was hazy. Even the spectre of OFSTED, when examined, meant only the requirement to respond to a report.[42] For many schools, the extent of their unfulfilled obligations suggested generally that religious education was unlikely to stand out. Moreover, a vague action plan could timetable religious education as one of the last areas to be tackled within a four-year plan. The sanctions if nothing happens before the next inspection remain uncertain. Indeed, several educators I spoke to took for granted that in many schools legal requirements would remain only partially fulfilled by the time of the next OFSTED inspection:

> I was at a conference recently where people said, well the first round of [OFSTED] reports were dead easy because schools aren't doing it every day. ... You could simply say they're not fulfilling their statutory requirements, you don't have to get into any judgements whether what they're doing is or is nor worship, and if it's any good. The feeling is that if OFSTED survives to the second round of inspections then all schools will more or less be doing something every day and that's when you'll get the really heated arguments about whether something is or isn't worship. [Inspector Religious Education, London council]

A more immediate form of coercion concerns ministerial action as a result of complaint.[43] The establishment of a complaints structure was seen by initiators of the 1988 provisions as a key aspect of the legislation, its corresponding lack in the 1944 Act being identified as a reason for the high levels of previous, sustained non-compliance. This reliance on a complaint to enforce the legislation is, however, skewed in its implications since it means that some aspects of the Act are more likely to be enforced than others. The requirement, for instance, on rural, mono-cultural areas to include to some degree 'all of the principal religions represented in the country' (1/94, para. 35) might be a less likely candidate for complaint than the mandate that Christianity predominate in multi-cultural urban areas where Christian activists are present to ensure its execution.

The main group, however, on whom coercion is exercised are young people. As long as they are registered pupils, they have no formal right or even freedom to opt out of daily collective worship and religious education unless their parents write a letter. Although children are not compelled by the law to pray, attendance alone is not sufficient. 'Taking part in collective worship implies more than simply passive attendance' (1/94, para. 59), although it is unclear how much more can be expected.[44]

This coercion is rooted in conservative discourse's denial of young people's religious autonomy (and the assumption of a single, familial faith). Young people, even of eighteen, cannot choose whether to participate in religious worship or study. Any sense that they may have separate wishes and religious identity to their parents is denied by the statutory provisions which, throughout, refer to safeguarding *parental* rights and interests. In the light of young people's relative autonomy in other areas, most obviously their right post-sixteen to leave secondary education, their inability to absent themselves from daily prayer is an interesting anomaly.

Perhaps the closest analogy is the inability of young men under eighteen to consent to sexual acts with other men. Both the male age of consent, as well as the enforcement of prayer and religious education suggest a paternalistic imperative to enforce the norm, to protect young people from their own potentially corrupting desires. Given a choice, young people may experiment with atheism, even with other religions, to their own future detriment and regret. But beyond that, the enforcement of Christian prayer and religious education is also a way of perpetuating a particular community. Young people's identity as belonging, both to their school and to their nation, is maintained and reinforced by the shared experience of prayer and heritage learning. Yet the maintenance of this community accentuates the exclusion of others; the articulation of school with Christian faith reproduces the other as outsider.

However, the efficacy of articulating Christianity to education cannot be assumed. First, many schools may remain reluctant to coerce young adults to attend prayers. Second, the requirement to attend, if it is perceived as coercive, may generate antagonism and hostility rather than a sense of community, particularly since compulsion in this area contradicts young people's self-perception as emerging adults.

Resources

The final means of generating effects I wish to explore is through the deployment of resources. Principally, and not surprisingly, the legislation generated resources for parents opposed to secular, multi-cultural or multi-faith education. This form of advantage took several forms. First, it focused time, attention, teaching skills and money on what was seen by right-wing Christians as a fundamental aspect of the curriculum in a way that furthered the values they uphold. This is not to say such parents have no criticisms. Many on the Christian right feel the legislation has not gone far enough, albeit a step in the right direction.

Second, the reforms have given conservative Christian education greater legitimacy. Instead of the claim for Christian education being perceived as a fringe demand, the centrality of Christianity to British tradition has been legislatively entrenched, with local syllabuses across the country asserting this 'fact'. Thus parents and teachers can use the language of the legislation to demand compliance (Hart, 1993: 13–14).

Third, the legislation specifically provides parents with a procedure through which complaints can be made. In doing so, the government has provided the Christian right with a further incentive to rigorously monitor religious education and prayer since there is a route for action. One Labour councillor interviewed suggested that as a result of the 1988 Act, religion in schools had become an agenda item in many evangelical churches:

> One of the items is making your local school meet the terms of the Act. The local evangelical churches, that is part of their general agenda for the 90s really. ... The Christians are trying to join PTAs [Parent Teacher Associations], and they do feel empowered by the legislation, and they do feel their expectations have been raised. [London Labour councillor]

By offering a way for the Christian right to gain a political profile, the 1988 Act has opened the way to a more American-style religious politics.

Yet, in considering the resources made available by the legislation, it is important not to see this as an entirely one-sided process. Opponents, too, were facilitated and, of course, incited by the law into taking action. Discussing the way in which the law can function as a resource for its opponents problematises the notion of resistance. For if the latter involves *obstructing* change, how does this square with oppositional tactics which *rely* on change to generate the means for their initiatives to take effect? While some opponents of change looked back to an idealised vision of multi-faith coalescence, and simply refused to implement the law, transgressing its boundaries, others explored how they could integrate governmental changes within a 'forward-looking' framework, which nevertheless continued to deploy a multi-faith discourse.[45] Indeed, progressive educators drew on the requirement that other religions be included in the syllabus to support a multi-faith perspective. However unlikely this was to be meaningfully supported by central government, it nevertheless provided some recognition of Britain's status as a multi-faith society that could be utilised by different religious communities. Similarly, the procedures established to gain exemption enabled schools for the first time since 1944 explicitly to provide a single, lawful, non-Christian or multi-faith assembly.

The legislation also worked in another way to empower other faith communities. By drawing attention to, and accentuating, Christian dominance within British maintained schools, separatist claims for other faith schools were strengthened. The 1988 Act offered ideological resources for those from all faiths who wished to maintain their separateness. It also acted as a factor in drawing progressive religious educationalists together to protest or minimise Christian hegemony. Indeed, it may be liberal or progressive *Christian* participants in interfaith work who felt most politically disempowered. In my interviews, several Christian educationalists expressed dismay at the Acts for undermining their ability to partake as equal partners within a broad, multi-faith curricular process.

In their oppositional deployment of the 1988 religious provisions, actors also drew on power emanating from elsewhere. For instance, the discursive authority and resources head teachers and governing bodies gained as a result of LMS (Local Management of Schools) was used to assert an independence that would not submit to 'immoral' legislation. Within a context of continuous government onslaughts and surrender, religious education became an issue around which schools could attest their political conviction, asserting a foundational right – freedom of thought – more basic than compliance with the law.

Defiant heads and schools were also, paradoxically, able to draw on government inspections as a resource to disseminate their position. As repeated inspections identified a high level of non-compliance, feelings of solidarity – indeed, alternative forms of belonging – were reinforced.[46] The media, too, assisted in fulfilling this role through their coverage of annual inspection reports and high profile stories such as 'Major's old head takes on Tories over God'.[47] Thus, institutions which in other circumstances have proven more useful to the right (Cooper, 1994a), helped diffuse fears that particular schools or authorities were adopting isolated positions that left them vulnerable.

In contrast, the right were limited by the resources generated through the legislation. Complaints procedures proved slow and cumbersome, and government departments reluctant to interfere. The individualistic orientation of taking out a grievance necessitated a wholesale campaign really to put pressure on non-complying schools or 'illegal' syllabuses; but the level of political support required for this to take place did not exist. As a result, despite anxiety about OFSTED and the possibility of a challenge, schools tended to feel few repercussions would befall their failure to implement the law.

In addition, central government and the right may have underestimated the extent to which their religious politics lacked support among educational professionals. Given the relatively marginalised character of their position, more needed to be done to solidify Christianity than simply to pass a law demanding its affirmation. Government might state in a circular the 'special status of Jesus Christ', but given the strength of alternative religious beliefs and discourses, including perceptions of religious freedom and independence from the state, this by itself proved insufficient.[48]

Instead, government religious discourse provided a tool for those organising against the religious right and affirming a multi-faith politics. Progressive forces rearticulated elements of conservative discourse to provide an adversary for their own framework. The more central government emphasised the special position of Christianity, the more opponents could argue for a multicultural, humanist approach on the basis of the problems government policy would generate.

Conclusion

In this exploration of power and religious education legislation, I have focused on the mechanisms through which the Acts and attendant circulars generated effects. Yet, as I have suggested, there is a danger of *assuming a priori* the effects of particular forms of power. In the context of religious education, for example, it is tempting to speculate that Christianity has become more pervasive, and other faiths further subordinated as a result of government policy. However, actual effects are much more equivocal. Government action led in many ways to a re-entrenchment of progressive practice and transgressive activity as educational workers battled to protect their own normative practices. In response, central government launched its own counter-offensive, attempting to limit the room for manoeuvre or local autonomy. Yet, the struggle of central government to capture micro-power techniques was also limited by internal dissent. The Christian right may have been able to convert their agenda into legislation, albeit with some compromises. However, ambivalence among government officials, inspectors and other politicians as well as educational workers meant the extent to which it was implemented and enforced remained equivocal (Cooper, 1995b).

While the process of governance does not require a uniformity of intention, the serious lack of central and local co-ordination combined with high levels of non-compliance suggest both the Christian right and central government proved unable to capture local educational power technologies.[49]

Thus, although the Christian right appeared in the ascendancy, able to shape – at least to a degree – government policy, their failure to operationalise religious education law as far as they wished may have proven their downfall. By repeatedly engaging in unsuccessful offensives, they highlighted their inability to construct a new religious settlement in Britain. At the same time, their own political agency shaped the counter-offensives of opponents. While the right may in the long run be seen as having failed, their legacy in helping to frame the terms through which religion, heritage and national identity are debated – structuring the discursive field – should not be overlooked. As Ewald (1992: 170) argues, discipline involves everyone speaking the same language; for this reason norms are important since they help society communicate with itself. By focusing attention on Christianity, the Christian right constructed a normative centre to what had become a decentred, fragmented issue. While they did not generate agreement, they achieved the potentially beneficial outcome (for them) of people talking about the same thing.

The introduction of legislation dealing with religion in schools and the struggle this generated thus provides a useful case study through which to explore a Foucauldian-influenced paradigm of power. Foucault's emphasis on a shifting, tactical set of relations, his focus on micro-techniques of governance, provides a useful frame for analysing the technologies of governmental power as well as the constantly changing equilibrium of forces engaging and responding to each other. Foucault's work also helpfully emphasises the contingency and unpredictability of effects, the displacement (at least in part) of intentionality and the value of inverting received wisdoms.

In this chapter, I have attempted to show how these principles can help elucidate the practice and implications of a particular set of legislative provisions. In doing so, however, I have also reworked elements of Foucault's paradigm of power. By focusing on power as the generation of effects, I remove any assumed linkage between power and domination/asymmetry[50] and thus erase the conceptual inevitability of resistance or conflict. I also focus on a wider range of power technologies than many Foucauldians through considering coercion and the deployment of resources. The latter is particularly important in identifying the means by which subjugated forces can assert their demands and generate effects.

NOTES

1. The research for this chapter is part of a larger project, the Power of Law within Municipal Politics, carried out by myself and Ann Stewart, funded by the Economic and Social Research Council as part of their Local Governance Programme, award no. R000232035. The objective of our project was to explore the contradictory, unpredictable and often surprising results of legal change particularly in their impact upon institutional power relations. Within the project one area of focus was education, and within that religious education law. My interest in the latter was provoked by the attempt to legislate a new religious consensus and the levels of opposition this engendered. It also offers an interesting paradigm through which to explore Foucauldian ideas about power.
    This chapter draws on field research on religion in schools, including interviews with approximately twenty people involved in education (as councillors, governors, heads, Local Education Authority (LEA) inspectors, teachers, and education officials) from four urban authorities in different parts of Britain. Interviews took place between September 1993 and May 1994.

2. See Lords, 26 February 1988, col. 1453. For discussion of the amendment's introduction, see also Hart (1993); Poulter (1990).

3. This inverts Foucault's conception of 'subjugated knowledges' (1980f: 82) which tends to refer to naive knowledges, disqualified as inadequate, and usually articulated or linked to marginalised communities, such as prisoners and mentally ill patients. Whether traditional approaches to religious education and prayer were truly subjugated is debatable. The point I wish to make here is their *perception* as being such. For further analysis of the Christian right's self-presentation as a marginalised minority, see Herman (1994).

4. For a discussion of the more general theoretical issues involved, see Foucault (1980f: 99).

5. This is not to deny the political importance of domination. However, restricting power to it can marginalise the less overtly coercive ways through which certain relations, interests, desires, and agendas prevail, and, indeed, are produced.

6. This is a fifth methodological point which I do not wish to focus on here.

7. One could argue this is an example of disciplinary power colonising law. However, I would argue this requires a distinction between the two which is oversimplistic.

8. Clearly, each of these effects in turn generate other effects. I try in this chapter to follow some of these chains, however, in many instances the subsequent effects remain unknown; for example, the extent to which the changes have impacted upon young people's perceptions of religion.

9. In setting out technologies of power in this way, I do not mean to suggest that they operate as discrete forms. A better way, perhaps, of seeing them is as different facets of the same phenomena. Legislation operates discursively, coercively, as a resource, and means of discipline. At a less general level, the creation, for instance, of grievance procedures operates to discipline teachers and governing bodies as well as providing a resource for parents dissatisfied with the way the Act is being implemented.

10. Adopting this approach, ideology is differentiated from material practice. This is not to deny that frameworks of meaning are shaped by social practices and embedded within them. They do not float on wind currents as disembodied thoughts. However, while we may only be able to determine meaning through analysing practices, this does not make the two synonymous.

11. Others have explored the ways in which physical layout and agency combine to reinforce each other, such as the control exerted by a teacher within the classroom.

12. This does not have to be by the subject of the coercion.

13. Differing provisions exist for pupils in grant-maintained, voluntary controlled, voluntary aided and special agreement schools.

14. However, if prayers are 'mainly' rather than 'wholly' Christian, the inclusion of non-Christian material must be justified (see Hull, 1993).

15. The 1993 Act includes in certain circumstances a fifth group – the governing bodies of certain grant-maintained schools.

16. For a discussion of the relationship between Christianity and public morality, see Jackson (1992: 103–5).

17. See Ashbourne, Lords, 26 February 1988, col. 1467; Coombs, Commons, 23 March 1988, cols 402–3.

18. At different points in the debates attacks are made on a relativist position which refuses to differentiate between truth and falsehood in the normative beliefs of different faiths. Advocates and supporters of the legislation have also emphasised the general value and contribution of Christianity to social life. See, for instance, letter from head, *The Times Education Supplement*, 17 June 1994, who states, as a result of Christian values, England remains 'the most kindly, tolerant and law-abiding society in the world'.

19. All children are required to learn and understand Christianity's historical significance. Thus, although it is possible for schools to get exemptions from Christian worship, the same is not available for religious education.

20. A comparable example of this is S. 28 Local Government Act 1988 which, in prohibiting local authorities from 'promoting homosexuality', legislated lesbian and gay households as 'pretended families'. For a more general discussion of this role of law, see Smart (1989).

21. For example, see Cox, Lords, 26 February 1988, col. 1456. See also Haldane (1986) for an attack on cultural pluralism within the state sector.

22. For a useful discussion of different approaches to religious education in the US, see Mueller (1986).

23. For instance, see Ron Dearing, chair, School Curriculum and Assessment Authority, who stated that for young children classroom work should focus on the traditions pupils brought with them (the *Guardian*, 6 July 1994).

24. For example, see Swinfen, Lords, 26 February 1988, col. 1473.

25. See Bishop of London, Lords, 21 June 1988, col. 666.

26. The asymmetry of treatment between children of different faiths is explicit throughout the legislative provisions. For instance, in applying for exemption from 'broadly Christian collective worship', Circular 1/94 states that 'care should be taken to safeguard the interests of any parents of children for whom broadly Christian collective worship would be appropriate' (para. 71). However, in the more common situation where a determination has not been issued, the Circular states that '[P]upils who do not come from Christian families should

be able to join in the daily act of collective worship even though this would, in the main, reflect the broad traditions of Christian belief' (para. 65).

27. Racialised references are relatively obscure. While the implicit meaning of articulating nation to Christianity is a white subject, parliamentary debate made reference to the existence of black Christians, although they tended to be (relatively) exoticised within parliamentary discourse.

28. For example, see Blatch, Lords, 26 February 1988, cols 1465-6.

29. Differentiation between faiths, or rather between Christianity and other faiths, formed a primary objective for proponents of the legislation. The regulation of worship and religious education in the 1988 Act was intended to separate and categorise, to produce knowledge that privileged difference rather than emphasising commonality.

30. For a discussion on the ways different discourses intersect, see Palmer and Pearce (1983).

31. For a more critical perspective on this point, see Jackson (1992).

32. For instance, see Chris Wright, *The Times Education Supplement,* 19 August 1994, who argues that pupils need to master basic ideas, not engage in sophisticated, academic speculations regarding the nature of faith.

33. However, it is interesting that despite adopting this approach, the model syllabuses produced reveal the extent of similarities between religions. This may reflect real commonality or the power of educational discourse in its presentation of religion.

34. What this was actually identified as being undoubtedly would vary. In addition, the perception of teachers might not necessarily reflect the wishes of many (Christian) parents.

35. See Hart (1993) on the ways in which pressure can be exerted on schools without deployment of formal grievance procedures.

36. This again reinforces the notion that Christian parents should be able to choose not to send their child to a school in which worship includes non-Christian elements. The same right is not available to any other parent.

37. A major fear was that if the report was damning it would affect parents' choice of school. The per capita basis of funding schools under Local Management of Schools meant loss of pupils could lead to a downward spiral that might end with closure.

38. Religious knowledge is also being produced by government ministers. A shift has taken place from Christianity as a spiritual discourse to a legal one in which religious decisions are made by government lawyers rather than priests.

39. Determinations were used by many schools in order to maintain multi-faith or separate worship already in existence. However, the process established by the Act forces these practices into monitored, narrow frameworks or alternatives that cannot be altered except with permission from SACRE.

40. One of the ideological implications of this aspect of the law is the assumption children come from mono-faith households. There is no discussion or provision for children whose parents are of different faiths. Thanks to Carl Stychin for raising this point.

41. Within Ss 68 and 99 the Education Act 1944 confers powers on the Secretary of State to give directions if a local authority acts unreasonably or fails to discharge its duty. This power was mentioned by almost nobody I interviewed. According to the *The Times Education Supplement,* 17 June 1994, Ilkley Grammar School

in West Yorkshire were told by the DFE that they had twelve months in which to implement the law on collective worship. This was an official direction under S. 99, although it appeared unclear why this school was chosen.

42. Many schools also draw on arguments of impossibility, for example, lack of space to hold full assemblies. See also *Haydon* v. *Kent* [1978] QB 343.

43. The relationship between the complaints process and disciplinary forms of power is discussed earlier.

44. Children who receive permission from their parents to withdraw from collective worship may be legitimately forbidden by their school from attending assembly while worship is taking place (1/94, para. 86).

45. One might question the extent to which this functioned as a counter-discourse. Nevertheless, like all discursive struggles where discourse and counter-discourse mirror each other, a degree of closure is generated causing other discourses to remain unarticulated. It is also worth noting that only certain 'counter-discourses' were produced. For instance, the emphasis of proponents of the legislation that this *is* a Christian country remained scarcely challenged.

46. Even OFSTED has come out against the legislation, particularly the legislation on collective worship as being unworkable.

47. *Independent on Sunday*, 18 September 1994.

48. See Tamney (1994) who argues that the conservative project to promote religion in schools is likely to fail because Christian leaders are shifting to the left, the strength of multi-culturalism, the humanist influence, and the perceived inconsistency of religion with other educational values.

49. Indeed, co-ordination of micro-powers has been more effective operating against central government incursions.

50. Power *may* involve asymmetries and frequently does; however, conceptually it does not have to.

Bibliography

Works by Foucault (including edited collections)

(1965) *Madness and Civilization: A History of Insanity in the Age of Reason* (London: Routledge).

(1970) *The Order of Things: An Archaeology of the Human Sciences,* trans. A.M. Sheridan (London: Routledge).

(1972a) *The Archaeology of Knowledge,* trans. A.M. Sheridan-Smith (London: Routledge).

(1972b) 'The Discourse on Language', in Foucault (1972a) (New York: Pantheon Books).

(1977a) *Discipline and Punish: The Birth of the Prison,* trans. A. Sheridan (Harmondsworth: Penguin).

(1977b) *Language, Counter-memory, Practice: Selected Essays and Interviews by Michel Foucault,* ed. D.F. Bouchard (Ithaca, NY: Cornell University Press).

(1978) *The History of Sexuality, Volume 1: An Introduction,* trans. R. Hurley (Harmondsworth: Penguin).

(1979) 'Power and Norms', in M. Morris and P. Patton (eds) *Michel Foucault: Power Truth, Strategy* (Sydney: Feral Publications).

(1980a) 'Prison Talk', in Foucault (1980f).

(1980b) 'Body/Power', in Foucault (1980f).

(1980c) 'Two Lectures', in Foucault (1980f).

(1980d) 'Truth and Power', in Foucault (1980f).

(1980e) 'The Eye of Power', in Foucault (1980f).

(1980f) *Michel Foucault: Power/Knowledge: Selected Interviews and Other Writings 1972–1977,* ed. C. Gordon (London: Harvester Wheatsheaf).

(1980g) 'The Order of Discourse', in R. Young (ed.) *Untying the Text: A Poststructuralist Reader* (London: Routledge).

(1982) 'Afterword: The Subject and Power', in Dreyfus and Rabinow (1982).

(1984a) 'What Is Enlightenment?', in Foucault (1984g).

(1984b) 'Nietzsche, Genealogy, History', in Foucault (1984g).

(1984c) 'What Is an Author?', in Foucault (1984g).

(1984d) 'On the Genealogy of Ethics: An Overview of Work in Progress', in Foucault (1984g).

(1984e) 'Politics and Ethics: An Interview', in Foucault (1984g).

(1984f) 'Polemics, Politics and Problematizations', in Foucault (1984g).

(1984g) *The Foucault Reader,* ed. P. Rabinow (Harmondsworth: Penguin).

(1984h) 'Preface' to Deleuze and Guattari (1984).

(1985) *The Use of Pleasure: The History of Sexuality, Volume 2* (Harmondsworth: Penguin).

(1986) *The Care of the Self: The History of Sexuality, Volume 3* (Harmondsworth: Penguin).

(1988a) 'The Minimalist Self', in Foucault (1988f).

(1988b) 'Critical Theory/Intellectual History', in Foucault (1988f).

(1988c) 'An Aesthetics of Existence', in Foucault (1988f).

(1988d) 'Practising Criticism', in Foucault (1988f).

(1988e) 'The Masked Philosopher', in Foucault (1988f).

(1988f) *Michel Foucault: Politics, Philosophy, Culture: Interviews and Other Writings 1977–1984* , ed. L.D. Kritzman (London: Routledge).

(1988g) 'Technologies of the Self', in Martin et al. (1988).

(1988h) 'The Political Technology of Individuals', in Martin et al. (1988).

(1988i) 'The Ethic of Care for the Self as a Practice of Freedom', in J. Bernauer and D. Rasmussen (eds) *The Final Foucault* (London/Cambridge, Mass.: MIT Press).

(1989) *Foucault Live (Interviews, 1966–84)* (New York: Semiotext[e]).

(1991a) 'Questions of Method', in Burchell et al. (1991).

(1991b) 'Governmentality', in Burchell et al. (1991).

(1991c) *Remarks on Marx* (New York: Semiotext[e]).

Foucault, M. and Deleuze, G. (1973): 'Intellectuals and Power', *Telos* 16: 103–9.

Secondary Works

Adler, M. (1958) *The Idea of Freedom* (New York: Doubleday).

Alcoff, L. (1988) 'Cultural Feminism versus Poststructuralism: The Identity Crisis in Feminist Theory', *Signs: Journal of Women in Culture and Society* 13 (3): 405–36.

Alcoff, L. (1990) 'Feminist Politics and Foucault: The Limits to a Collaboration', in A.B. Dallery and C.E. Scott with P.H. Roberts, *Crises in Continental Philosophy* (New York: State University of New York Press).

Allison, D.B. (ed.) (1985) *The New Nietzsche* (Cambridge, Mass.: MIT Press).

Armstrong, T.J. (1992) *Michel Foucault Philosopher* (Hemel Hempstead: Harvester Wheatsheaf).

Ashley, R. (1988) 'Untying the Sovereign State: A Double Reading of the Anarchy Problematique', *Millennium*, 17 (2): 227–62.

Ashley, R. (1989): 'Living on the Border Lines: Man, Poststructuralism and War', in Der Derian and Shapiro (1989).

Ashley, R. and Walker, R.B.J. (1990) 'Reading Dissidence/Writing the Discipline: Crisis and the Question of Sovereignty in International Studies', *International Studies Quarterly* 34: 367–416.

Baker, K.M. (1994) 'A Foucauldian French Revolution?', in Goldstein (1994a).

Baldick, C. (1983) *The Social Mission of English Criticism 1848–1932* (Oxford: Clarendon Press).

Barrett, M. (1991) *The Politics of Truth: From Marx to Foucault* (Cambridge: Polity Press).

Bartelson, J. (1995) *A Genealogy of Sovereignty* (Cambridge: Cambridge University Press).

Bartky, S. (1988) 'Foucault, Feminism and the Modernization of Patriarchal Power', in Diamond and Quinby (1988).

Benhabib, S. (1992) *Situating the Self: Gender, Community and Postmodernism in Contemporary Ethics* (Cambridge: Polity Press).

Benhabib, S. (1995) 'Subjectivity, Historiography, and Politics', in Benhabib et al. (1995).

Benhabib, S., Butler, J., Cornell, D., Fraser, N. and Nicholson, L. (1995): *Feminist Contentions: A Philosophical Exchange* (London: Routledge).

Bernauer, J. (1990) *Michel Foucault's Force of Flight: Towards an Ethic for Thought* (New Jersey: Humanities Press).

Bernauer, J. and Mahon, M. (1994) 'The Ethics of Michel Foucault', in Gutting (1994).

Bhabha, H. (ed.) (1990) *Nation and Narration* (London: Routledge).

Bordo, S. (1990) 'Feminism, Postmodernism, and Gender-Scepticism', in Nicholson (1990).

Bordo, S.(1993) *Unbearable Weight: Feminism, Western Culture and the Body* (Berkeley: University of California Press).

Bowles, G. and Klein, D. (1983) *Theories of Women's Studies* (London and New York: Routledge).

Boyce, D.G. (1991) *Nationalism in Ireland*, 2nd edn (London and New York: Routledge).

Bradshaw, B. (1989) 'Nationalism and Historical Scholarship in Modern Ireland', *Irish Historical Studies* xxvi: 104 (November): 329–51.

Brown, C. (1994) 'Critical Theory and Postmodernism in International Relations', in Groom and Light (1994).

Buckley, A. (1991) 'Uses of History Among Ulster Protestants', in G. Dawe and J.W. Foster (eds) *The Poet's Place: Ulster Literature and Society Essays in Honour of John Hewitt, 1907–1987* (Belfast: Institute of Irish Studies).

Bull, H. (1977) *The Anarchical Society: A Study of Order in World Politics* (London: Macmillan).

Burchell, G., Gordon, C. and Miller, P. (eds) (1991) *The Foucault Effect: Studies in Governmentality* (Hemel Hempstead: Harvester Wheatsheaf).

Butler, J. (1987) 'Variations on Sex and Gender: Beauvoir, Wittig and Foucault' in S. Benhabib and D. Cornell (eds) *Feminism as Critique: On the Politics of Gender* (Minneapolis: University of Minnesota Press).

Butler, J. (1990a) 'Gender Trouble, Feminist Theory, and Psychoanalytic Discourse', in Nicholson (1990).

Butler, J. (1990b) *Gender Trouble: Feminism and the Subversion of Identity* (London: Routledge).

Butler, J. (1991) 'Imitation and Gender Insubordination', in Fuss (1991).

Butler, J. (1992) 'Contingent Foundations: Feminism and the Question of "Postmodernism"', in Butler and Scott (1992).

Butler, J. (1993a) *Bodies That Matter: On the Discursive Limits of 'Sex'* (London: Routledge).

Butler, J. (1993b) 'Sexual Inversions', in Caputo and Yount. (1993).

Butler, J. and Scott, J.W. (eds) (1992) *Feminists Theorize the Political* (London: Routledge).

Butterfield, G. (1944) *The Englishman and his History* (Cambridge: Cambridge University Press).

Cain, M. (1993) 'Foucault, Feminism and Feeling: What Foucault Can and Cannot Contribute to Feminist Epistemology', in Ramazanoglu (1993).

Canning, K. (1994) 'Feminist History after the Linguistic Turn: Historicizing Discourse and Experience', *Signs* 19 (2) (Winter): 368–404.

Caputo, J. and Yount, M. (eds) (1993) *Foucault and the Critique of Institutions* (Pennsylvania: Pennsylvania State University Press).

Carter, B., Harris, C. and Joshi, S. (1987) 'The 1951–55 Conservative Government and the Racialisation of Black Immigration', *Immigrants and Minorities* 6: 335–47.

Carter, B., Harris, C. and Joshi, S. (1993): 'The 1951–55 Conservative Government and the Racialisation of Black Immigration' in W. James and C. Harris, *Inside Babylon: The Caribbean Diaspora in Britain* (London: Verso).

Chartier, R. (1994) 'The Chimera of the Origin: Archaeology, Cultural History, and the French Revolution', in Goldstein (1994a).

Clegg, S.R. (1989) *Frameworks of Power* (London: Sage).

Cohen, E. (1991) 'Who Are "We"? Gay "Identity" as Political (E)motion (A Theoretical Rumination)', in Fuss (1991).

Cooper, D. (1994a) *Sexing the City: Lesbian and Gay Politics Within the Activist State* (London: Rivers Oram Press).

Cooper, D. (1994b) 'Productive, Relational and Everywhere? Conceptualising Power and Resistance within Foucauldian Feminism', *Sociology* 28: 435–54.

Cooper, D. (1995a) *Power in Struggle: Feminism, Sexuality and the State* (Buckingham: Open University Press).

Cooper, D. (1995b) 'Defiance and Non-Compliance: Religious Education and the Implementation Problem', *Current Legal Problems 1995* 48 (2): 253–79.

Cousins, M. (1987) 'The Practice of Historical Investigation', in D. Attridge, G. Bennington and R. Young (eds) *Post-Structuralism and the Question of History* (Cambridge: Cambridge University Press).

Cousins, M. and Hussain, A. (1984) *Michel Foucault* (London: Macmillan).

Crossley, N. (1995) 'Body Techniques, Agency and Intercorporeality: On Goffman's *Relations in Public*', *Sociology* 29 (1): 133–49.

Curtis, L.P., Jr (1994) 'The Greening of Irish History', *Eire-Ireland* 29 (2): 7–29.

Davidson, A.I. (1986) 'Archaeology, Genealogy, Ethics', in Hoy (1986).

Dean, M. (1994) *Critical and Effective Histories: Foucault's Methods and Historical Sociology* (London: Routledge).

Deane, S. (1991) 'Wherever Green Is Read', in M. Ni Dhonnchadha and T. Dorgan (eds) *Revising the Rising* (Derry: Field Day).

Deleuze, G. (1985) 'Nomad Thought', trans. D.B. Allison, in Allison (1985).

Deleuze, G. (1988) *Foucault,* trans. S. Hand (Minneapolis: University of Minneapolis Press).

Deleuze, G. (1992) 'What Is a *dispositif?*', in Armstrong (1992).

Deleuze, G. and Guattari, F. (1984) *Anti-Oedipus: Capitalism and Schizophrenia,* trans. R. Hurley et al. (London: Athlone Press).

Dennett, D.C. (1991) *Consciousness Explained* (London: Penguin).

Der Derian, J. (1987) *On Diplomacy: A Genealogy of Western Estrangement* (Oxford: Blackwell).

Der Derian, J. and Shapiro, M. (eds) (1989) *International/Intertextual Relations: Postmodern Readings of World Politics* (Lexington, Mass.: Lexington Books).

Deveaux, M. (1994) 'Feminism and Empowerment: A Critical Reading of Foucault', *Feminist Studies* 20 (2): 223–47.

Dews, P. (1987) *Logics of Disintegration: Post-Structuralist Thought and the Claims of Critical Theory* (London: Verso).

Dews, P. (1989) 'The Return of the Subject in Late Foucault', *Radical Philosophy* 51: 37–41.

Diamond, I. and Quinby. L. (eds) (1988) *Feminism and Foucault: Reflections on Resistance* (Boston, Mass.: Northeastern University Press).

Diprose, R. (1994) *The Bodies of Women: Ethics, Embodiment and Sexual Difference* (London: Routledge).

Di Stefano, C. (1990) 'Dilemmas of Difference: Feminism, Modernity and Postmodernism', in Nicholson (1990).

Dreyfus, H.L. and Rabinow, P. (1982): *Michel Foucault: Beyond Structuralism and Hermeneutics* (London: Harvester Wheatsheaf).

Dreyfus, H.L. and Rabinow, P. (1986): 'What Is Maturity? Habermas and Foucault on What Is Enlightenment', in Hoy (1986).

During, S. (1992) *Foucault and Literature: Towards a Genealogy of Writing* (London and New York: Routledge).

Ewald, F. (1992) 'A Power Without Exterior', in Armstrong (1992).

Fanning, R. (1986) '"The Great Enchantment": Uses and Abuses of Modern Irish History', in J. Dooge (ed) *Ireland in the Contemporary World* (Dublin: Gill and Macmillan).

Fanning, R. (1988) 'The Meaning of Revisionism', *Irish Review* 4: 15–19.

Fennell, D. (1988) 'Against Revisionism', *Irish Review* 4: 20–4.

Feyerabend, P. (1975) *Against Method* (London: Verso).

Flax, J. (1990a) *Thinking Fragments: Psychoanalysis, Feminism and Postmodernism in the Contemporary West* (Berkeley: University of California Press).

Flax, J. (1990b) 'Postmodernism and Gender Relations in Feminist Theory', in Nicholson (1990).

Flynn, T. (1994) 'Foucault's Mapping of History', in Gutting (1994).

Forbes, I. (1987) 'Warfare Without War: Intervention in the International System', *Arms Control* 8: 52–67.

Foster, R.F. (1986) 'We Are All Revisionists Now', *Irish Review* 1: 1–5.

Foster, R.F. (1988) *Modern Ireland 1600-1972* (London: Penguin).

Foster, R.F. (1993): *Paddy and Mr. Punch: Connections in Irish and English History* (London: Allen Lane).

Frankfurt, H.G. (1971) 'Freedom of the Will and the Concept of a Person', *Journal of Philosophy* LXVIII (1): 5–20.

Frankfurt, H.G. (1988) 'Identification and Wholeheartedness', in Frankfurt, H.G. *The Importance of What We Care About* (Cambridge: Cambridge University Press).

Fraser, N. (1989) *Unruly Practices: Power, Discourse and Gender in Contemporary Social Theory* (Cambridge: Polity Press).

Fraser, N. (1995a) 'False Antithesis', in Benhabib et al. (1995).

Fraser, N. (1995b) 'Pragmatism, Feminism, and the Linguistic Turn', in Benhabib et al. (1995).

Fryer, P. (1984) *Staying Power: The History of Black People in Britain* (London: Pluto Press).

Fuss, D. (ed) (1991) *Inside/Out: Lesbian Theories, Gay Theories* (London: Routledge).

Gane, M. and Johnson, T. (eds) (1993) *Foucault's New Domains* (London: Routledge).

Geras, N. (1995) 'Language, Truth and Justice', *New Left Review* 209: 110–35.

Gilligan, C. (1982) *In a Different Voice: Psychological Theory and Women's Development* (Cambridge, Mass.: Harvard University Press).

Goldberg, D. (ed.) (1990) *Anatomy of Racism* (Minnesota: University of Minnesota Press).

Goldberg, D. (1993) *Racist Culture: Philosophy and the Politics of Meaning* (Oxford: Blackwell).

Goldstein, J. (ed.) (1994a): *Foucault and the Writing of History* (Oxford: Blackwell).

Goldstein, J. (1994b) 'Foucault and the Post-Revolutionary Self: The Uses of Cousinian Pedagogy in Nineteenth-Century France', in Goldstein (1994a).

Goodman, L.E. (1987) 'Determinism and Freedom in Spinoza, Maimonides, and Aristotle: A Retrospective Study', in F. Schoeman (ed.) *Responsibility, Character and the Emotions* (Cambridge: Cambridge University Press).

Gordon, C. (1991) 'Governmental Rationality: An Introduction', in Burchell et al. (1991).

Gordon, C. (1993) 'Question, Ethos, Event: Foucault on Kant and Enlightenment', in Gane and Johnson (1993).

Grant, R. and Newland, K. (eds) (1991) *Gender and International Relations* (Milton Keynes: Open University Press).

Green, T.H. (1956 [1881]) 'Liberal Legislation or Freedom of Contract', in A. Bullock and M. Shock (eds) *The Liberal Tradition* (Oxford: Clarendon).

Grimshaw, J. (1993) 'Practices of Freedom', in Ramazanoglu (1993).

Groom, A.J.R. and Light, M. (eds) (1994) *Contemporary International Relations: A Guide to Theory* (London: Pinter Publishers).

Gutting, G. (ed.) (1994) *The Cambridge Companion to Foucault* (Cambridge: Cambridge University Press).

Haber, H.F. (1994) *Beyond Postmodern Politics: Lyotard, Rorty, Foucault* (London: Routledge).

Habermas, J. (1984) *The Theory of Communicative Action Volume 1* (Boston, Mass.: Beacon Press).

Habermas, J. (1986) 'Taking Aim at the Heart of the Present', in Hoy (1986).

Habermas, J. (1987a) *The Philosophical Discourse of Modernity: Twelve Lectures,* trans. F. Lawrence (Cambridge: Polity Press).

Habermas, J. (1987b) *The Theory of Communicative Action Volume 2* (Boston, Mass.: Beacon Press).

Haldane, J. (1986) 'Religious Education in a Pluralist Society', *British Journal of Education Studies* 34 (2): 161–81.

Hall, S. (1991) 'Old and New Identities, Old and New Ethnicities', in King, A. (ed.) *Culture, Globalization and the World System: Contemporary Conditions for the Representation of Identity* (Basingstoke: Macmillan): 40–68.

Hall, S., Critcher, C., Jefferson, T., Clarke, J. and Roberts, B. (1978) *Policing the Crisis: Mugging, the State and Law and Order* (London: Macmillan).

Harding S. and Hintikka, M. (eds) (1983) *Discovering Reality: Feminist Perspectives on Epistemology, Methodology and the Philosophy of Science* (Dordrecht: Reidel).

Harris, C. (1987) 'British Capitalism, Migration and Relative Surplus Population', *Migration,* 1 (1): 47–90.

Hart, C. (1993) 'Legislation and Religious Education', *Education and the Law* 5: 7–17.

Hartsock, N. (1983) 'The Feminist Standpoint: Developing the Ground for a Specifically Feminist Historical Materialism', in Harding and Hintikka (1983).

Hartsock, N. (1990) 'Foucault on Power: A Theory for Women?', in Nicholson (1990).

Harvey, D. (1989) *The Condition of Postmodernity: An Enquiry into the Origins of Cultural Change* (Oxford: Blackwell).

Herman, D. (1994) *Rights of Passage: Struggles for Lesbian and Gay Legal Equality* (Toronto: Toronto University Press).

Hesse, C. (1994) 'Kant, Foucault, and *Three Women*', in Goldstein (1994a).

Himmelfarb, G. (1992) 'Telling It as You Like', *TLS* (16 October): 12–15.

Hinsley, F.H. (1973) *Nationalism and the International System* (London: Hodder and Stoughton).

Hockaday, A. (1987) 'Warfare Without War: Intervention in the International System: Observations on Ian Forbes's Paper', *Arms Control* 8: 68–72.

Hoffman, M. (1988) 'Conversations on Critical International Relations Theory', *Millennium*, 17, (1): 91–5.

Hollis, M. and Smith, S. (1991) *Explaining and Understanding International Relations* (Oxford: Clarendon).

Holmes, C. (1988) *John Bull's Island: Immigration and British Society 1871–1971* (London: Macmillan).

Horton, J. and Mendus, S. (eds) (1994) *After MacIntyre* (London: Polity Press).

Hoy, D.C. (ed.) (1986) *Foucault: A Critical Reader* (Oxford: Blackwell).

Hull, J. (1993) 'The Fundamental Distinction: A Review of DFE Draft Circular X/94 Religious Education and Collective Worship ii October 1993' (Unpublished).

Hull, J. (1994) 'The New Government Guidelines on Religious Education', *British Journal of Religious Education* 16: 66–9.

Hunt, A. and Wickham G. (1994) *Foucault and Law: Towards a Sociology of Law as Governance* (London: Pluto Press).

Hunter, I. (1988) *Culture and Government: The Emergence of Literary Education* (London: Macmillan).

Hutton, P.H. (1988) 'Foucault, Freud and the Technologies of the Self', in Martin et al. (1988).

Jackson, R. (1992) 'The Misrepresentation of Religious Education', in M. Leicester and M. Taylor (eds) *Ethics, Ethnicity and Education* (London: Kogan Press).

Jay, M. (1984) *Marxism and Totality: The Adventures of a Concept from Lukács to Habermas* (Cambridge: Polity Press).

Jenkins, K. (1991) *Re-Thinking History* (London and New York: Routledge).

Joshi, S. and Carter, B. (1984) 'The Role of Labour in the Creation of a Racist Britain', *Race and Class* XXV (3): 53–70.

Joyce, P. (1994) *Democratic Subjects: The Self and the Social in Nineteenth Century England* (Cambridge: Cambridge University Press).

Joyce, P. (1995) 'The End of Social History?', *Social History* 20 (1) (January): 73–91.

Juss, S.S. (1993) *Immigration, Nationality and Citizenship* (London: Mansell)

Kay, D. and Miles, R. (1992): *Refugees or Migrant Workers? European Volunteer Workers in Britain 1946–1951* (London: Routledge).

Keeley, T. (1990) 'Toward a Foucauldian Analysis of International Regimes', *International Organization* 44: 83–105.

Keohane, R. (1984) *After Hegemony: Cooperation and Discord in the World Political Economy* (Princeton: Princeton University Press).

Keohane, R. (ed.) (1986) *Neorealism and Its Critics* (New York: Columbia University Press).

Keohane, R. (1988) 'International Institutions: Two Approaches', *International Studies Quarterly* 32 (4): 379–96.

Keohane, R. (1989) *International Institutions and State Power: Essays in International Relations Theory* (Boulder, Co.: Westview Press).

Krasner, S.D. (ed.) (1983) *International Regimes* (Ithaca, NY: Cornell University Press).

Krishna, S. (1993) 'The Importance of Being Ironic: A Postcolonial View on Critical International Relations Theory', *Alternatives* 18 (3): 285–417.

Kuhn, T.S. (1970) *The Structure of Scientific Revolutions*, 2nd edn (Chicago, Ill.: University of Chicago Press).

Laing, R.D. (1960) *The Divided Self: A Study of Sanity and Madness* (London: Tavistock).

Larrabee, M.J. (ed.) (1993) *An Ethic of Care: Feminist and Interdisciplinary Perspectives* (London: Routledge).

Layder, D. (1990) *The Realist Image in Social Science* (London: Macmillan).

Layder, D. (1994) *Understanding Social Theory* (London: Sage).

Layton-Henry, Z. (1984) *The Politics of Race in Britain* (London: Allen and Unwin).

Lemert, C.C. and Gillan, G. (1982) *Michel Foucault: Social Theory and Transgression* (New York: Columbia University Press).

Linklater, A. (1990) *Beyond Realism and Marxism: Critical Theory and International Relations* (London: Macmillan).

Little, R. and Smith, M. (eds) (1991) *Perspectives on World Politics* (London: Routledge).

Lloyd, M. (1993) 'The (F)utility of a Feminist Turn to Foucault', *Economy and Society* 22 (4): 437–60.

Lloyd, M. (1996a) 'Foucault's "Care of the Self": Some Implications for Feminist Politics', in C. O'Farrell (ed.) *Foucault, the Legacy: Conference Proceedings* (Queensland: Queensland University of Technology Press).

Lloyd, M. (1996b) 'A Feminist Mapping of Foucauldian Politics', in S. Hekman (ed.) *Feminist Interpretations of Michel Foucault* (Pennsylvania: Pennsylvania State University Press).

Lukács, G. (1971) *History and Class Consciousness* (London: Merlin Press).

Macey, D. (1994) *The Lives of Michel Foucault* (London: Vintage).

MacIntyre, A. (1981) *After Virtue* (London: Duckworth).

MacIntyre, A. (1990) *Three Rival Versions of Moral Enquiry* (London: Duckworth).

MacLean, J. (1988) 'Belief Systems and Ideology in International Relations', in R. Little and S. Smith (eds) *Belief Systems in International Relations* (Oxford: Basil Blackwell).

Magill, K. (1996) *Freedom and Experience: Self-Determination Without Illusions* (London: Macmillan).

Marcus Aurelius (1983 [*c*. AD 150]): *The Meditations of Marcus Aurelius*, trans. G.M.A. Grube (Indianapolis: Hackett).

Martin, L., Gutman H. and Hutton P. (1988) *Technologies of the Self: A Seminar with Michel Foucault* (Amherst: University of Massachusetts).

McNay, L. (1992) *Foucault and Feminism: Power, Gender and the Self* (Cambridge: Polity Press).

McNay, L. (1994) *Foucault: A Critical Introduction* (Cambridge: Polity Press).

Megill, A. (1987) 'The Reception of Foucault by Historians', *Journal of the History of Ideas* 48: 117–41.

Miles, R. (1989) 'Nationality, citizenship and migration to Britain, 1945–1951', *Journal of Law and Society* 16 (4): 426–42.

Miles, R. (1993) *Racism after 'Race Relations'* (London: Routledge).

Miles, R. and Phizacklea, A. (1984) *White Man's Country: Racism in British Politics* (London: Pluto Press).

Mill, J.S. (1987) 'On Bentham', in Ryan (1987).

Miller, J. (1993) *The Passion of Michel Foucault* (London: HarperCollins).

Morgenthau, H. (1948) *Politics Among Nations* (New York: Knopf).

Mueller, L. (1986) 'Religious Rights of Children: A Gallery of Judicial Visions', *New York University Review of Law and Social Change* 14: 323–40.

Nardin, T. (1983) *Law, Morality and the Relations of States* (Princeton, NJ: Princeton University Press).

Nicholson, L.(ed.) (1990) *Feminism/Postmodernism* (London: Routledge).

Nietzsche, F. (1956) 'The Genealogy of Morals', in *The Birth of Tragedy and the Genealogy of Morals*, trans. F. Golffing (New York: Anchor Doubleday).

Nietzsche, F. (1983) 'On the Uses and Disadvantages of History for Life', in *Untimely Meditations*, trans. R.J. Hollingdale (Cambridge: Cambridge University Press).

Noiriel, G. (1994) 'Foucault and History: The Lessons of a Disillusion', *Journal of Modern History* 66 (September) 547–68.

Norris, C. (1993) *The Truth About Postmodernism* (Oxford: Blackwell).

O'Brien, P. (1989) 'Michel Foucault's History of Culture', in L. Hunt ed. *The New Cultural History* (Berkeley and Los Angeles: University of California Press).

O'Farrell, C. (1989) *Foucault: Historian or Philosopher?* (London: Macmillan).

Okin, S.M. (1989) *Justice, Gender and the Family* (New York: Basic Books).

Osborne, P. and Segal, L. (1994) 'Gender as Performance: An Interview with Judith Butler', *Radical Philosophy* 67: 32–9.

Owen, D. (1994) *Maturity and Modernity: Nietzsche, Weber, Foucault and the Ambivalence of Reason* (London: Routledge).

Palmer, J. and Pearce, F. (1983) 'Legal Discourse and State Power: Foucault and the Juridical Relation', *International Journal of the Sociology of Law* 11 (4): 361–83.

Pawson, R. (1989) *A Measure for Measures: A Manifesto for Empirical Sociology* (London: Routledge).

Phelan, S. (1989) *Identity Politics: Lesbian Feminism and the Limits of Community* (Philadelphia: Temple University Press).

Phelan, S. (1990) 'Foucault and Feminism', *American Journal of Political Science* 34 (2): 421–40.

Poster, M. (1982) 'Foucault and History', *Social Research* 49 (1) (Spring): 116–42.

Poster, M. (1984) *Foucault, Marxism, and History* (London: Polity Press).

Poster, M. (1992 'Foucault, the Present and History', in Armstrong (1992).

Poulter, S. (1990) 'The Religious Education Provisions of the Education Reform Act', *Education and the Law* 2:1 11.

Probyn, E. (1993) *Sexing the Self: Gendered Positions in Cultural Studies* (London: Routledge).

Rajchman, J. (1991) *Truth and Eros: Foucault, Lacan, and the Question of Ethics* (London: Routledge).

Rajchman, J. (1992) 'Foucault: the Ethic and the Work', in Armstrong (1992).

Ramazanoglu, C. (ed.) (1993) *Up Against Foucault: Explorations of Some Tensions Between Foucault and Feminism* (London: Routledge).

Rattansi, A. and Donald, J. (eds) (1992) *'Race', Culture and Difference* (London: Sage/Open University).

Riley, D. (1988) *'Am I That Name?': Feminism and the Category of 'Women' in History* (London: Macmillan).

Riley, D. (1992) 'A Short History of Some Preoccupations', in Butler and Scott (1992).

Rochlitz, R. (1992) 'The Aesthetics of Existence: Post-Conventional Morality and the Theory of Power in Michel Foucault', in Armstrong (1992).

Rorty, R. (1989) *Contingency, Irony, and Solidarity* (Cambridge: Cambridge University Press).

Rose, N. (1989) *Governing the Soul: The Shaping of the Private Self* (London: Routledge).

Rosenau, P. (1990) 'Once Again into the Fray: International Relations Confronts the Humanities', *Millennium* 19 (1): 83–110.

Rothstein, R.L. (1991) 'On the Costs of Realism', in Little and Smith (1991).

Rudé, G. (1972) *Debate on Europe 1815–1850* (New York: Harper and Row).

Ryan, A. (ed.) (1987) *John Stuart Mill and Jeremy Bentham: Utilitarianism and Other Essays* (Harmondsworth: Penguin).

Saggar, S. (1992) *Race and Politics in Britain* (London: Macmillan).

Said, E. (1983) *Orientalism* (Harmondsworth: Penguin).

Said, E. (1993) *Culture and Imperialism* (London: Chatto & Windus).

Samuel, R. (1991) 'Reading the Signs', *History Workshop* 32 (Autumn): 88–109.

Samuel, R. (1992) 'Reading the Signs II', *History Workshop* 33 (Spring): 220–51.

Sawicki, J. (1991) *Disciplining Foucault: Feminism, Power and the Body* (London: Routledge).

Sayer, A. (1994) *Method in Social Science: A Realist Approach*, 2nd edn (London: Routledge).

Sayers, S. (1985) *Reality and Reason: Dialectic and the Theory of Knowledge* (Oxford: Basil Blackwell).

Scott, J. (1988) *Gender and the Politics of History* (New York: Columbia University Press).

Scott, J. (1991) 'The Evidence of Experience', *Critical Inquiry* 17 (4): 773–97.

Shapiro, M. (1992) *Reading the Postmodern Polity: Political Theory as Textual Practice* (Minneapolis: University of Minnesota Press).

Simons, J. (1995) *Foucault and the Political* (London: Routledge).

Smart, C. (1989) *Feminism and the Power of the Law* (London: Routledge).

Solomos, J. (1993) *Race and Racism in Contemporary Britain*, 2nd edn (London: Macmillan).

Soper, K. (1993) 'Productive Contradictions', in Ramazanoglu (1993).

Speigel, G. (1991) 'History and Post-modernism', *Past and Present* 135 (July): 189–208.

Spinoza, B. (1910 [1677]) *Ethics* (London: Dent).

Stone, L. (1991) 'History and Post-modernism', *Past and Present* 131 (May): 217–18.

Sylvester, C. (1994) *Feminist Theory and International Relations in a Postmodern Era* (Cambridge: Cambridge University Press).

Tamney, J. (1994) 'Conservative Government and Support for the Religious Institution: Religious Education in English Schools', *The British Journal of Sociology* 45: 195–210.

Taylor, C. (1984) 'Foucault on Freedom and Truth', *Political Theory* 12 (2): 152–83.

Thacker, A. (1993) 'Foucault's Aesthetics of Existence', *Radical Philosophy* 63: 13–21.

Thiele, L. (1990) 'The Agony of Politics: The Nietzschean Roots of Foucault's Thought', *American Political Science Review* 84 (3): 907–25.

Tickner, A. (1992) *Gender in International Relations: Feminist Perspectives on Achieving Global Security* (New York: Columbia University Press).

Trachtenberg, M. (1985) 'Strategists, Philosophers and the Nuclear Question', in R. Hardin, J.J. Mearsheimer, G. Dworkin and R.E. Goodie (eds) *Nuclear Deterrence. Ethics and Strategy* (Chicago: Chicago University Press).

Tress, D.M. (1988) 'Comment on Flax's "Postmodernism and Gender Relations in Feminist Theory"', *Signs, Journal of Women in Culture and Society* 14 (1): 196–200.

Tyler, C. (1991) 'Boys Will Be Girls: the Politics of Gay Drag', in Fuss (1991).

Vernon, J. (1994) 'Who's Afraid of the "Linguistic Turn"? The Politics of Social History and Its Discontents', *Social History* 19 (1) (January): 81–97.

Visker, R. (1995) *Michel Foucault: Genealogy as Critique* (London: Verso).

Voltaire (1980) *Letters on England,* trans. L. Tancock (Harmondsworth: Penguin).

Walker, R.B.J. (1993) *Inside/Outside: International Relations as Political Theory* (Cambridge: Cambridge University Press).

Walkerdine, V. (1990) *Schoolgirl Fictions* (London: Verso).

Waltz, K. (1959) *Man, the State and War* (New York: Columbia University Press).

Waltz, K. (1979) *Theory of International Politics* (London: Addison-Wesley).

Walzer, M. (1989) *The Company of Critics: Social Criticism and Commitment in the Twentieth Century* (London: Peter Haben).

Watson, G. (1982) 'Free Agency', in G. Watson (ed.) *Free Will* (Oxford: Oxford University Press).

Wight, M. (1977) *Systems of States* (Leicester: Leicester University Press).

Wilson, M.D. (ed.) (1969) *The Essential Descartes,* trans. E.S. Haldane and G.R.T. Ross (New York: Meridian).

Wokler, R. (1994) 'Projecting the Enlightenment', in Horton and Mendus (1994).

Wolf, S. (1990) *Freedom Within Reason* (Oxford: Oxford University Press).

Woodward, J. (1988) *Understanding Ourselves: The Uses of Therapy* (London: Macmillan).

Young, R. (1990) *White Mythologies: Writing History and the West* (London: Routledge).

Young, R. (1995) 'Foucault on Race and Colonialism', *New Formations* 25 (Summer): 57–65.

Index